Religion and Gurus in Traditional and Modern India

Religion and Gurus in Traditional and Modern India

Uday Mehta

KALPAZ

First Published, 2018

Published by

Kalpaz Publications
C-30, Satyawati Nagar,
Delhi – 110052
E-mail: kalpaz@hotmail.com
Ph.: 9212142040

Printed at: G. Print Process, Delhi

Cataloging in Publication Data—DK
Courtesy: D.K. Agencies (P) Ltd. <docinfo@dkagencies.com>

Puniyani, Ram, author.
Religion and gurus in traditional and modern India / Uday Mehta.
pages cm
Includes bibliographical references.
ISBN 9789351282808

1. Gurus—India. 2. Hinduism. 3. Religion and sociology—India. I. Title.

LCC BL1202.P86 2018 | DDC 294.5 23

Contents

Introduction

The Context

"Religion and Gurus in traditional and Modern India" is a consolidation of a series of publications and essays in the area of sociologoical apparaisal of religion, syncretism and modern gurus and godmen in India over period of last few decades. My interest in this area emerged from the fact that the sociology of religion is a relatively less explored area. At the same time there has been some path breaking work by the late Prof. G.S. Ghurye in his well known work "Sadhus of India, Gods and Men". Some important contributions have come from the late Prof. Radhakumar Mukherjee and the late D.P. Mukherjee. Extensive work in this field was also done by the late Dr. K. M. Kapadia and then by late Dr. A. R. Desai. In current times, Prof. Yogendra Singh's contribution is noteworthy. One cannot forget Prof. T. N. Madan's work in the field either.

Unfortunately we find that the historical thrust that was evident in understanding the sociology of religion, evident in the works of the late Profs. Mukherjee and Ghurye, the late D.P. Mukherjee, and late Drs. K. M. Kapadia and A. R. Desai is completely lost under the influence of western and particularly established branch of American sociology, with its exclusive focus on the structural- functional approach for a long time. As a result, historical and analytical studies have almost withered away from Indian sociology.

Ours is a humble attempt in this direction to revive this earlier thrust of enquiry in sociological appraisals.

In this book we have attempted to look at the present and historical context. With the rise of communal forces in the post 1980s, it was difficult to ignore the socio-economic and political situation. The rise of political parties like the BJP and Shiv Sena and their increasing foothold in all spheres of life compelled me to understand and examine religion and its manifestations in Indian society. Post 1980s one sees consolidation and strengthening of the hold of communal forces in many parts of the country, the extent of which can be examined by the self imposed curfews that were witnessed during the broadcast of Ramayana and Mahabharat serials on national television. The sentiments were further propelled by Ramjanmabhoomi yatra initiated and popularised by the B.J.P. and its affiliated organizations, as Sant Sammelan, Bajrang Dal, Vishwa Hindu Parishad with the active connivance of the R.S.S. It found over whelming response and its influence could be seen extensively in both urban as well as rural areas. In some of the northern states like Uttar Pradesh and even in Gujarat there was unprecedented communal tension finding manifestation also in a series of communal disturbance in these as well as other states. Mumbai which is otherwise known for its cosmopolitan outlook and communal harmony witnessed such communal tension, culminating in a major communal riot in 1992, which resulted into a polarization of communities never witnessed earlier.

This extensive mass support for the Ramjanmbhoomi Yatra and the B.J.P. also emerged from other socio-economic factors. As a result of the agrarian reforms initiated since independence, such as the zamindari abolition, land ceiling, tenancy reforms and other developmental measures, the other backward classes (OBCs) were acquiring a much stronger economic, social as well as political base in rural India. This campaign for the Ramjanmabhoomi yatra provided them a fresh opportunity to consolidate their base and extend their political influence in rural as well as urban areas. Some got opportunities also to consolidate their financial base from the support they acquired as a result of the state policy of building up a self-sustaining and independent economic growth. It also made possible financial support from the state for the Indian entrepreneur class by promotion of their industrial base with launching of extensive small and medium industrial projects in many parts of the country. This rising strata of OBCs found a golden opportunity by joining the bandwagon of communal forces to gain a political hold in rural as well as urban India.

The neoliberal policy and economic reforms with their thrust on free market economy also were instrumental in the state directly or indirectly lending support to divisive forces. Hence, since the eighties the country has witnessed a new social, political and economic scenario with the state losing interest in upholding the secular and egalitarian constitutional commitment of the earlier era. This also coincided with the emergence of a new breed of rulers in society, the godmen and women, gurus and their acquiring an extensive mass base. In this historical backdrop there is a need to examine the role of these godmen and women in influencing and molding Indian society. The role of modern Godmen and women, gurus etc in consolidating the communal forces in society cannot be underestimated and therefore is in need of a more systematic and exhaustive appraisal.

Apart from conducting an enquiry into the role of godmen and gurus, my interest in the study of religion was also prompted by some other equally serious considerations. The all pervasive influence of religion in Indian society is widely known and is not a new phenomenon. Since Vedic times, religion has exercised a profound influence in all spheres of the Indian society. There are several salient factors, originating probably in the agricultural mode of production, the dominant role of the polity, the persistence of village communities, the dominance of the state, external invasions etc, and there could be many more historical factors that could explain the predominant role of religion in Indian society and even its persistence in modern Indian society. This overwhelming influence of religion in Indian society right from probably the pre-vedic period and its persistence over the medieval to modern period has also contributed in my undertaking an enquiry in this crucial area.

The inspiration for explaining this vital aspect of Indian society also comes from the need to review the dogmatic understanding of the Marxist interpretation of the role of religion and an exclusive focus on its reactionary character, as the opium or a sigh of the oppressed. Some eminent sociologists also visualized that over a period of time, with the advancement of science, technology and industrial development, religious influence would decline and eventually may even wither away. But instead of declining, religion has become far more dominant globally. For example, American President Bush's sympathy for Christian religious fundamentalism and emergence of phenomena of the moral majority movement. This kind of religious fundamentalism exercises significant influence in American society and polity.

Apart from this observation, it should also be noted that religion in the modern society is also playing a dual role. While its reactionary aspects have been highlighted, one has to keep in mind its progressive influence, its relevance as a protest against the establishment, and the injustice and exploitation of the oppressed. In Latin American revolutions, the role of liberation theology could not be overstressed. But for the impact of the priests working among the oppressed, the radical transformation experienced by several Latin American nations like Nicaragua, Equador, Bolivia, Brazil would not have been possible. Similarly, the contribution of liberal and Sufi traditions in Islam and their impact in Muslim as well as other nations like India cannot be under- estimated. Hence, there is an urgent need to focus on these liberative aspects of religious traditions, especially in the context of Indian society.

Lastly, I also strongly feel that all pervasive influences of religion, in its multiple forms, also deserve serious attention. It is my humble contention that unless we understand the root causes of religious appeal, our appraisal confined to the role of the established institutional structures of different religions would not help us understand the deeper motivating factors of this phenomenon.

In this sense, the relevance of religion cannot be exhausted only in terms of its explanation as a sigh of the oppressed or a soul of the soulless world, or even as a protest against sufferings inflicted on overwhelming majority of humanity by the present monopolistic capitalist financial system dominant all over the world today. The roots of its appeal appear to us much deeper than normally visualized. Human beings tend to be creative by nature. Man can't live without breeding and material survival is a must, a pre-condition for any progress or development. But the essence of being is much more than what over-presumption of material survival could suggest.

Unless we take this essence of being into count, we would not be able to explain how medieval saints like Kabir, Tukaram and several others can exercise such powerful influence on our minds even today. This appeal is universal. The same yardstick would be applicable to impact of the Sufi or Christian saints' writings. Apart from this, the increasing alienation experienced with the intense, all-pervasive commoditization of all aspects of human life – aspirations, emotions, all creative expressions - under this market dominated, global neo-liberal regime, encroaching on individual freedom in every sphere of creative activity, ranging from the literature to all forms of arts, films, and even sports, has undoubtedly immensely contributed in heightening the appeal of religion in modern society.

The sharp increase in economic disparities with the prolonging of the monopoly of finance capital with its unsatiable drive for accumulation of capital has in no small way contributed in aggravating this phenomenon of alienation in modern society, harmful to the formation of the social bonds so necessary for human well being. It isolates us from one another. In effect, there are two worlds, that of the rich and that of the rest of us. The rich exert power over us and by doing so, deny us our full humanity. Schutz says: "The concept of alienation clarifies both the extent and the significance of what is lost for those subordinated in social power structures. Not only is their full self-initiative denied...but the full development of their faculties and intentions in all other realms of life is thereby stifled and more or less permanently stunted. People...manifest behaviors ranging from withdrawal to social or intellectual incompetence, from distraction to aimlessness or apathy, from anger, confusion, depression and anxiety to obsession and neuroses and, in some, violence of one kind or another" (Analytical Monthly Review No.12 March 2012. The great Inequality - Michael D.Yatas. P.14).

Thus, multiple forms of alienation, with its intensity, pervasiveness and gravity, certainly pave way for the increasing spread and influence of all varieties of religious fundamentalism along with a genuine desire based on the creative, constructive and altruistic urges of mankind for seeking solutions from religion that could satisfy their deeper aspirations.

The Book

The present volume consists of eight essays. The first four essays deal with the role of Hinduism in modern Indian society and syncretism in the Indian context. The other two articles are on gurus in India. The other four essays are focused on the four leading godmen of western India. These four essays are based on our findings based on field investigation conducted mostly during the years and in 2010. Our study on Rajneesh was done much earlier during the late 1980s.

The first essay on the role of Hinduism, while keeping in view the experiences in this country since the last three decades, seeks to bring out that what is being projected as Hinduism in recent years is actually a concept based on a crude amalgam of various contradictory set of beliefs, rituals and practices. The new Hindu phenomena have acquired strength as a result of the widening of the social base of political Hinduism in the post-independence period. The backward castes or more appropriately the other backward classes who benefitted from the initial phase of agrarian reforms have now entered new socio-religious spheres which were till recently reserved for the upper caste Hindus and have developed stakes in them. This phenomenon is also described as a process of political sanskritization. The large scale mobilization required for the Ramjanmabhoomi Yatra, in all probability would not have been possible without the actual involvement of the large masses.

The charismatic thrust and contrast of the new Hinduism becomes strikingly evident if one compares it with the dominant spirit of the nineteenth century religious reform movement and the medieval Bhakti movement in India. Raja Ram Mohan Roy, in the ninentheenth centruy in India, opposed the caste system, idol worship, religious separatism, child marriage and the practice of sati. He advocated remarriage of widows, inter-caste marriages, English education and freedom of speech. He founded the Brahmo-Samaj based on this line of reforms.This spirit of reforms based on liberality, democracy and egalitarianism is also quite evident in the preachings of social reformers such as Gokhale, Ranade, Agarkar and others in western India.

Nevertheless, while keeping in mind the distinct contribution made by the nineteenth century religious reform movements, one should not overlook the fact that the Bengal renaissance as well as its counterpart in Maharashtra were essentially sponsored by upper caste elites who were initially exposed to western liberal ideas, values and aspirations based on democratic. Although they came in sharp conflict with Sanatan orthodox Hindu religious protagonists, their impact was by and large confined to certain selected intellectual circles.

In sharp contrast to this upper caste sponsored religious reform movements, Jotirao Phule through the Satyashodhak Samaj founded by him in 1873 stood for more egalitarian reforms keeping in view the interests of the lower castes, particularly peasant castes. Modern intellectuals such as Phule developed an ideology which sought to use a revitalized Hindu tradition as the spiritual and moral centre around which the liberal modernism of the west could be created. This is also dubbed as "eastern morals and western science". The upper caste elites accepted the Aryan theroy of race which had implication of identifying them ethnically with their British conquerors rather than a majority of their countrymen, which traced civilization in India from the Aryan conquest and which provided a new pseudo-scientific justification for the caste hierarchy. They also developed an economic theory which looked to the capitalist development of India freed from the destructive bonds of British imperialism. Hence, they opposed foreign exploitation without considering the exploitation of workers by the nation's capitalists or that of peasants by landlords and the lower bureaucracy.

Against this presumption, Phule argued that a majority of Indians were dark skinned non-Aryans. The majorities of Indians were peasants and had no hope either in the near or distant future of becoming members of the bureaucratic elite or capitalists, large or small. The liberal modernization of Hindu culture and the capitalist development of India did not conform to their interests.

In this context, it is interesting to note that the internal conditions created as a result of the introduction of the modernization by the British in the 19th century paved way for the emergence of religious reform movements which in a sense also articulated the aspirations of the rising bourgeois, and the decadence and utter bankruptcy of the capitalist system in resolving any of the basic economic, political, social or cultural problems. The crisis of legitimacy, it has created conditions giving rise to a new aggressive religious fundamentalism particularly since the last few decades.

The modern version of Hinduism itself is based on the concoction and distortion of earlier historical traditions and an unfortunate identification of nationalism with Hinduism since the 19th century, with sufficient room for the future distortion. Hinduism, as popularly percieved today, is a downright reactionary formation and rules out any possibility of the emergence of any form of liberation theology within its folds.

The second essay on syncretism while dealing with a variety of interpretations of this widely prevalent phenomenon, seeks to bring out its relevance in the Indian context. In the case of India, syncretism of adoption of religious traditions has been an all-embracing phenomenon. Sila Khan in this context proposes a more interesting classification of syncretic traditions in this country. As per the proposition, syncretic traditions among religious communities in this country could be classified into four distinct categories:

(1) Divine power or charisma may attract devotees, regardless of their origin, around a particular religious figure. For example, the worship of a Sufi saint like Moinuddin Chisti by Hindus and that of a goddess performed by Muslims, with the hope of securing boons.

(2) There is in some situations a tendency to cling to one's former beliefs. For instance, some Muslims continue to worship a Hindu deity they did before their conversion.

(3) All over the sub-continent, a number of Muslim saints are still regarded as the guardians and protectors of Hindu or Jain Shrines. Angar Shah, for instance, at the entrance of the Jain sacred complex of Shatrunjaya Palitana in Gujarat. Vavar is the guardian deity of the god Ayappa at the shrine of Sabarmala in Kerala.

(4) Apart from this, there are syncretic shrines where Hindu and Muslim elements seem to co-exist within one single tradition and where the saints have a dual identity, for instance, the legend of Satya Pir in Bengal or Ramdev Pir.

Much of the violence, as Rama Shyam in her unpublished Ph.D. dissertation suggests, stems from religious inference. Such bigotry fails to take into account the day-to-day interaction in the human society that translates into mutual aid akin to the inner nature of human beings. Upholding this principle, terms as syncretism pose a challenge to the euro-centric way of looking at faith. Ashish Nandy's (1990) argument also revolves around two aspects of south Asian religion: Faith and ideology. By faith he implies religion as a way of life, a tradition that is 'definitionally' non- monolithic and operationally plural. By religion as ideology, Nandy means religion as a sub-national, national or cross-national identifier of populations contesting for or protecting non-religious, usually political or socio-economic interests. Such religious ideologies then get identified with one or more texts, rather than the ways of life of the believers. Ashish Nandy in his critique of religion as ideology also holds the view that secularism in India is not only irrelevant but has proved harmful to Indian society. He blames secularism and modernity for the new religious violence witnessed by this country in recent years. Nandy advocates that the Indian secular state has much to learn about morality from Hinduism, Islam and Sikhism, while Hinduism, Islam and Sikhism have nothing to learn from the secular state in this respect. As an alternative to secularism,

Nandy stands for the recovery of India's traditional religious tolerance. Likewise, Hindu nationalism, Nandy argues is nothing but an offshoot of Nehruvian state imposed secularism which leaves people no choice.

Nevertheless, as Akeel Bilgrami suggests, nationalism is more a omnibus and vague formulation to analyse. There are a variety of ingredients that go into a particular nationalism at different stages and sometimes even at the same stage. One cannot lump together Palestinian nationalism with Zionists or for that matter German nationalism. It can have instinctive ties to social democracy, liberal democracy, autocracy or fascism.

Similarly, the monolithic, majoritarian, Brahminic version of Hinduism as popularized by the Sangh Parivar is not just an offshoot of or a reaction to state-imposed secularism or modernity, as its construction process goes a long way into the recesses of Indian history and has helped perpetuate the most remarkably resilient, non-egalitarian social formation in the world. It is actually the product of sustained efforts over centuries on part of the upper castes to sustain their hold over the Hindu rashtra.

Likewise, Nandy and several other scholars pleading for syncretism or luminal movement, idealize indigenous religious tradition, its tolerance and its extensive acceptance among masses. Indian society, historically, right from an early period, has not only witnessed multiple religious and social traditions, but also clashes of traditions at different levels at various historical junctures right from the vedic period till the advent of the British rule in this country. Nandy's justification of and blanket support to Hinduism, as it is widely understood, is a predominantly upper caste, Brahminic version, popularized in the medieval period, especially after the advent of the Muslim rule in this country. This was projected as an ideological construction in the context of the vulnerability of the orthodox Brahminic traditions, in the face of the growing popularity of the Bhakti movement and the egalitarian values of Islam as projected by Sufi saints.

The third essay of this study focuses on the role and relevance of the Gurus and Sants, as Romila Thaper so aptly suggests, the cult of denouncers in Indian society since vedic times. The organized groups of renouncers in the post-vedic period, as she argues, were neither negating the society to which they belonged nor trying to radically alter it, but rather they were seeking to establish a parallel society.

Inherent in this attempt was the notion of dissent, but its articulation was often ambiguous.

The denouncers do not necessarily represent a religious sect but often an order constituting an alternative lifestyle, in many ways contradictory to that of his original social group.

The mid-first millennium has largely seen the breakup of tribal society and the emergence of the monolithic centralized state power, the emergence of a host of sects such as Nirganthas, the Ajivikas and later the Buddhist, as well as the various Carvaka sects. The main body of monks came from the lower social orders such as artisans, fishermen, hunters and basket-weavers. The tantric-yogic combination was predominant in the relatively less Hinduised border regions around Assam, being a channel by which foreign elements were assimilated into Hinduism, giving rise to the sub-stratum culture of obscure families and castes and their assimilation into the political and economical vortex of the western tradition via the system of land grants. The Siddhacharyas of this cult were mostly from the lower castes and this would be also true of the Nathpanthis. This sub-stratum culture was opposed to the orthodox tradition, an opposition which came to be symbolically expressed in tantric rituals, much of which is a reversal of Brahminic values.

Bhakti-Movement

The Bhakti movement which largely prevailed during the medieval period also deserves close appraisal as it sharply differs from the earlier cults of denouncers. It also needs special attention as its major proponents pose a striking contrast to the cults of godmen, gurus and other varieties that emerged during the post-independence period. Although the initiation of the Bhakti movement could be traced to the sixth and seventh centuries with Alwars and Nayanas in South India, in medieval India its spread was for more extensive and it exercised a deeper impact in many parts of the country.

In Maharashtra, several devotional sects came up, of which the warkari sect proved to be the most influential.

The devotional cult of Vitthal, it is significant to note, was not monopolized by any one sect. It has incorporated various sects like the Nath, Dutt, Chaitanya, Anand and Sufi.

From Dyaneshwar to Tukaram, no saints from the Warkari sect felt the need of kingly or princely support, or were interested in any kind of gift of land. They did not depend on the generosity of the wealthy. Through their own living example, the performance of *kirtans* and expounding of philosophy and religion, they carried on their work with a missionary zeal. But once a religious movement becomes well organized, it gives rise to vested interests that alienate the leaders from the followers. This is why the Maharashtrian saints did not start *Maths*. Tukaram had exhorted Kirtankars not to accept food where they performed *kirtan* and renounce all kind of pride and hypocrisy.

Kabir is the most outstanding exponent, often ambiguous, of the Bhakti movement in Northern India. He stressed on the fundamental equality of man as reflected in the earlier writings of the Siddhas and the Nath Panthis and this tradition continued in the later sixteenth and seventeenth century writings of Guru Nanak, Dadu, Dayal and other saints as those of Bihar.

While Kabir, Raidas, Rohan, Dadu and others believed in the basic equality of all specially in the position of the Brahman contrast to in the caste hierarchy. In other words in Bhakti movement there are two contradictory current, ie.. At the religious level there is no discrimination based on caste in terms of one's devotion is God, but in secular society secular distinctions were not disapproved.

Basically, the saints expressed disapproval of social distinctions by seeking to identify themselves with the sufferings of the common man, although they choose to express themselves in religious terms.

Sufi saints also played a similar role during the medieval period. They opposed the tyranny of the powerful. They preached against social inequality and struggled against the prevalent orthodoxy and blind faith. Their following also predominantly came from the lower strata, irrespective of religion.

In the concluding remarks, this essay seeks to bring out the sharp difference between the ancient cult of renouncers and the medieval Bhakti movement saints and the modern gurus. Renouncers in the ancient Indian society, right from the Upanishad to the Mauryan and Gupta periods, played a significant role in articulating the socio-economic and political transformation that was taking place in Indian society at various historical junctions. Not only they articulated this trend of transformation, they also registered their dissent by evolving an alternate style of living, a parallel philosophy or school of thought, entering into debate with what they considered the outdated established religious school. The protest started with challenging vedic formulation, animal and human sacrifice associated with Yagna, to a philosophy that Buddhists call the middle path, which facilitated trade and commerce and also provided some semblance of solace by starting Sanghams based on equality, simplicity and high ethical values vis-a-vis the destruction of the tribal communities that took place with the emergence of the state as an established institution in early Indian society. Similarly other schools or sects as Lokayat, Siddha and Nath cults and some other tantric sects also articulated the sentiments of the lower strata of Hindu society and in a sense also could channel their discontent and register their protest against the dominance of upper castes and their established schools of religious philosophy.

The medieval Bhakti movement also, beginning with the Alwars and Nayarats - devotional cults in South India, subsequently culminated in practically all parts of the country. It circulated the dissent, protest and the desire for reform of the lower strata against the oppression and domination of upper and particularly Brahmin castes in Indian society. Medieval saints, most of whom came from the lower strata, popularised Bhakti by the use of vernacular media, simplifying devotional practices, and by encouraging women to participate in religious worship. Bhakti saints set up a unique precedent by their lifestyle. Practically all of them led a simple life, most of them earned their own living, preached simplicity and never accepted any gift, even food, from their followers. They even despised kings, nobles and such other dignitaries and by and large taught that they are the root cause of people's misery. They set up a strikingly different model of religious pursuits, which included austerity, honesty, transparency, simplicity of language and life style and exclusive stress on lower strata and women for worship.

Modern godmen, however, pose a strong contrast to them with their fabulous wealth, support from corporates and the political and administrative hierarchy, their huge institutional set up, their corrupt practices, and hypocracy, appearing more as charlatans compared to the medieval saints.

The fourth article in this series talks about the prolific growth of godmen, gurus, sants and bapus. Apart from godmen and gurus, there are other numerous categories such as palmists, astrologers, vastu shastris, chhaya shastris, tantrics, visionaries and others who command a large following.

Post 80s, India seems to have witnessed an extensive spread of this phenomenon. It is not accidental, given that the post 80s period has witnessed profound change in economic policy and the political and social orientation of our major political parties, especially of the Indian National Congress. Thus the decisive shift in Congress policy and an open overture to placate Hindu sentiments was certainly instrumental in consolidating the Hindutva forces and also indirectly landing support to the growing popularity of the major godmen and women who have hardly any inhibition in exhibiting their pro-Hindu and anti-Muslim bias.

Modern godmen and gurus invariably drop hints of their miracles, supernatural powers and ability to resolve all problems faced by their devotees, in contrast to the simplicity, humbleness and the absence of any such pretensions among the Bhakti saints of medieval India. The fourth essay in this volume deals with the modern godmen and their origin in the guru phenomenon in this country. The guru phenomenon seems to be a peculiar feature in Asia, especially in the Indian society. This essay, while attempting to trace the origin of the guru phenomenon argues that early vedic literature does not refer to the Lord guru, as the vedic religion essentially revolves around sacrificial rituals associated with yagna. During the Upanishad period, when the focus turned to the pursuit of knowledge, the ashram system was established. The acharya who taught students in such gurukuls was also called the guru.

Mangalvadi holds following five sociological factors as being of special significance for the acceptance of guruism, namely:

(1) The nature of education in Aryan society
(2) The esoteric nature of Upanishad and later Indian religious scriptures
(3) The class or caste system with Brahminic dominance in religious affairs and sporadic reactions to it
(4) The authoritarian structure of Indian family life and the repressive puritanism of Indian society and
(5) The absence of printed books.

The guru in the Upanishad tradition is a realised individual, one who is intellectually supposed to know the Vedas and experientially dwells on the absolute Brahman. The epics, in contrast, highlight the divinity of the guru and the consequent reverence and worship of him.

The ascendency of the Brahmin class along with the heterodox teachers of Buddhism and Jainism gave impetus to the ascetical groups within Hinduism. The indispensability of the gurus is stressed in all Smriti literature.

It is in the tantric tradition that the gurus acquire extraordinary importance. In tantric tradition, the diksha or initiation of a pupil gains utmost significance and without the guru, there cannot be any initiation. In the Natha Siddha tradition too, the guru occupies supreme position. Both these cult traditions are influenced by the tantric traditions. Among the Bhakti saints in the medieval period too, the Nath sect's influence is evident.

With the advent of the British rule, the guru phenomenon based on the earlier Nath, Sidha and other tantra sects and subsequently evident in the medieval Bhakti movement lost its earlier prominence. The British administration and scholars were inclined towards accepting the dominant social and cultural ethos of the traditional Indian society based on the supremacy of the Brahmin experts.

Apart from that, even Indian scholars and social reformers who were exposed to Western ideals, development and value system based on the liberal and democratic framework of European and particularly the British society, also projected classical vedic ideals and the social order as having all ingredients of such a liberal outlook. The evils of Indian society were knowingly or unknowingly attributed to the impact of the alien systems of the Mughals and others.

The national movement and a large number of our national leaders from the Indian National Congress subscribed to such an outlook. The nationalist leaders who also by and large came from the higher castes and better off sections of Indian society also found it quite convenient to adopt and advocate such an outlook. Such a back drop hardly left any space for the rival religious or cultural groups as was the case in the medieval and earlier phases of Indian society to project and propagate their alternate religious and social positions and practices. Thus, the guru phenomenon thrived in this cultural and religious interface.

In the earlier post-independence period too, when India had attained a comparatively new threshold of economic, political and social development, one hardly notices any significant spread of the guru phenomena. It is essentially during the last three or four decades that one witnesses an extensive spread of the guru phenomena all over the country. The wide spread growth of the guru phenomena is largely linked with the rapid and growing influence of the Hindutva forces in this country. Several other factors have also contributed to the rapid and amazing spread of gurus or godmen in the recent years. We can only enumerate some of the significant factors which we think have played a more vital role in this direction.

Electronic media, with its extensive spread since the 1980s with the relay of the serials Ramayana and Mahabharat also significantly boosted the appeal of communal forces which gained a larger foothold in Indian society.

Apart from this, the forces unleashed by neoliberalism with its exclusive stress on unregulated market mechanism have also facilitated the spread and popularity of the guru phenomena. The world of gurus and gurumais, with its infinite variety of appeals cultivated by its seasoned operators has become a big attraction cutting across caste and class borders and thereby has successfully created a huge market. The devotional audio and video cassettes that fuel this phenomena alone fetch over crores of rupees annually in the Indian market. If one takes into account the huge amounts of money generated through T.V. and other serials based on the almost infinite variety of mythological figures, probably the financial market created and total profit generated from such programmes would exceed the total capital generated from all other entertainment markets put together.

As Prof. Panikar has aptly argued, since independence the extensive spread of religiosity and commoditization of religion largely account for the rapid rise of the guru-gurumai phenomena in the last more than three decades in India.

The state patronage, open admiration and presence of the prominent political leaders, at the central as well as state level, at such events irrespective of their allegiance to any particular political party is also responsible for the rise and institutionalization of the guru/gurumai cults in India. The corporate sector has also extended large scale support by the presence and sponsorship by industrial magnates and business tycoons of Ramkathas, Bhagwat Saptahs, Shiv Parayans, Radha-Krishna celebrations, Gayatri Yagnas, and similar religious discourses and festivals initiated by modern godmen all over the country. Apart from this, other major factors instrumental in the rapid rise and popularity of the modern guru-gurumai phenomena are the increasing insecurity, alienation, despair experienced by practically all sections of the Indian population cutting across caste and class lines as a result of cut- throat competition and the inflated consumerism let loose by the global policy of neo-liberalism based on an unregulated market mechanism.

The subsequent four essays are based on the studies conducted on four eminent godmen, gurus or sants in western India. Though they are from western India, they are known nationally as well as internationally. These include Morari Bapu, Asaram Bapu, Bhagwan Rajneesh and Aniruddha Bapu. Rajneesh expired sometime back but his Ashram in Pune is still an attraction and a centre of inspiration for many Indian as well as western disciples.

The fifth essay in this volume makes an exhaustive assessment of Acharya Rajneesh's work and his distinct contribution along with the glaring contradictions in his philosophy and practices.

Rajneesh's radical presentation, freshness of style, especially his outrageous messages attracted a wide variety of people - the inquisitive, the adventurous, liberals and radicals, young and old, men and women. They saw in Rajneesh a modern man, critical, sexually liberated, a person of a different sensibility and also an anti-establishment guru.

Although Rajneesh denounced all established religions, two major currents of thought which decisively influenced his perspective are Buddhist philosophy and tantric practices. But his teachings have very little in common with the original preachings of Buddha. Rajneesh was actually more influenced by Zen Buddhism which also became an integral part of Mahayana Buddhism, the idealist distorted version of original Buddhism, or the doctrine of void, a slate of emptiness propounded by Nagarjuna which also become an integral part of Mahayana teachings.

Rajneesh with his advocacy of Shunavoda or the state of void as a perfect state of bliss actually followed in the footsteps of the Mahayanist School. Thus, Rajneesh's calling himself '*Osho*' at the final phase of his life was nothing but a crude mockery of all that Buddha stood for. Similarly, Rajneesh's interpretation of the tantra has a close link with the tantric Buddhists who believed that *sukha* is not possible at all without the body. Rajneesh finds the possibility of perfect bliss on the basis of our ordinary experiences of pleasure based on basic physical impulses. His entire thesis on sex to super consciousness also rests on this foundation. As Rajneesh insists, 'If you wish to be liberated, be ever devoted to it.' This understanding of the tantrism is again a gross distortion of the original basis of the tantric philosophy.

Sudhir Kakar's observations in this context succinctly convey the reasons which must have prompted Rajneesh to adopt tantra as an integral part of his teachings, as this was convenient to boost his image as a 'rebel' against Hindu religious orthodoxy. Moreover, it also helped establish his advocacy of sex as a source of divinity. Tantra could also fit into the conceptual framework he evolved to attract his western disciples. In the process he contradicted the basic tenets of his preachings but that hardly bothered him. His concept of Nirvana, void or a state of perfect bliss borrowed from Zen or Mahayana Buddhism flatly contradicts dehavada, the proto materialist basis of tantric philosophy.

It is not surprising to find that Rajneesh could get away with several gross contradictions and inconsistencies in his teachings. This was possible for the simple reason that an average Indian (or for that matter even western) listener knowns so little about religious scriptures or various schools of philosophy that it hardly requires much effort to exploit his or her ignorance and gullibility.

Rajneesh is not the only one, most of the godmen in India as well as other countries have managed to thrive by taking advantage of the innocence of their average followers and playing upon their psychological needs of dependence, emotional insecurity, intense sense of alienation, frustration and anxieties, all of which are becoming so wide spread in modern society.

The sixth essay, an appraisal of Morari Bapu, has been guided by various considerations. Morari Bapu is unique in many ways. He is a modern guru and claims no following in terms of disciples. Unlike several gurus of his stature, he is easily accessible, and does not claim any special power for miracles. He also suggests that he does not believe in superstition. He has no pretention of tracing his legacy from any distinct guru parampara (tradition) or any well established lineage, his past in terms of his childhood, family background , social and financial status, educational performance etc. There are hardly any pretensions in his life style, habits, family life and routine activities.

He is widely admired as a unique exponent of Tulsidas's Ram Charit Manas. His presentation is simple and lucid. His command over Gujarati language, his sharp memory, his sense of humour, his musical recitation, his grasp of Gujarati literature, his physical fitness to conduct recitals for hours and also modesty are quite impressive, despite the fact that he comes from a small, backward village of Saurashtra, from a poor family background and limited educational qualifications. Nevertheless, it is important to note that there is a close correspondence of his rising curve of popularity for Katha recital and the extensive campaign for Ramjanmabhoomi and the construction of the Ram temple in Ayodhya, culminating in the destruction of the Babri Masjid in the early 1990s. Thus, it also reflects on the Hindu revivalist upsurge with the increasing popularity of the discourse on the Ram Charit Manas in the last more than four decades.

There is a gross contradiction between Morari Bapu's preaching of the cherished ideals of truth, love, compassion and non-violence as the core of the Tulsi Ram Charit Manas as he upholds and the practice of the covert or overt connivance with the state in Gujarat under Narendra Modi's regime of unleashing an unprecedented communal carnage in 2002 which led to a pogrom against Muslims. Even after over a decade of the communal riot, Muslims are still exposed to all kinds of insecurity and hostility in many parts of the state. We have focused on Morari Bapu especially because he has acquired a wide reputation as a promoter of communal harmony and sympathy for the cause of minorities.

The second section exclusively deals with the archeological findings about the society, material culture, geographical locations of towns and Sri Lanka and other vital data of that period. This appraisal seems essential to us as our presumptions and popular myths of this period deserve severe examination.

The third section deals with the riddle of the Ramayan. There are not only hundreds but thousands of versions of the Ramayan which are popular not only in different regions of this country, but also in many parts of Asia. Hence brief perusals of this wide variety of versions of Ramayan deserve serious consideration.

The fourth section provides a profile of Morari Bapu. We have attempted to provide a faithful account of Morari Bapu's distinct achievements, unique traits as a modern guru, his biographical sketch and other details as made available from the website on Bapu and from his biographies.

The fifth section deals with the gross contradiction between the preaching and practice of Morari Bapu. Morari Bapu's public image and contention about commitment to the Gandhian values of non-violence, truth, love and compassion (which he also claims are the values upheld by Tulsi Ramcharitmanas) and the gross distortions and violations in the application of these ideals. Tulsi's Brahminic bias and his adherence to the Hindu dharma shastras' code of degradation of position of women and lower social strata of Indian society and upholding of chaturvarna and karma principles (siddhant) based on the hierarchical caste system are quite visible in his works. Morari Bapu also does not show any hesitation in identifying with BJP and VHP's communal agenda on the erection of the Ram mandir in Ayodhya on the spot where the Babri masjid is demolished and on similar demands like abolition of article 370 on Kashmir from the Indian constitution.

The seventh essay in this volume provides the critical appraisal of Gujarat-based Asaram Bapu who also commands a large following from the western as well as northern states of India. Asaram Bapu is unique in terms of his preaching, and partly also practice, from the many other traditional as well as modern saints in India. The other saints in India either owe allegiance to a particular religious sect, or to some distinct religious or spiritual legacy. Several other saints have also specialized in religious discourse in terms of recital of some epic narration and have become popular for the discourse on Ram katha, Bhagvat katha, Shiv puran or Bhagvat gita. After independence, the Swami Chinmayanand focused on teachings of Vedanta and especially imparting knowledge, with his unique interpretation of Bhagvat Gita and its spiritual message.

Asaram Bapu is strikingly different from this galaxy of other saints in the sense that he does not follow any fixed pattern in any of his discourses. He neither sticks to any particular religious scriptures nor he dwells at length on vedic or upanishadic teaching, nor he follows the actual content of the Bhagvat Gita. He does not even casually mention Tulsi Ramcharitmanas or Bhagvat Gita. If at all reference is given to any of these religious scriptures, it is so incidental or casual that one can't take such references seriously. This becomes evident from the interesting titles of his major audio and video cassettes, such as:

(1) *Madhu Jeevan Kaise Banayein?* (How to make life sweet?)
(2) *Jeevan Unnat Kaise Banayein?* (How to make lifeprosperous?)
(3) *Sansar Musafirkhana Hai* (Our life is like a retiring room)
(4) *Geeta Bhagvat Saar* (Essence of Bhagvat Geeta)

Similarly he has a series of video cassettes on *mantra jaap* (recital of mantra-magical spell).

Bapu is in a sense like the many other gurus of such variety who have mastered the technique of hypnotizing their audiences. Their grasp of mass psychology or audience expectation is so deep that they could play on the audience's sentiments, and easily bring them under their spell.

The focus of our study on Asaram Bapu was his well established Ashram in Surat. The present Surat Ashram is located at a distance of fifteen kilometers from Surat station. The ashram is spread across around 25 acres and is located near the bank of the Tapti river. The location is very peaceful and pleasant. The initiation of this ashram could be traced to 1985. When the ashram was started, it had only one room made of ordinary clay. Now it has become a huge palace. It seems it started with the acquisition of the government land, and gradually the ashram encroached upon the farmers land located in the vicinity. Earlier this area was not within the limits of the Municipal Corporation, but now since it has come under the corporation, there is lot of pressure from different quarters for the removal of illegal encroachment of land by Ashram. There are quite a few cases in the high court regarding this encroachment. Such illegal occupation and land encroachment is not an isolated case. This seems to be true of practically all the huge Ashrams built by Asaram in many parts of the country and legal battles with the farmers, village panchayats or corporations in such locations have become common features of such establishments.

During the Holi celebration which our field investigators witnessed, around three to five lakh people from different parts of the country visited this ashram, many of them staying for over three days. Preparation for this festival is very well managed which requires great administrative efficiency, resources, man power, tents, parking place, elaborate arrangements for food, stay, water, sanitation, toilets along with huge publicity and marketing skills.

Modern godmen and gurus also derive very rich dividends from such celebrations. Such celebrations also provide an opportunity to exercise political influence and enable such gurus to sort out their personal problems under this context.

Most of the modern gurus and godmen with their huge establishments or empires have been also accused of big scandals. For example, Satya Sai Baba, Swami Mukatanand, Bhagwan Rajneesh and even Shankaracharyas apart from the Mahants or religious heads of *akhadas* or religious organizations, especially in Ayodhya and other places, have been shrouded with gossip, scandals, corruption and crimes. In the chapter on AsaramBapu we provide a brief account of the major scandals surrounding his Ahmedababd, Surat and Chindwara Ashrams. The mysterious death of 2 children in Chindwara Ashram incited a police enquiry. Similar incidents have also been reported from the Ahmedabad ashram and other parts of Gujarat. The sudden departure of a very trusted disciple and medicinal stores claiming cure for all kinds of ailments are other areas of corruption reported. The outrage and protest regarding all the malpractices get unrelenting support cutting across party lines, ranging from the prominent BJP leaders such as ex-prime minister Atal Bihari Bajpai and Lalkrishna Advani to George Fernandes, ex-prime minister Chandrashekhar to Shiv Sena leader Uddhav Thackray.

The essay concludes with the observation that how the trinity of Hindu saints, political leaders and the state with the implicit connivance of Asaram Bapu need not be an accidental phenomenon.

The last essay of this volume is devoted to the study of Shree Aniruddha Bapu, a prominent Maharastrian saint who also is strikingly different in the galaxy of the modern godmen. Unlike other godmen or gurus, Aniruddha Bapu does not claim to have any distinct religious affiliation or initiation from any known or even unknown guru. One hardly finds even any hint of his receiving blessing from any guru. There is no reference of his religious association with any particular sect or religious school. There are no records of either he or his family having any inclination for the worship of Shirdi Sai Baba. Yet he emerges as a godman, reincarnation of Shirdi Sai Baba and also of Ram on his own, without any spiritual lineage.

Aniruddha Bapu's ways are quite unorthodox. Trained as a medical doctor, he enjoyed smoking and theatre. Not donning attire similar to other religious gurus separates him from the usual godmen. His old pals from Nair Hospital noted that he was a prolific reader and thinker and had wide-ranging interests apart from the medicine like literature, politics, history and philosophy.

Unlike other recent godmen or gurus, a sizeable number of his followers come from a middle class Brahmin background. Aniruddha Bapu is a Brahmin and a proud one who is highly conscious of his caste and the distinct caste attributes. Similarly, Bapu also differs from the rest of godmen in terms of his unique programme of disaster management activities, medical camps and welfare, educational and sports activities in interior tribal areas in Maharashtra. His style of functioning is distinct from other godmen and gurus in India. Similarly, unlike other godmen or gurus, Aniruddha Bapu is known not only for his religious or spiritual eminence but as a visionary who is extensively interested in analyzing the national and global political and economic scenario, including the international correlation of power blocks. His exhaustive appraisal of the possibility of the Third World War, its initial spark in the Palesitne-Israel war, and all major powers joining the global war, and India entering and leading and ultimately emerging as a victorious power in the final scenario is unique and appeals not only to the right leaning follower but also to proponents of nation state theories. Aniruddha Bapu also drops hints about the possibility of his playing a major role in terms of guiding and providing effective strategy for winning the battle (the comparison obviously being with Krishna who led the battle of Mahabharat resulting in the Pandavs' victory over the Kauravs).

This exhaustive appraisal clearly brings out the distinct traits of Aniruddha Bapu in comparison with other godmen and gurus in India. We find it quite interesting to compare and contrast Shree Aniruddha Bapu and the late Rajneesh on academic eminence and sharp intellect, the latter also being a unique modern guru of the twentieth century. The contrast between the two is sharp, with Aniruddha Bapu being a brilliant student, highly qualified with an excellent academic record - a gold medalist who gained his MD specialising in rheumatology. He also has a good command over three languages - English, Marathi and Hindi. He is also a great scholar of Indian scriptures as well as modern medical science, history of different civilizations and the backdrop of the two World Wars with good insight into the international and national scenario. His scientific approach and rational frame of mind is very much visible in the systematic and effective holistic training course provided. The standard text book brought out by Shree Aniruddha Academy of Disaster Management is evidence of him being a shrewd modern guru unlike Rajneesh who was a liberated unorthodox modern guru. In contrast to Rajneesh, Aniruddha Bapu is highly traditional and orthodox in his outlook, in terms of his interpretation of the Indian religious scriptures and dogmatic adherence and promotion of the Sanatani Brahminic philosophy and values.

Concluding remarks

Religion, globalization and alienation bring out the recent trend of religious revivalism along with the neo-liberal policy perused by monopoly finance capital under the hegemony of the United States of America. We are also of the view that the recent appeal of religious fundamentalism should also be viewed in the context of the total alienation of the individual from his being in terms of withering away of any space for his private existence in this phase of the decadence of global capital.

Finally, we would like to stress that there are glaring contrasts between the modern godmen and gurus and the medieval saints who flourished from the11th to almost the 16th century in many parts of India. The traditions set up by medieval saints such as Kabir, Nanak, Dadu, Ravidas, Garibdas, Charandas, Miralhar and others in northern India and Varkari saints like Gyandev, Namdev, Eknath and Tukaram in Maharashtra or Narsi Mehta in Saurashtra are strikingly different from the style of functioning and precedents set up by modern godmen and gurus in the last four decades in India.

The medieval saints' role as aptly summed by Malik was dissent, protest, reform or at times even rebellion against the conservative, conventional and dogmatic preachings and practices of the upper caste and especially Brahmin pandits who monopolized rights over Vedic and other religious scriptures and exploited and oppressed the lower castes, women and other toiling strata with the full connivance of the ruling strata. The medieval saints, with their simple lifestyle, modesty, honesty, selfless devotional mode of worship, and the simple, poetic rendering of religious scriptures in regional languages such as Hindi, Marathi, Gujarati and their invocation to all strata inclusive of women, children and the lowest sections of Indian society to worship and participate in religious rituals and ceremonies challenged the monopoly of the Brahmin pandits and their interpretation of the Vedas. In sharp contrast to the modern godmen and gurus, medieval saints lived a simple life, with transparency and earned their livelihood often by their traditional craft based on manual labour. They consciously avoided building up an institutional complex around them and expected similar simplicity, transparency and devotion from their followers. They never posed as a divine being and did not demand such worship from their followers.

Modern godmen and gurus however build empires around them and maintain close links with the political and administrative hierarchy, corporate magnates and elites in modern Indian society. Transparency and simplicity are totally alien to them and quite a few of them are involved in litigation over the land often illegally occupied by them for their Ashrams. They are involved in various scandals ranging from sex to murder, to property disputes and conspiracy in the process of expanding their empire, often illegally. Their wealth is fabulous and it is not possible to estimate or arrive at any correct figure of their wealth. Similarly, it is difficult to provide any clear picture of their manipulation of income, tax evasion and the types of diversions of the huge funds at their command. Obviously without the blessings of the political and administrative machinery it is impossible to get away from such fraudulent practices.

As a matter of fact we can sum up by stating that modern godmen and gurus ideally represent the rotten, corrupt system that prevails in this country.

1

The Role of Hinduism in Modern Indian Society

India has witnessed a massive upsurge of traditional as well as modern religio-mystical cults of godmen, swamis, gurus, shastris, bapus and bhagats particularly during the last three decades. Some of these cults operate at local, district or regional level while some have established an extensive network at national as well as international levels. Along with the new cults, the hold of various traditional religious sects has acquired new dimensions in recent years. The increasing politicization of religion in the last few years has also posed a serious dilemma with regards to the role of religion in modern Indian society.

It is not only in India but even in western countries, particularly even in industrially advanced nations like the U.S.A. that the new as well as traditional religious movements have gained an unprecedented momentum in recent years. The growing influence of religion in U.S.S.R. and China has also been widely reported. The powerful influence of the church in Polish solidarity movements and the Buddhist impact on the Vietnamese liberation struggle has also been acknowledged. The dominant role of the church in overthrowing the authoritarian regime in Philippines and the Buddhist monks' hold in the recent reactionary political upheaval in Ceylon cannot be overstressed. The decisive influence of Islamic fundamentalism in the Iranian revolution and several other Muslim countries has been sufficiently highlighted while the emergence and significance of liberation theology in Latin America would call for an independent appraisal.

The persistence and extension of religious influence in advanced western countries, in colonial and post-colonial nations of Asia, Africa and Latin America, and even in so called socialist societies has raised some basic questions with regard to the significance of religion in human society. Many sociologists and anthropologists on the basis of their studies of primitive as well as modern societies have come to the firm conclusion that it is impossible to visualize any present or even future society devoid of the presence of religion in some form or the other. They feel that the need for religion would be felt in all human societies, irrespective of their cultural or technological levels, or socio-economic systems as religion fulfills some basic urges, emotional needs and provides a sense of security to individuals. Several critics in this context have also pointed out the hollowness of the Marxist dictum of reducing the significance of religion as an opiate for the oppressed and exploited strata.

The Marxist View

It is true that vulgar Marxist appraisals have focused exclusively on the role of religion as opium for the poor, highlighting its reactionary significance for the toiling people. Nevertheless, such a dogmatic assertions should not be confused with historical, dynamic and objective approach evolved by Marx and Engels in their critique of religion.

A close perusal of the views expressed by Marx and Engels on religion as reflected in their various works mentions their observations on the radical significance of early Christianity, its peculiar origin and Jesus as messiah of the oppressed, and in their writing on the pesant war in Germany highlighting Munzer's effective use of image of early Chirastianity for raising the morale of the poor peasants. Their works on Hegel's philosophy of right, the Holy Family, the Jewish question among others reveal their deep concern for all relevant facts, their dynamic approach, examination and modification of their interpretations in the light of fresh appraisal and exposure to new situations, and the least dogmatic assertions, as the dominant features of their perspective on religion.

Marx and Engels in all probability were influenced by Tylor's view in tracing the origin of religion in the primitive man's sense of awe and fear in the face of an inexplicable nature, or religion emerging as fantastic reflection in man's mind of those external forces that control their daily life. It was however Engels who first pointed out that "while both magic and religion have their origin in humanity's lack of control over the forces of nature, religion however also reflects humanity's lack of control over the social forces that resulted from class domination."

References

Siegel, Paul N; The Meek and the Militant, PP 21-26, Oxford University Press 1987, pp. 21- 26.

Thapar, Romila: The Hindus and Their Isms - Syndicated Moksha? P 14, Seminar, September 1985, p. 14.

Mukherjee, Nirmal & Banerjee, Ashis: Neo-Nationalism. P 26, Seminar, September 85, p. 26.

Damodaran K: Man and Society, Delhi 1970, pp. 75, 84.

Omvedt, Gail: Cultural Revolt in a Colonial Society, Bombay 1976, p 99

Damodaran, K. Op. cit p. 88.

Kappen, S: In Search of a New God, Illustrated Weekly, June 9, 1985, p. 27-28.

2

Syncretism in the Indian Context: A Sociological Appraisal

Syncretism essentially implies the permeability and fluidity of religious situations. The Dictionary of Sociology as suggested by Fairchild defines syncretism as "The process of amalgamation of conflicting, or at least different, parties or principles of cultures - more specifically assimilation of foreign groups. The foreign elements disappear as psychological and cultural entities into the majority and the majority adopts both the individual and a selection and adoption of their cultural traits."

Generally speaking, syncretism has been associated with folk religion with reference to the practices of primitive societies. It has also been equated with popular religion, more evident in relatively non-modern societies.

Syncretism: A Variety of Interpretations

Both the views presented above as per Rama Shyam reflect a deep prejudice regarding the sociology of religion. Fairchild's explanation of the disappearance of the foreign elements somewhere suggests only the immigrants or minorities getting synchronized. One has seen in the case of India how syncretism or adoption of religious traditions has been an all embracing phenomenon. Even the second view of syncretism being mostly evident in non-modern societies also appears to be rather high-browed and tilted in favor of the world religions (Roy Burman, 1993 70[1]).

As rightly suggested by Peter der Veer (1994 P208[2]), as a broad process every religion is syncretistic since it constantly draws upon heterogeneous elements to the extent that it is often impossible for historians to unravel what comes from where. Eliade (1987[3]) also opines that social presupposition for the rise of syncretism can be the co-existence of various groups.

Roy Burman further classifies syncretism in terms of the power dimension. According to him syncretism could be classified into five categories: (a) Defensive Syncretism (b) Aggressive Syncretism (c) Recessive Syncretism (d) Adaptive Syncretism and (e) Pragmatic Syncretism. These categories are based on the nature of relationships and patterns of interaction among the various groups exposed to this process. [4]

While referring to syncretism, Peter Vander points out that in India syncretism is a trope in discourse of multi-culturalism and that scholarly discussion of syncretic phenomena such as Hindu worship of Sufi saints usually omits consideration of conflict or of the processes of expansion and contraction.[5]

Concepts Contesting Syncretism

While referring to syncretism, Mayaram argues that it tends to ignore the multiplicity of meaning which human agency seeks to comprehend the cosmos around. It restricts itself to a binary opposition of syncretism and anti-syncretism. Hence Mayaram prefers to use the term liminality - a term that takes into account a third space that seeks to transcend the binary mode of thought and understanding. In a sense, it also does away with the sacred-profane categorization through a peculiar combination of reverence and irreverence to the gods. This is evident in traditions where gods, as she suggests, are made fun of through poetic burlesque (In Mayaram's account, Bhim is associated with much of the comic relief in the Mewati The mahabharat (Mayaram, Shaila:

'Re-Thinking Meo Identity : Cultural Fault Line, Syncretism, Hybridity or Liminality in Comparative Studies of South Asia, Africa and the Middle East, Vol. XVII No.2, 1997)[6].

Liminality as a concept has been developed by Victor Turner in re-thinking approaches to anthropology. Drawing from William

Dilthey's theories, Turner expounded the thesis that the fundamental basis of human knowledge was the lived experience of human beings. Turner suggests that though we may attempt to understand society in terms of its structures and their functions, yet what forms meanings is the way people interact and experience within this structure. Hence an understanding of the relationship between thoughts, symbols, actions and interactions is the key to the making of people and their experiences. Within this framework, Turner talks of the things that happen between the structures - instances of heightened emotions and their impact. He defines these as the liminal and interstitial spaces where people come out of the routine. He departs significantly from traditional anthropology in that in his analysis is not so much what happens within the confines of social structures but what happens between and outside them that is important.

Linking the concept of liminality to rituals and festivals, Turner puts forward the idea of communities - people spontaneously emerging as social groups with love for each other and a sense of solidarity.

According to Turner, communities come into play during 'collective religious or political phenomena'. He explains that people who are normally divided and antagonistic can come together and transcend their differences in their common experience or humanity which in this case is defined within the liminal spaces. For Turner, these spaces may be a threat to social structures and cohesion, but he celebrates them to represent the positive potential that reaffirms solidarity and social bonds between people.[7]

Another concept which comes closer to this controversy is that of 'hybridity' evolved by Homi Bhabha (cited in Mayaram, 1997) that expresses the inter-cultural encounter. Hybridity implies how two entities combine to produce a third, with specific reference to cross cultural kinship/marriage. However, even this concept, as argued by Mayaram, falls into the trap of the pure verses the 'hybrid', thus implying a racial understanding of the universe. [8]

Sila Khan proposes a more interesting classification of syncretic traditions accordingly to their significance with regards to various quotidian practices among religious communities.

(1) Divine power or charisma (Shakti in the Hindu tradition, barkat in the Islamic) may attract devotees, regardless of their

origin, around a particular religious figure. For example, the worship of a Sufi saint like Moinuddin Chisti by Hindus and the worship of a goddess performed by Muslims with the hope of securing a boon.

(2) There is in some situations a tendency to cling to one's former beliefs. For instance, some Muslims continue to worship a Hindu deity as they did before their conversion.

(3) All over the sub-continent a number of Muslim saints are still regarded as the guardians and protectors of a Hindu or Jain Shrine - Angar Shah for instance, at the entrance of the Jain sacred complex of Shatrunjaya near Palitana in Gujrat. Vavar is the guardian deity of the god Ayyappa at the shrine of Sabarimalai in Kerala.

(4) Apart from this, there are syncretic cults where Hindu and Muslim elements seem to co-exist within one single tradition and where the saints have a dual identity. Sila Khan illustrates this phenomenon through practices recorded by scholars in different places. For example, the Legend of Satya Pir in Bengal recorded by Roy and the celebrated cult of the Panch Pir or Ramdev Pir. [9]

Syncretic cults are very prominent in the villages of Sunderban in West Bengal where the vagaries of nature take a heavy toll. Similarly cults related to healing practices are also abundant.

Since time immemorial syncretic practices are common around agricultural cycles as food abundance is the basis of human existence.

Important shrines similarly continue to remain decisive meeting points of religious communities in the Indian landscape. These shrines determine the importance of sacred places vis-a-vis religious syncretism and continue to be the centre of power, interaction and legitimacy in the realm of the lived religious experiences of people.

Cultural syncretism is also quite evident in art forms and festivals. Kabirpanthis, for instance, celebrate in Kabir's hymns the single God. Similarly the Sikhs reintegrate the teachings of Kabirpanthis into Hinduism in their Adi Granth and also the hymns of Sufi saints.

The Mount Mary festival celebrated in the month of September in Mumbai also attracts huge crowds for days together coming from all religious communities in India.

The Relevance of the Syncretic Discourse

The appraisal of the discourse on syncretism is quite important against the backdrop of extensive violence and communal disturbances in the last two decades in India. Much of the violence, as Rama Shyam suggests in her unpublished Ph.D. dissertation, stems from religious intolerance. Such bigotry fails to take into account the day-to-day interactions in human society that translates into an ethos of mutual aid akin to the innate nature of human beings. Upholding this principle, terms like syncretism or liminality pose a challenge to the Euro-centric way of looking at faith. Nandy argues (1990. 71) that the Eurocentric perception gradually came to be associated with the dominant culture of the colonial states in the region. It subsumes under it a set of clear polarities, centre vs. periphery, true faith vs. its distortions, civil vs. primordial and great traditions vs. local or small traditions.

Rooted in the secularization debate, Nandy's (1990) argument revolves around two aspects of South Asian religions: Faith and ideology. By faith he implies religion as a way of life, a tradition that is by definition non-monolithic and operationally plural. He prefers to use the term definitionally because unless a religion is geographically and culturally confined to a small area, it has a way of life, in effect, to turn into a confederation of a number of ways of life which are linked by a common faith that has some theological space for the heterogeneity which everyday life introduces (Nandy, 70). It is in this light that he establishes the difference between Iranian and Indonesian Islams, two cultures which can be divided by the same faith, two forms of Islam that are interlocking, not isomorphic, in relation to each other. By religion as ideology, Nandy means religion as a sub-national, national or cross-national identifier of populations contesting for or protecting non-religious, usually political or socio-economic interests. Such religions as ideologies then get identified with one or more texts, rather than ways of life of the believers and come to denote the relatively purer forms of the religion.

It is this religion as ideology approach that the secularization debate aspires to counter. However, in attempting to do so, it discounts the multiplicity of meanings that emerge out of daily social interactions and human situations. What becomes evident is the discomfort of the notion of secularism with the fluid definitions of self characteristic to many South Asian cultures. Nandy suggests that such a self which can be conceptually viewed as a configuration of selves invokes and reflects the configurative principles of religions as faith and is incompatible with the idea of secularism that chalks out an area in public life where religion is not admitted. Qualifications of this aspect of religion lie in slogans like "We are Indians first, Hindus second". Religion is constantly relegated to the private background by the public arena which has no space for faith.[10]

Similarly as Rama Shyam argues, the sociology of religion has come a long way from rigid categorization in terms of great tradition of urban elite and little tradition of folk. But despite ample instances of refuting the claims of the "either/or" configuration, we find that this tendency wields sway over much scholarly writings.

Syncretism comes across as a process that is ongoing and very much a part of all religious traditions. It is, as Veer (1994) indicates, an aspect of religious interactions over time. Every religious tradition goes through certain adaptations and accommodations. It originates, takes root and develops through an exchange of belief systems over a period of history, while moving from one locale to the other. It needs to be driven home that despite efforts at homogenizing religious beliefs, what has sustained is the syncretic appeal of religious experiences that bring people of different faiths together in a celebration of their mass consciousness that surpasses the normative dogmas usually laid down in scriptural texts or orthodox directives. One feels closer to the spirituality of the divine and seeks comfort in what Rabindranath Tagore calls the religions of man.[11]

When it comes to every day religious experiences, scriptural directives are modified, as Rama Shyam suggests, suiting the more practical needs of human beings. This leads to complete dissolution of the boundaries between the so called 'great' and 'little' traditions. Theocracy gives way to spiritualism and the quest for happiness and solace translates into the quest for the divine and this amalgamation finally results in a form of religion that emerges from the daily lives of human beings and it is virtually impossible for institutionalized or codified doctrines - that are supposed to remain constant - to deal with such spontaneity of social upheavals. (This appraisal of syncretism is entirely based on the unpublished thesis of Rama Shyam submitted for Ph.D. in Tata Institute of Social Sciences. Chapter-II of the dissertation.)

Ashish Nandy in his critique of religion as ideology also holds the view that secularism in India is not only irrelevant but has proved harmful to Indian society. He blames secularism and modernity for the new religious violence witnessed by this country in recent years. He characterizes secularism as a child of modernity and colonialism as a product of Western science and rationality. It functions as the ideology of the modern state, which Nandy thinks of as a source of most contemporary problems. He argues that it is the secular state and its elite, with its instrumental rationality and a moral and manipulative technocratic managerial ethos, that has been responsible for the greatest atrocities of this century from the Third Reich to the Gulags, from Hiroshima to the anti-Sikh riots in Delhi. Thus, Nandy's rejection of secularism, as Joseph Tharamangalam sums up, is rooted in a two-fold critique, a critique of modern culture and society that approvingly and respectively draws on the Gandhi of Hind Swaraj and a critique of the secular state. Nandy advocates that the Indian secular state has much to learn about morality from Hinduism, Islam and Sikhism, while Hinduism, Islam and Sikhism have nothing to learn from the secular state in this respect. As an alternative to secularism, Nandy stands for the recovery of India's traditional religious tolerance. The greatest representative of such tolerance was Gandhi, but it is still widely practiced by the masses of non-modern, peripheral believers, in contrast to the modern, secular rationalists and the semi-modern zealots.[12]

Nandy further argues that secularism has its own principles of tolerance and intolerance. He also thinks that the imported idea of secularism has become increasingly incompatible with the fluid definitions of the self shared by several South Asian cultures. Such more fluid definitions of the self, he feels, are more compatible with religion which as faith depends more upon a distinctive set of the non-self and anti-selves. Nandy argues that the anti-selves are counter points without which the self just cannot be defined in the major cultures of South Asia.

Akeel Bilgrami, while focusing on Nandy's work, aptly brings out that such a contemporary critique of Nehru begins by drawing a fundamental distinction between religions as faiths and ways of life on the one hand and as constructed ideologies on the other. This is intended as a contrast between the more accommodating, non-monolithic and pluralist religious folk traditions of Hinduism and Islam and the Brahminical BJP and the fundamentalist Muslim League versions of Islam, which amount to constructed religious ideologies, that is, intolerant of he terodoxy within themselves as well as of each other. Nandy's target obviously is modernity itself, with its modern conception of nationhood and its state craft, which is the source of such ideological constructions that distort those more innocent aspects of religion as "ways of life".

Likewise, Hindu nationalism, Nandy argues, is nothing but an offshoot of Nehruvian state-imposed secularism which leaves people no choice. Thus, secular tyranny breeds Hindu nationalist resistance with its own form of tyranny.

As Bilgrami suggests, nationalism is a far more omnibus and vague formulation to analyse than Nandy or the Hindu Nationalists allow. There are a variety of ingredients that go into a particular nationalism at different stages and sometimes even at the same stage. One can't lump together Palestinian nationalism with Zionist or for that matter German nationalism. It can have instinctive ties to social democracy, liberal democracy, autocracy or fascism. In India too, nationalism exhibits different characteristics during its anti-imperialist struggle phase to the post-Independence stage with its major thrust on capitalist consolidation.

Similarly, the monolithic, majoritarian, Brahminic version of Hinduism as popularized by the Sangh Parivar is not just an offshoot of or a reaction to state-imposed secularism or modernity, as its construction goes a long way into the recesses of Indian history and has helped perpetuate the most remarkably resilient, inegalitarian social formation in the world. As Bilgrami suggests, it is the product of sustained efforts over centuries on part of the upper castes to sustain their hold over the Hindu psyche.[13]

Likewise, Nandy and several other scholars pleading for syncretism or a liminal movement idealize indigenous religious tradition, its tolerance and its extensive acceptance among masses. Indian society, historically, right from an early period, has not only witnessed multiple religious and social traditions, but also clashes of traditions at different levels at various historical junctures, right from the Vedic period till the advent of the British rule. Nandy's justification and blanket support to Hinduism betrays his bias and indifference to the subaltern traditions in India. Hinduism, as it is now widely understood, is a predominantly upper caste, Brahminic version popularized in the medieval period, especially after the advent of Muslim rule. This was projected as an ideological construction in the context of the vulnerability of the orthodox Brahminic traditions in face of the growing popularity of the Bhakti movement and the egalitarian values of Islam as projected by Sufi saints.

Our slightly elaborate appraisal of Nandy's critique of secularism and its irrelevance for India is imperative as those who exclusively uphold the importance of syncretic and liminal practices also knowingly or unknowingly extend concurrence to such presumptions about the irrelevance of secularism in the Indian context and disapprove of its application in this country under the pretext that the concept is Euro-centric. Unfortunately those who advocate such arguments are not aware or quite conveniently ignore the fact that there is no monolithic model of secularism that could be applied to Europe. Within Europe too, social, political and religious traditions are so different that it is impossible to locate any uniform process or model of secularism for these nations. Even within one nation, historically, the process of secularization has proceeded in such an uneven manner that one cannot mechanically apply a uniform abstract model for even a single country. There are upward and downward curves in the secularization process and it is impossible to mechanically fit them in a uniform pattern. We have no intention of belittling the great significance of syncretic practices in India. As a matter of fact, it is because of the extensive prevalence and appeal of syncretic religious practices in India that communal forces have not been able to strike deeper roots despite the open indulgence and blatant promotion of the communal divide by practically all mainstream political parties in recent years.

People who throng such shrines or dargahs in large numbers visit them largely for the fulfillment of their worldly material aspirations, ranging from desire for progeny to employment, success in examinations, desired life partner, physical or mental health to material prosperity. Aspirations for spirituality, divinity or mental peace certainly could be an important element of their visits to such sacred spots. But it would be extremely difficult to make clear cut distinctions between the two expectations.

In our concluding observation, we would like to point out two glaring instances where communal passions were raised to a point which vitiated the communal amity at the national level. The first is the recent case of Amarnath Yatra in Jammu and Kashmir where the debate over the control of Amarnath Trust and ownership of land around the shrine took such bitter turn that the whole state was divided on communal lines and the deep unrest around this issue aggravated communal tension and antagonism across India.

The second is the case of the Babri Masjid demolition and the national campaign for the construction of a Ram temple in its place. For almost over a decade communal tension and bitterness were created and the BJP successfully exploited this opportunity for registering a massive victory in parliament and several other states in the late 1990s. Even now attempts are made to utilize this issue for electoral purposes.

It is widely recognized that at the local level of networks, Hindus and Muslims interacted and enthusiastically participated in the Amarnath Yatra which was a classic illustration of communal harmony where both communities depended on each-other. Similarly it is noted by many scholars that many temples in Ayodhya are looked after by Muslims and Ayodhya never had any problem of communal antagonism. In both cases, communal forces and mainstream political parties including the Indian National Congress were instrumental in aggravating communal tension with their populist policy.

Our contention in citing these two glaring instances of communal tension and divide is that despite a long history of syncretic traditions and communal amity in these two places, political forces were quite successful in wiping out such syncretic traditions and disturbing communal harmony at the national level, leaving permanent scars with the nation facing the consequences of such opportunistic indulgence. Hence, unless we keep in mind the socio-economic and political forces operating at the macro-level, our exclusive focus on syncretic traditions at the micro-level would not help us properly comprehend and find a solution to the problem of communal peace and harmony. Syncretic traditions are very important and as we noted earlier, but for the deeper roots they have acquired in India since the medieval Bhakti and Sufi movements, communal forces would have succeeded in shaking the prevailing democratic set up and replacing it probably with creation of the "Hindu Rashtra".

References

1. Roy Burman, J.J. : "Syncretism and some reference to the Disputed Shrine of Ayodhya", Journal of the Indian Anthropological Society 28 (1) : 69-82, 1993
2. Veer, Ven der Peter: "Syncretism, Multiculturalism and the Discourse of Tolerance, PP-196-211 in Steward and Shaw (Ed) Syncretism/Anti-Syncretism: The Politics of Religious Synthesis. London and New York, Routledge, 1994
3. Eliade, Mircea (Ed): "Syncretism" in the Encyclopedia of Religion "Volume i 14 PP 218/227 New York. Macmillan Publishing Company, 1987
4. Roy Burman Ibid.
5. Veer Ibid.
6. Mayaram, Shaila : "Rethinking Meo Identity:Cultural Fault Line, Syncretism, Hybridity or Liminality in Comparative Studies of South Asia, Africa and the Middle East" Vol. XVII, No.2, 1997
7. Turner, Victor : "The Centre Out There : Pilgrim's Goal" in History of Religions 12 (3) – 191-230, 1973
8. Mayaram, Ibid
9. Khan, Dominique - "Liminality and Legality" A Contemporary Debate among the Imam Shahis of Gujrat PP 209-232 in Ahmad, Imtiaz and Reifeld, Helmut (ed). Lived Islam in South Asia: Adaptation, Accommodation and Conflict. Delhi Social Science Press, Sila 2004
10. Nandy, Ashish 1990: "The Politics of Secularism and the Recovery of Religious Toleration" in Das, Veena (ad). Mirrors of Violence: Communities, Riots and Survivors in South Asia. New Delhi Oxford University Press.
11. Veer, Ibid.
12. Nandy, Ashis, Ibid.
13. Bilgrami, Akeel: Two Concepts of Secularism, published in Economic and Political Weekly, July 9, 1994 PP. 1937-53.

3

Gurus in India: A Historical Perspective

Religion, since almost the pre-Vedic period, has exercised tremendous influence on Indian society. Religious influence is evident in practically all aspects ranging from art, dance, music, theatre, sculpture and painting to the all important events of Hindu life such as birth, marriage, death, and even to other social, political as well as economic spheres of Indian society. If it was true of traditional Indian society, even in modern Indian society, the impact of religion in some form or the other hardly needs elaboration.

Cults of Renouncers in Indian Society

In this section we focus on the relevance and role of the gurus, sants etc, or, as Romila Thapar so aptly suggests, the cult of renouncers in Indian society since the Vedic times. In her paper titled "Renunciation: The Making of a Counter-Culture", she argues that the organized groups of renouncers of the post-Vedic period were neither negating the society to which they belonged nor trying to radically alter it, but rather they were seeking to establish a parallel society. Inherent in this attempt was the notion of dissent but its articulation was often ambiguous. In early India this role is enmeshed with the complexities of caste and with the nature of dissent.

The renouncer does not necessarily represent a religious sect but often an order constituting an alternative lifestyle, in many ways contradictory to that of his original social group. For instance, he cannot observe caste norms, must be celibate, cannot own property, and may be requested to break various food taboos.

The focus, as she suggests, is on the social manifestations of these groups and their role in historical change. Initially, it seems, asceticism arose from groups which questioned the ritual of sacrifice as the means of acquiring magical power. Proponents of asceticism believed that tapas and dhyana were more effective. Gradually the idea was extended to more than magical power to absolute freedom. This was seen primarily as the freedom of the soul or consciousness to achieve a state of ecstasy, to receive knowledge from experience and meditation rather than from the claim of revelation.

The Mid-First Millennium B.C. and Proliferation of Sects

The mid-first millennium B.C. saw a proliferation of sects in the Ganges valley. Many of these were pariwajakas wandering in groups under the direction of a teacher or loosely affiliated to sects, but preferring to wander by themselves, alone. The wanderers were often dissidents. The question of the orthodox tradition had started prior to this period but what was new was the emergence of various sects such as Nirganthas, the Ajivikas and later the Buddhists as well as various Charvaka sects. The dissidence of these groups was however qualitatively different since they were not individual dissenters but had organized their dissent into sects whose identity was based on an opposition to the orthodox doctrines as expressed in the notions of the sanctity of the Vedas, the authority of the Brahmins, Varnashram dharma and the worship of the Gods.

The proliferation of sects has been explained due to the breakup of tribal society and its consequences. The cushioning effect of kinship was declining with the impersonal relations of post-tribal society coming to the fore. The increasingly hierarchical ordering of society had been hostile to the wanderers. This was further reiterated by the growth of towns and cities during this period with the anonymity and alienation encouraged by urban institutions. Inevitably there was a breach of methods of adjustment. The introduction of technology also brought profound change in prevailing socio-economic structure. Its description as the age of transcendence was not accidental. Economic prosperity made possible by the new situation permitted the maintenance of such large groups of renouncers. The Buddha spent more years at Rajagriha and Shravasti than anywhere else and the early and important monasteries were located at both these towns and at Kaushambi. The earlier Jaina tirthankar Parshvanath is also associated with towns. It was the towns which provided the renouncers with an audience and later patronage.

The main body of monks came from the lower social orders such as artisans, fishermen, hunters, and basket-weavers. Similarly, the Mathura inscriptions of the pre-Gupta period indicate support for the Jains, also coming from trading groups, artisans and castes low on the social scale.

The Tantric-Yogic Combination

The Tantric-Yogic combination was predominant in the relatively less Hinduized border regions around Assam, these being a channel by which foreign elements were assimilated into Hinduism, giving rise to the substratum culture of obscure families and castes and their assimilation into the political and economic vortex of the great tradition via the system of land grants. The Siddhacharyas of this cult were mostly of low castes. The association of Tantricism with yoga was in all probability an undercurrent of one strand in the ethos of renouncers since early times. This would be true also of Nathpanthis. The substratum culture was opposed to the orthodox tradition, an opposition which came to be symbolically expressed in Tantric rituals, much of which is a reversal of Brahman values.

Thus, as Romila Thapar so aptly brings out, the appearance of renouncers as an organized section of society occurs historically at periods of change when there emerge within society not only religious but social and economic sanctions to maintain such groups. For example, the growth of urban centers and the expansion of the agrarian economy. The religious impetus may come from the need to institutionalize a way of life that is new (the Ajivikas, Jains and Buddhist Sanghas), as a strategy for proselytizing (the Dasnami Sanyasis and the Bairagis), or as a means of crystallizing a popular religious ethos and providing it with status (the Tantric sects and Yoga). Not all such sects were opposed to orthodoxy but the technique of using social heresy was employed to organize a religious identity, and the sects therefore registered various degrees and stages of non-conformity. The Buddhist, Jains and Ajivika monks were opposed to Brahminical orthodoxy but the expression of their dissidence took on a puritanical form in which certain social mores were ultimately strengthened but the manifestations of Brahminical religion were discarded. The groups influenced by Tantricism accepted some of the religious symbols but discarded many of the social mores. The Dasnami Sanyasis supported Brahminical orthodoxy but did not conform to the Brahminical view of sanyasa in the setting up of monastic centers.

The renouncers, as she argues, were above and beyond the conventional laws, for they conformed to their own laws and these were often in contradiction to the accepted social laws. This gave them added prestige as it also gave them freedom to protest against the laws of normal society. The form which their protest took was the flouting of social convention. The accommodation of this protest and the investing of it with charisma and moral authority have been in a sense characteristic of Indian society.[1]

Romila Thapar's appraisal provides a vivid and critical understanding of the cult of renouncers in the context of the socio-economic and political transformation experienced by Indian society right from the Vedic to the post-Vedic and Mauryan period.

The Bhakti Movement

The Bhakti movement which largely prevailed during the medieval period also deserves close appraisal as it sharply differs from the earlier cults of renouncers. It also needs special attention as its major proponents pose a striking contrast to the cults of Godmen, gurus and other varieties of saints that emerged since post-independence. Although the initiation of the Bhakti movement could be traced to the sixth and seventh centuries with the Alwar and Nayanar movements in South India, in medieval India its spread was far more extensive and it exercised a deeper impact in many parts of the country.

Indian scholars, Marxists as well as others, have exhaustively and critically examined the significance of the Bhakti movement. Within Marxist circles also there are sharp divisions and evaluations differ widely. We don't see any relevance of referring to such controversies in this appraisal. Our attempt here is only confined to a brief appraisal of the major thrust of the teachings of the leading Bhakti saints in Southern, Western and Northern India and their impact on the medieval Indian society.

The Bhakti Movement in South India

The Bhakti movement in South India, especially in the Tamil region began sometime in the middle of the sixth Century A.D. and continued till almost up to the tenth century A.D.. As brought out by G.S. Harayan and V. Kesavan, this movement represents a new wave of Aryan or Hindu influence. The two main currents of the Bhakti movement are Shaivism and Vaishnavism, and their saints are known as the Nayanars and Alwars respectively. The movement created cultural links by cutting across political boundaries and promoted a new Tamil consciousness. It coincided in time with the rise of a new feudal monarchy in the South. Initially, it had to confront the already established orders of Jainism and Buddhism. But the growth of Shaivism was so rapid that the kings became its patrons and even went to the extent of persecuting the followers of the heretical sects. Thus Brahminism returned with a vengeance along with its institutional base in temples. The support for temples came from the grant of agrarian settlements in the adjoining areas. In a sense, as suggested, rivalry between the Bhakti movement and the heretical sects also reflected the conflict for socio-political dominance between the land-owning and trading classes. It also should be noted that the Bhakti movement eventually took over Jainism and Buddhism not only because of royal patronage but also due to its use of several media that evoked popular enthusiasm, such as song and dance, and its egalitarian and democratic ethos so vividly expressed in poems and other writings of Nayanar and Alwar saints in the initial stage. This was strikingly different from the rigidity of the classical Brahminical approach. As the authors contend, the Bhakti movement in the South did deviate a great deal from the orthodox philosophy of Brahminical Hinduism and provided impetus to intellectual activity at both secular and spiritual levels. There was a rejection of abstract metaphysical as well as caste regulations. This could be seen in the fact that untouchables and outcastes have also been recognized as saints. Vedic ritualism was thus considerably changed and diluted by the addition of several other folk, local and regional elements. It made the individual and groups aware of some basic equal rights that they could claim at the cultural and religious levels. Similar freedom was also extended to women who had been denied such rights before.

The Warkari Movement in Maharashtra

In Maharashtra, several devotional sects came up of which the Warkari sect proved to be the most influential. Dyaneshwar, Namdeo, Ekanath and Tukaram were the major exponents of the Warkari sect. The Warkari sect was mainly concerned with the Shudras and the untouchables. It was thought necessary to chalk out a practical path as the Jains and other sects like Mahanubhavas emphasized ascetism which had hardly any attraction for common people. A path had to be found which would not disturb their day-to-day duties and household responsibilities and yet enable them to attain spiritual progress. The path of devotion did not mean either retirement or renunciation and not even spending one's time in performing bhajans all the time. These saints never accepted any conflict between day-to-day life of house holders and their spiritual pursuits. The Maharashtrian saints exhorted their followers to immerse themselves in the pursuit of their occupational and family life without losing sight of spiritual life in any way.

The devotional cult of Vitthal was not monopolized by any one sect. It had incorporated various sects like the Nath, Datta, Chaitanya, Anand and Sufi. Vitthal was worshiped as a deity and poetry (padas) of Dyaneshwar, Eknath Bhagvat, Namdeo and Tukaram were accepted as authoritative literature and that is how centers associated with Vitthal and Dyaneshwar, Eknath and Tukaram are acclaimed as holy centers of pilgrimage which have contributed to the solidarity between persons belonging to different castes, regions and sub-regions within Maharashtra.

From Dyaneshwar to Tukaram, no saints from the Warkari sect felt the need of kingly or princely support, nor were they interested in any kind of gift of land. They did not depend on the generosity of the wealthy. Through their own living example, the performance of kirtans and the exposition of philosophy and religion, they carried on the work with a missionary zeal. But once a religious movement becomes well organized, it gives rise to vested interests that alienates the leaders from the followers. That is why the Maharashtrian saints did not start

Maths. Tukaram had exhorted kirtankars not to accept food where they performed kirtan and renounce all kinds of pride and hypocrisy.

Soon after Tukaram's death, the devotional movement was on the wane, probably due to the revivalist trends which were reflected in the thinking of Hemadri, Vidyaran and Narasingh Saraswati that became dominant since the period of Ramdas.

Nevertheless, the saints contributed to the sophistication of the Marathi language and that is why Marathi literature can boast of a long tradition. The Sanskrit Gita was translated into Marathi by Gyaneshwar for easy access to people.

The Bhakti Movement in North India

While referring to the Bhakti movement in North India, Savitri Chandra aptly remarks that scholars have paid little attention so far to the social context of the Bhakti movement which developed in North India from the fifteenth century. If some critics regard the Bhakti movement as a reaction to Mughal oppression, others see it as a Hindu reform movement that arose in order to counter the challenge of Islam. Yet others see the radical wing of the Bhakti movement as representing the protest of the influential growing number of artisan groups which came into existence as a consequence of urban life developing under the Turks.

Kabir is the most outstanding exponent of the Bhakti movement in Northern India. He laid stress on the fundamental equality of man as reflected in the earlier writings of the Siddhas and the Nath Panthis and this tradition continued in the later sixteenth and seventeenth century writings of Guru Nanak, Dadu Dayal and other saints as those of Bihar. Such social ideas, especially those of Kabir, invited sharp reaction from both Hindu and Muslim orthodoxy as they were very radical for that period. Bhakti literature indicates the absence of abstract philosophical ideas; ideas instead are placed in a simple language which made a deep and direct appeal to the common man. Kabir often expressed these ideas by making fun of the Brahmins or other established strata in Indian society.

While Kabir, Raidas or Rohan Dadu and others believed in the basic equality of all, especially in terms of access to religious scriptures, Surdas and Tulsidas upheld the position of the Brahmin in the caste hierarchy. In other words, there are two contradictory currents in the Bhakti movement; i.e., at the religious level there is no discrimination based on caste in terms of one's devotion to God, but in secular society, social distinctions were not disapproved. Of course, all of them maintain that the intrinsic qualities of the varnas rather than birth status should be stressed. These ideas did make an impact on society because the exclusive rights of the Brahmins were diluted and after the sixteenth century, the low caste saints were respected by all sections of society. Kabir disapproved of beggary and emphasized the virtues of working for oneself. For most northern medieval saints, it was evident that the trader cum money lender was exploiting the poor and other officials including the divans and the king perpetuated injustice and the suffering of the masses. Bhakti saints also do not approve of asceticism of those orthodox sects which advocate renunciation of the world. For the Bhakti saints true devotion implies seeking god within oneself, in the routine daily life and their approach based on mysticism is fundamentally humanistic and individualistic. Hence, logically the rejection of a formal and organized religion based on authoritarianism was natural. However, such sacred books as the vedas and the Quran were not entirely rejected, but knowledge based on personal experience was given preference. They stated quite clearly that various rituals and practices were evolved by the privileged in order to control the common man. This approach also perpetuates the animosity between the Hindus and the Muslims. The various saints differ in their attitude towards the scriptures and the role of the priests. Unlike Kabir, Tulsidas and Surdas do not disapprove of the Vedas. Dadu as the dissenter who did not consider himself to be either a Hindu or Muslim invited hostility from both sides. On the other hand, Kabir, Raidas and Nanak, during the fourteenth, fifteenth and sixteenth centuries, considered scriptural knowledge secondary to personal knowledge and devotion to God.

Basically, the saints expressed disapproval of social distinctions by seeking to identify themselves with the sufferings of the common man, although they chose to express themselves in religious terms. The movement was thus ideologically against the prevailing socio-economic ideas and institutions which had sharpened the distinctions between the haves and have-nots.[2]

Sufi Saints also played a similar role during the medieval period. They opposed the tyranny of the powerful. They preached against social inequality and struggled against the prevalent orthodoxy and blind faith. Their following also predominantly came from the lower strata, irrespective of religion. Miyan Mir, Baba Farid, Shaikh Salim Chishti and Nizamuddin Auliya are some of the prominent Sufis who are respected by all for their humanistic preaching.

Godmen, Gurus in Post-independent India

In post-independence India, as we mentioned earlier, there is a prolific growth of godmen, gurus, sants and bapus. Apart from godmen and gurus, there are other numerous categories such as palmists, astrologers, vastu shastris, chhaya shastris, tantriks, visionaries and others who command a large following. They have proved to be the largest audience pullers as their discourse is attended by lots of people cutting across caste-class borders.

The Post-Eighties Spread

The post-eighties have witnessed an extensive spread of this phenomenon. It is not accidental that the post eighties period has witnessed a profound change in economic policy and the political and social orientation of our major political parties. The Indian National Congress under the late Mrs. Indira Gandhi's rule also openly adopted a strategy of Hindu appeasement and on the economic front opted for liberalization in the eighties, giving up its earlier thrust on self-reliance and attaining development through expanding the role of the public sector and protection to domestic industries. This shift in policy should also be viewed in the context of the structural crisis of the world capitalist economy since the end of the sixties, its repercussions on the Indian economy, our energy crisis in the late seventies and the pressure of the world's monetary institutions for greater access for the growing Indian market. It is also not surprising that since the eighties, the ruling parties also stopped giving even lip-sympathy to the earlier pronouncement of a socialist pattern of society and a pro-poor stance. Thus the decisive shift in Congress policy and the open overture to placate Hindu sentiments have to be viewed in the context of its open advocacy of world monetary institutions, i.e., pro-American policy since the eighties, culminating in its criminal silence on the demolition of the Babri Masjid in 1993 under the Narasimha Rao Government. Thus the changing scenario since the eighties and especially after 1990 when India openly opted for the new economic policy of structural adjustment advocated by the World Bank and IMF has to be kept in view while examining the government policy of promoting the Hindutva agenda.

The decisive influence of the shift to the so-called market oriented liberalization policy as advocated by American imperialism could also be seen in the type of godmen and gurus who exhibit all the features of an effective marketing manager of a successful CEO in the corporate world.

Keeping this perspective in view, we will try to sum up the broad features of modern godmen or gurus that have dominated the scene since the eighties and nineties.

(1) The number is so large, it is impossible to keep track of them as many of them operate at a local level, some district, state and interstate while some operate at the national and global level.

(2) Many of them operate through some formal committee or trust but they monopolize the entire control.

(3) A sizeable number of them operate through institutions like the ashrams established by them and also engage in social welfare activities and provide various types of social services such as educational and relief operations, charitable dispensaries, modern hospitals, educational institutions etc.

(4) It is very difficult to have a correct estimate of the wealth acquired by them, cash as well as estates, the businesses they control, their total income and its distribution and also their modes of investment. Recently newspaper stories of their investment in the stock market and of being cheated by some followers were published but it is a matter of serious investigation.

(5) Their sources of accumulation of wealth are also not known. Most of them, especially in Gujrat and Mumbai, are more like kirtankars with proficiency in story narration based on Tulsi Ramayan and epics like Mahabharat and Gita. By and large source material is based on purans such as Bhagwat Puran with occasional reference to Upanishads and Vedas.

(6) Bhagwat Katha or religious discourse at times is only a small part of the total narration. Most of the time they talk of current problems, family situations, decadence because of

western culture, glorification of imaginary Hindu, Vedic, traditional value systems, institutions, family structure, spiritual values and the past glory and greatness of the Indian or Hindu nation.

(7) Most of them know several languages. Apart from the mother tongue, they speak well in Hindi with a limited knowledge of English and Sanskrit. Almost all of them know and quote from Sanskrit shlokas, Gita, Purans and lucidly explanation for the same. These are some characteristics common to all popular gurus.

(8) All of them stress the prime importance of attending kirtans. According to them, kirtans alone could pave the way for moksha, liberation, would give peace of mind, could resolve their followers' problems and Gods also would come to their rescue provided they regularly attend kirtans and internalize the guru's teachings.

(9) All of them are good orators, understand mass psychology, people's mind-sets and their problems, and have the art of presenting solutions acceptable to the audience.

(10) Katha, pravachans and discourse are intertwined with music, songs, poetic recitals, and jokes to the extent that the katha's actual content proceeds very slowly with many types of interjections.

(11) The people in the audience often search for a guru and once found, the guru is endowed with all ability for liberation. It's believed that the guru can find a solution for all their woes. This results in trust in the guru, worship of the guru, and the guru being regarded as God or as God's incarnation on earth.

(12) The disciples' expectation from satsangs and gurus are all based on worldly problems ranging from health to marriage, obtaining progeny, and especially male progeny, higher education, finding a suitable job, wealth, success in occupation, business etc. The Guru too understands such expectations and responds appropriately. There is hardly anything spiritual about this. Peace of mind is important but it's required here only to obtain better health, better family or business management.

(13) All these godmen or gurus invariably suggest some herbal treatment or some simple remedies for various ailments and also for serious health problems. They also suggest some yogic exercises.

(14) Their discourse is always in a very loud language full of anecdotes, stories, humor and entertainment. They also use various other devices. Bhajans at short intervals is a popular technique. It could be folk or classical and is often based on Bollywood tunes and expression of bhakti, especially Krishna-Gopi raas in a highly romantic style. Most of them also expect audience participation with clapping and dancing as if they also are in a state of trance, some of them do act or feel that they are in a state of semi-romantic, semi-devotional state of ecstasy.

Music forms a very important part of the discourse of practically all gurus. The guru sings but is also accompanied by a band of musicians and singers. This technique is described in psychotherapy as dissociation which is highly effective and is very cleverly used by all successful gurus.

Most of them invariably drop hints of their miracles, supernatural powers and ability to cure or resolve all problems. Very often, it is also common practice in case of some eminent gurus to present half a dozen or more disciples who would narrate how miraculously they have been cleared of fatal illness or have resolved their family or business crisis.

Some of the gurus are in such heavy demand that their discourse dates have to be booked much in advance, may be an year or more. From booking the date to arranging the program, publicity, accommodation, pandals, travel, lodging and boarding for the guru and his followers and guests - organizers have to arrange all this much in advance.

Apart from this, the guru may also charge a fee for his discourse which could be exorbitant. Even when they go abroad, the same pattern is followed.

Most of the established gurus maintain extremely good political, administrative and corporate connections. They are highly influential and often are in close touch with higher-ups in political and corporate circles. They often help them and also get favors in return for the assistance they are able to render due to their eminent public position.

The dais from where they address public gatherings is usually opulent, with a prominent display of gods and goddesses, usually Ram, Sita, Krishna, Radha, Hanuman, Shiv-Parvati, Vishnu-Laxmi, in the form of posters or expensive statues or idols.

On the basis of our observation of various T.V. channels that broadcast such devotional programs all the time, we found that now we have gurus of all age groups. Some could be as old as in their eighties while many are middle aged and also a sizeable number are very young and quite attractive. One almost gathers the impression that they must be spending a lot of time in selecting their wardrobe: expensive dresses, even different types of rings, for every discourse. One can see they have special costumes and very often when they speak about Radha and Krishna's raas leela, from their gesture and the way young girls respond through gestures and dance, the ambience is more seductive than spiritual.

It is also widely reported that most of them are womanizers. About their financial practices, their investment in stock markets and other such speculative or profitable avenues is widely suspected. Their involvement in various scandals, even criminal, is also reported.

In our concluding remarks, we wish to point out the sharp difference between the ancient cult of renouncers and medieval Bhakti Saints and the modern gurus. Renouncers in ancient Indian society, right from the Upanishad to the Mauryan and Gupta period, played a significant role in articulating the socio-economic and political transformation that was taking place in Indian society at various historical junctures. Not only did they articulate this transformation but registered their dissent by evolving an alternate style of living, evolving some parallel philosophy or school of thought, entering into debate with what they considered outdated established religious schools. The protest started with challenging vedic formulations, animal and human sacrifices associated with Yagna, to a philosophy that Buddha called the middle path which facilitated trade and commerce and also provided some semblance of solace by starting a sangham based on equality, simplicity and high ethical values vis-a-vis the destruction of the tribal communities that took place with the emergence of the state as an established political institution in early Indian society. Similarly other schools or sects as Lokayat, Siddha and Nath cults and some other Tantric sects also articulated the sentiments of the lower strata of Hindu society and in a sense also could channel the discontent and register the protest of the lower strata against the dominance of upper castes and their established schools of religious philosophy.

The medieval Bhakti movement too, beginning with the Alwar and Nayanar movements in South India and subsequently culminating in the medieval period in practically all parts of the country also articulated the dissent, protest and the desire for reform of the lower strata against the oppression and domination of upper and particularly Brahmin castes in Indian society. Medieval saints, most of whom came from the lower poor strata, popularized Bhakti by the use of vernacular media, by simplifying devotional practices, and by encouraging women to participate in religious worship. The Bhakti saints set up a unique precedent by their lifestyle. Practically all of them led a simple life, most of them earned their own living, preached simplicity and never accepted any gift, even food, from their followers. They even despised kings, nobles and such other dignitaries and by and large preached that they are the root cause of people's misery. They set up a strikingly different model of religious pursuits which included austerity, honesty, transparency, simplicity of language and life style and exclusive stress on lower strata and women for worship.

Modern godmen, however, pose a striking contrast to them with their fabulous wealth, support from corporate, political and administrative hierarchy, huge institutional setup, corrupt practices and hypocrisy, and appear more as charlatans compared to medieval saints.

It is no wonder that in modern Indian and also the global order, with its moral, intellectual and economic decadence, its thrust on the neo-liberal market economy with the American President George W. Bush ideally representing this decadence, the kinds of modern godmen or gurus we have are also perfect exhibits for such a system. This contrast also enables us to understand the contrasting role of the cult of renouncers and the medieval saints in Indian society.

The above observations are quite disturbing and probably too sweeping. But the operation of the many godmen and women deserves serious appraisal. The recent mysterious deaths of two children in

Asharam Bapu's Ahmedabad ashram and two more in Chhindwara district of Madhya Pradesh in his ashram schools are shocking.

In both Ahmedabad and Chhindwara, protests against the activities of the Asharam Ashram have acquired a massive form. In both places people in thousands displayed their hatred against this bapu by violent demonstration and mass hunger strike. Protest is also directed against the state government and the police officials with whose connivance Asharam bapu is able to conduct his legal and illegal activities.

These recent incidents in these states also indicate the imperative need for closer perusal of modern godmen and women's activities, the basis of their appeal, their mode and network of operation. Of course there would be quite a few of these spiritual gurus who are honest, committed and sincere in their beliefs and intentions. But a proper appraisal of their impact on society becomes all the more imperative.

We shall conclude our paper with the reproduction of a critique of godmen and women and Guru Das, a deity in Kerala.

A century back it was Swami Vivekananda who characterized Kerala as a lunatic asylum. It was the most deplorable social situation arising from the worst form of untouchability, highly irrational rituals, superstition led by caste-feudal forces that prompted Vivekananda's sharp comment. However the renaissance movement led by Sreenarayana and Ayyankali followed by initiatives on the part of democratic and left forces did succeed in transforming Kerala to a socio-political situation which was far better than that in other Indian states. Obviously, the formation of the first Kerala government led by the communist party after state re-organization took place in this historical context.

However, ever since the notorious liberation struggle of the late 1950s led by Congress mobilizing reactionary, casteist and religious fundamentalist forces with imperialist dollars and due to the ideological and political weaknesses of the left, the above mentioned progressive stream had been experiencing reversals which assumed a new dimension consequent on imperialist globalization since the 1990s. One manifestation of this has been the mushrooming of fake godmen and women or what is called the spiritual mafia in the guise of charity, philanthropy and religions throughout the length and breadth of the state. Along with funding, neo-liberalism with its ideology of post-modernism, whose affinity towards cult and identity are well known, has been propping up these fake godmen and women belonging to different religious denominations. Backed by immense foreign funds and sponsored by the various ruling fronts in Kerala, almost 2000 fake godmen and women are flourishing in various parts of the state. Invariably, under the cover of religion, charity and philanthropy, they are engaging in mafia land deals, fake money transaction, sex crimes, exortion and so on. The unparalleled growth of speculative finance and the all-round degeneration that it has created and above all the further decay of organized religion along with growing parasitism associated with imperialist crisis are all providing fertile fields for the growth of the spiritual mafia. As agricultural land is increasingly becoming a speculative asset, there is an unholy relationship between land mafia and fake godmen. More often, the latter prefer the company of ruling class political leaders, bureaucrats, police officials, film stars and of course, the wealthy.

While even official estimates put the number of fake godmen and women in the state at more than 1500 among whom 200 have an obvious criminal background, investigation has proceeded against only 25. Out of this, charge sheets have been prepared only in the case of three including Santhosh Madhavan and Himaval Bhadrananda. Though existing provisions of the law empower the police to frame cases on its own, the policy of appeasement towards different religious groups and sects by the government hampers investigating agencies to pursue the matter freely.

An interesting aspect is that while the government investigation is confined to small fry such as Santhosh Madhavan, the spiritual mafia such as Mata Amritanandmayi and K.P. Yohannan go scot free. For instance, Mata Amritanandmayi is reportedly running a financial empire worth Rs. 20,000 crores. The tentacles of this spiritual mafia have spread over everything from charity and philanthropy to rehabilitation and real estate throughout the country. It is just like a parallel government in spite of several criminal allegations against it. Another case is that of K.P. Yohannan who, with funds from USA and Germany, runs two institutions, Gospel for Asia and Believers' Church as cover organizations for his underworld financial and real estate deals. Even the Kerala government's own records put the recent funds that he earned from foreign sources at Rs. 1,040 crores. A part of this money is used for purchasing about 2500 cores of land in Kottayam district from the Goenka Group which is illegally possessing about 76000 acres of estate lands in various districts of Kerala in violation of the land lease agreement with the government. He is also reportedly operating a parallel telecommunications network at his headquarters in Tiruvalla with the connivance of those in power. No serious investigation is going on against his unlawful activities.[3]

References

1. Thapar, Romila: Renunciation. The Making of a Counter Culture\Essay from Ancient Indian Social History. Pg 63-104. Orient Longman Ltd. 1978. New Delhi.
2. Malik, S C (ed): Some Aspects of Dissent, Protest and Reform Ed by S.C. Malik Articles by M.G.S. Narayanan, V. Kesaran, G. B. Sardar and Savitri Chandra, Indian Institute of Advanced Study, Simla 1978.
3. James, P. J.: Proliferation of Fake Godmen and Women in Kerala. Pg 30-31, Red Star Journal of CPI (M) July 2008.

4

Modern Godmen: A Sociological Appraisal

Historical Background

Gurus have been with us since the Vedic period. Suddenly they have been in great demand in last three or four decades. As Mangalwadi aptly remarks, millions of people, young and old, rich and poor, illiterate and sophisticated, bow before them. Agnostics are baffled, sociologists surprised and psychologists made curious by this phenomenon. Gurus have become influential even in the decaying western culture ('World of Gurus', Mangalwadi).[1]

As a matter of fact, the rise and popularity of Gurus have to be viewed also in the broader context of the revival and resurgence of indigenous art, music, dance, medicine and language boosted by the official and non-official institutions, especially since independence.

The Origin and Relevance of Gurus

According to some observers, early Vedic literature does not refer to the word guru. Even the idea of a guru is absent as the Vedic religion essentially revolves around sacrificial rituals. The word was first used and the concept developed during the Upanishadic period when the emphasis shifted from sacrifice to gyaan as the means to liberation. A guru was needed to impart gyaan. During the Upanishadic era, the ashram system was also established. The acharya who taught students in such gurukuls was also called the guru.

With the advent of the Pauranik and Tantrik religions, the founder who initiated the sect or creed also began to be called guru. His followers who preached and propagated his doctrines were also referred to as gurus. For the followers of Tantrika sects, the giver of a mantra was a guru. The secret mantras were communicated in the ears of the disciples and were called Bija or the Guru Mantra. It was in these Pauranik and Tantric sects that the lineage of guruship was established. For the continuation of the lineage, it was considered essential that the guru be married and have sons.

While tracing the origin of the institution of the guru as a peculiar product of Indian society, Mangalwadi holds the following five sociological factors as of special significance for the acceptance of Guruism, namely (1) the nature and place of education in Aryan Society; (2) the esoteric nature of Upanishadic and later Indian religions, (3) the class or caste system with Brahminic dominance in religious affairs and sporadic reaction to it, (4) the authoritarian structure of Indian family life and the repressive puritanism of Indian society and (5) the absence of printed books.[2]

Peter Brant, another noted Western scholar explains the origin of the cult of gurudom in terms of psychological motives, authoritarianism and puritanism. Right from his earliest days the young Indian was expected to conform absolutely to his father's wishes and commands for the rest of his life. The average Indian is almost incapable of doing anything of which his father disapproves. In this situation, the guru can appear as rescuer. For with him, the whole conditional mechanism of happy slavery can come into operation without conflict. He is the father who has been chosen. In this way, the disciple remains free in his bondage, bound in his freedom. Taught to be non-attached, he can cut himself off from his family without guilt. [3]

Mangalwadi, on the basis of his own observation about the life style in the ashrams of the Divine Light Mission at Haridwar and New Delhi, also draws similar inferences. Young people were found to be doing manual labor almost slavishly but happily in this ashram. They cannot step out of the ashram nor answer the question of visitors without permission. Yet they testified that they had peace and contentment now, which they did not have before. The author, however, suspected that some of this peace came because of the fact that their three meals a day were guaranteed in the ashram and not necessarily so at home.[4]

The second factor, closely connected to the first, is also rooted according to Brent in the repressive puritanism of Indian society. The contempt of sexuality and the strict segregation of sexes led to repression of normal emotions. These feelings were often transferred towards a guru as to a deity, resulting in intense devotion. In the West, as Brent argues, they are free to work for the approval of those they love or respect and whom they would like to love and respect them. This is not the case with Indians who fit into the family situation and thier social stratum as inevitably as a part of a machine - for the average and particularly the middle-class Indian, there are often only two directions he can go to prove that he can love, that he can be loved. One is towards homosexuality, the other towards the guru. These are not of course, as Brent suggests, mutually exclusive. Instances of some widely respected gurus in India having sexual relationships with their young disciples were cited to substantiate such contention.[5]

The above observations of Mangalwadi and Brent, though quite valuable, provide only partial explanations for the emergence and popularity of the cult of gurudom in Indian society. For the better and more comprehensive understanding of the guru phenomenon, we would prefer to refer to a more vivid and descriptive account of the role of the guru in Vedic and post-Vedic society.

In ancient times, as brought out by William Cenkker, the transmission of learning was oral. Teachers repeated to their students texts that they themselves had received orally. In the whole of Vedic literature there is no reference to writing because that literature was transmitted entirely by the spoken word. The oral transmission of sacred literature continued longer in the Indian civilization than any other.

Later religious literature explicitly forbids the writing down of the Veda.

The Mahabharat, for example, condemns to hell anyone who would write the Vedas. The Narada Smriti claims flatly that learning the Veda from a book, unlike learning it from a teacher, is utterly worthless. There is an adage that the text must be learned from the lips of a teacher and not from a manuscript because religious education takes place through hearing and memorizing sacred wisdom. Kumarila Bhatta (eighth century C.E.) describes the learning of the Veda from written sources as equal to not comprehending it. The oral transmission of the Veda continued till the eleventh and twelfth centuries C.E. [6]

Further, the same author remarks, "The hymns of the Rig Veda are now classified according to families of authors.

" Each unit of the Rig Veda authored by a particular family possesses a significant homogeneity of authorship. While there existed no system that could be identified with a single teacher, the poets and philosophers of India's earliest religious literature did achieve a marked individuality. The religious preferences of each family of authors can be detected in the hymns by their reference to a cult of deities and by creation of a hereditary class of teachers. This enabled Indian society to make strides in education. In early times, as suggested, the teachers usually were householders and did not charge any fees for their teachings. Various types of teachers existed in ancient India: Guru, acharya and upadhyaya were the common types. The gurus after performing various rites gave instructions in the Veda. Upadhaya, although often called the first teacher, along with a disciple's parents, taught only some portion of the Vedas and expected some reward for his instruction.

The Gurus in the Upanishads

The guru in the Upanishads played a dual role of an intellectual and spiritual guide. A teacher as per the Upanishads is a self-realized person. The Mundak Upanishad describes the guru as one well-versed in the Vedas and absorbed in the Brahman. A significant portion of early Indian literature is enigmatic. The early teachers sharpened their skills in debates on the basis of the Sutra literature. The Chandogya Upanishad refers to the teacher as one who gives the direction. During the times when the Upanishads were composed, it was not unusual for teachers to be both householders and ascetics. In contemporary Jain and Buddhist education, only an ascetic can become a teacher. However, by the end of Upanishad period, it appears only an ascetic could be a teacher.

According to the Taittiriya Upanishad, the teacher is the first letter. The student is the last letter. Knowledge is the meeting place. Instruction is the link.

The unique contribution that the Upanishads make to educational method in religious development is the three fold operation of hearing (shravan), reflecting (manan) and concentration (nididyasana). The focus on hearing, reflection and concentration obviously acquires significance, especially in the context of oral transmission of religious knowledge in the ancient Indian society.

Meditation is, however, separated from the above threefold method. The Upanishads do not offer a technical definition of meditation. The Upanishads use various words for meditation, of which, it seems, the most common are upasna and vidya. Upasna virtually means to come near a thing or to approach the realization of the self through concentration on an object of meditation. Meditation may be made for instance, on a syllable, such as Om or on a more material symbol.

The Guru in the Upanishadic tradition is a realized individual, one who is intellectually supposed to know the Veda and experientially dwells on the absolute Brahman. The epics, in contrast, highlight the divinity of the guru and the consequent reverence and worship of him. Krishna in the Geeta is addressed as father, lord and most venerable guru. In the purans, it is stated that the guru was regarded as the highest divinity in a particular sect, the Bhagvata Puran which regards the guru as a deity who is worshipped because liberation comes only through him. In much of this literature, the guru's actions are equated with those of God.

The ascendency of the Brahmin class along with the heterodox teachers of Buddhism and Jainism gave impetus to the ascetical groups within Hinduism and the indispensability of the guru is stressed in all Smrti literature. But it is only among the gurus of the Tantra that this imperative was strong because as William suggests,

"Esoteric and secret aspects of their salvation process could be known only through the preceptor."[7]

The ideal teacher in the Upanishads is supposed to be a figure of intellectual astuteness while in Tantra his personality is presumed to be dominated by mysterious power.

Two Parallel Religious Traditions

In this context it would be pertinent to bring out two almost parallel religious traditions in Indian society since a very early period. These two trends may broadly be categorized as (i) Idealist and (ii) Proto-materialist or Atmavadi and Dehwadi traditions. The Atmawadi tradition is broadly represented by the Upanishadic and Smriti literature and the Dehwadi trend is evident in Tantric, Lokayat and similar traditions. The relevance of this basic distinction is needed for a proper understanding of the guru phenomenon in Indian society.

Tantric Tradition

The Tantra, as argued by N.N. Bhattacharya, categorically asserts that without diksha or initiation, all efforts are bound to be futile. This aspect has been elaborately treated in all Tantric texts. "The word diksha is derived from the root da (to give) and kshi (to destroy) and hence, as per the Tantric tradition, diksha confers divine knowledge and destroys sin. Most of the Tantric works provide that the knowledge conveyed by the guru must be kept secret. In the Tantras, any qualified person, irrespective of caste or sex, can act as guru and for this purpose, he or she may have to wait for years. He must possess a quiet mind and be well versed in scriptures. The disciple should solely rely on him and be ready to surrender everything to the guru. Buddhist tantras also have the highest praise for the guru, but also warn against false gurus who pretend to know the truth and give false instruction motivated by a greed for money.

According to the Mahanirvana Tantra, persons belonging to sects like Sakta, Shaiva, Vaishnav and Ganpatya may have sectarian gurus, but in order to become a kaula, initiation from a proper kaula teacher is necessary. There is a difference between diksha and updesh. While the former includes abhishek or complete consecration, the latter means communication of mantra during a solar or lunar eclipse, at a tirtha, Siddhakshetra or in a temple. On the day of initiation, the novice, after a bath, is supposed to offer gold or its substitute to the guru for the removal of his sin. Then the guru draws a Sarvatobhadra mandala on an altar, sanctifies the five makaras or the tatvas, places an auspicious jar and fills it with wine. The guru consecrates the novice by sprinkling holy water and uttering a mantra invoking the deities and then gives a new name to him as a symbol of his new life.

This type of initiation is quite in accordance with the entirety of the Indian tradition of initiation in which the idea of death and rebirth is the driving force. The rebirth of the initiate is often represented dramatically by a magical representation of the act of dying and being born from the womb.

Many features of the Vedic upanayan and Tantric diksha are, as suggested, sophisticated versions of the primitive tribal rites of initiation.

The importance of initiation at puberty becomes evident when we look at the primitive secret societies headed by tribal elders. These societies bear distinctive totems, traditions and rituals and in many cases have magico-religious functions. Admission to such a group is restricted to those who have undergone the appropriate rites and rituals.

The idea of primitive secret societies reminds one of the Buddhist Guhya Samaja. The name itself has the same meaning. Tantric converts to early Buddhism, although they professed a belief in the Buddha Sangha and Dhamma, did not give up the traditional beliefs and rituals which they used to practice in secret. The secret conclaves which thus grew within the monastic order developed, in course of time, into organization known as the Guhya Samajas. Their teachings and practices were not sanctioned in early Buddhism, but they were not slow to find means of obtaining the sanction. They tried to introduce their doctrines into Buddhism by composing a new Sangiti or collection or verses which came to be known as the Guhya Samaja tantra and by attributing these doctrines to Buddha, they were able to secure many followers within the Buddhist Sangha.[8]

The Siddhacharyas and the Buddhist-Tantric Influence

Within the fold of Buddhism there developed distinct Tantric ways, the aim of which was to attain siddhi or supernatural power. The followers of this path were opposed to Brahminism and the caste system. In fact, many of them came from the lowest castes. In different Tantric texts, there is reference to the Siddhas and sects like Siddhakula, etc. According to this tradition, there were 84 siddhas who were endowed with supernatural power which they achieved through meditation and physical exercises. Siddhas were also well known in the literature of medieval Indian alchemy for their valuable contribution. The lower ranks of Siddhacharyas are also evident from their names like Dombi, Sabari, Tanti, Camari, Teli and Kumari. They came from the castes of carpet carriers, leather-workers, washer men, oilmen, tailors, fishermen, wood-cutters etc. The Nath Siddhas are also included in the list. These Siddhacharyas did not bother for social distinctions and the caste system.

The Siddhas also believe in the divine power of the guru who initiates the disciples according to their potential. There are five kulas or brands of the Siddha culture: Dombi, Nati, Rajaki, Candali and Brahnani. These are symbols of five female forces or Shakti. The way of the Siddhacharya is basically that of Kaya Sadhana or the way of the body. According to Siddha, there are 32 nerves in the body through which the Shakti flows from its main centre below the naval region. The aim of the aspirant, in short, is the realization of Sahaj. Sahaj is the root of all existence, the source of eternal bliss and pleasures. When all the senses are merged in it, the aspirant has the feeling of absolute non-dualism. He then sees everything as an integral part of his own self.

Liberation here is conceived as not of soul. It is of body which can be attained within the span of human life. The followers of the siddha way use the term Jivanmukti. It means the attainment of immortality which is possible by kayasadhana or disciplining the body.

All believers in the Tantric kayasadhna, including the siddhas believe that the body is the microcosm of the universe. Mountain, sea, moon, sun, river all that of which in the world is composed are within the human body. It is by Hathayoga that one is able to have mastery over the body and mind; Shiva and Shakti reside in the body.

Tantrism and the Natha Siddha Tradition

Nathism originated among persons belonging to the lower ranks of Indian society. This tradition was influenced interestingly by Jainism and Ajivikism and on the other hand by Tantrism. The followers of Nathism had their centers all over North India, in Maharashtra in Western India, and also in parts of South India. In theoretical outlook they have been influenced by the Shaiva and Shakti Agamas. Practically their aim was to attain Siddhi or miraculous power and they characterized the method of attaining it as rahasya or esoteric. Nathism probably developed in the lower regions of the Himalayas. The Natha Siddhas had a general predisposition towards acute practices and acquisitions of supernatural practices and powers. Some of them also believed that by the yogic control over breath, disciplining of the body and the use of drugs made of mica and mercury it was possible to attain immortality. In many places in North India, the Nath Panthis are known as Kan-fat yogi because they were a peculiar earring known as Mudra or Kundala. They use Shiva symbols and observe the Shivratri festival and their religious theories and practices contain many Shakti-Tantric elements. Their deities include Niranjana, Sunya and Adinatha. In Nathism one finds diverse influences as Shaiva, Shakti, Buddhist, Jain and Ajivikas. Ingredients of Islam and Vaishnavism are also evident in the Nath way of life. Their religious discipline was based on Hathayoga. However, over a period one also finds among some Nathpanthis a trend influenced by the Brahminical fold.[9]

Medieval Period - The Bhakti Movement

The religious gurus of the medieval period were influenced by Sahaj ideals. Etymologically sahaj implies that which is same as human instinct itself. In popular version it was understood as God, by whatever name or attribute he may be characterized, resides in the heart of man. The realization of God as identical with one's own self has become the basis of all forms of Sahaj cult. This realization is called by the Sahajayani Buddhists as Mahasukha which is possible through the union of Sunyata and Karuna or Pragya and Upaya. The Natha panthis understand mahasukha in terms of immortality which is possible through Kayasadhana. All forms of Tantric teaching insist on the symbolic union of the male and female principle

- the efficient and material causes of creation
- within the body and this concept has influenced all types of medieval religious ideas.

The Sahaja ideal has also influenced Sikhism. Sikhism is anti-Brahminical; it has no room for communalism and the caste system. Like the Sahajiyas and the followers of the Tantric way, the Sikhs also believe in the absolute authority of the guru.

In the medieval age, several Vaishnav, Shaiva and Tantric sects launched religious reform movements and fought for the religious rights of the shudras and women.

Nevertheless, there were few exceptions in the medieval Bhakti-movements such as Tulsidas who championed Hinduism. He was critical of the Telis, Kumars, Chandals, Kiratas, Kolis and others belonging to despised castes who became gurus by just shaving their heads, meditating, observing vows and reading the purans and expected that the Brahmins should be subservient to them.

"Such observations of Tulsidas were a reflection upon the popularity of teachers like Rabidas, Dharna and others who belonged to the so-called lower castes and professions."[10]

Of the North Indian leaders of the religious reform movement, Ramanand of the 14th and 15th century belonged to the Vaishnav sect. In the Granth Sahib, one comes across a song attributed to him in whom he states that God (Rama) cannot be found in any external object, he is not in the Vedas, and one should seek him in one's heart. Among his disciples, Ravidas was a chamar (cobbler) by caste and profession, who attracted numerous disciples due to his liberal religious ideas. Kabir himself held Ravidas in high esteem. The Granth Sahib contains more than 30 songs composed by him. Jhali, Queen of Chittor, was his follower and the celebrated Mirabai was also his disciple. Thesena, another disciple of Ramanand, was a barber.

Apart from Ravidas, the most celebrated disciple of Ramanand, as widely accepted, was Kabir, born in 1398. He learnt from Ramanand the futility of the caste system, idolatry, pilgrimage, vows, fasts and all external formalities of religion and earned his livelihood by weaving. He advocated that everyone must work, he must earn to help others, but he should not accumulate wealth, should be truthful and accessible to all, he should realize the truth within himself, and that truth is in the form of love and compassion. One's religious system is different from another only in name, God may be called by any name and external formalities in a spiritual quest are meaningless.

One of the best exponents of the way of Kabir was Dadu (1544-1603) who was born in Rajasthan. His objective was to synthesize all forms of religion. The sect founded by him was known Parambrahma Sampradaya. He made a selection of devotional writing from all forms of religion and this compilation was unique. Dadu did not believe in any scripture. According to him, the realization of the self should be the aim of human life. His sons Garibdas and Maskindas and daughters, Nanibai and Mutabai composed many devotional poems. Of his disciples, Sundardas and Rajjab deserve consideration. Rajjab founded a sect, the teachers of which could be either Hindu or Muslim. Of the other medieval saints who pursued the ideals laid down by Kabir and Dadu, Dharamdas,born in Chapra in 1556, Laldas, coming from the meo tribe of Rajasthan, Puran Bhakt and Babalal of Punjab and Narsingh Mehta of Gujrat deserve special consideration.

Among the liberal religious teachers who flourished in North India in the first half of the 18th Century, Bhan Sahib, a follower of Kabir, formed a salvation army. His important disciples were Jivandas and Rabi Sahab. Charandas, who was born at Dehar near Alwar in 1703, started a sect of his own, was against caste system and all forms of superstitions. Shivanarayana born in 1710 in Belia district sought to synthethize Hindu and Muslim religious ideas. Jagjivan who flourished in the last quarter of the 17th century founded the Satyanam or Satnami sect. The Satnamis were against idolatry, untouchability and the caste system. Similar views were held by the Alakhnamis, a sect which flourished in Bikaner under the leadership of Lalgir.

In Maharashtra, saints like Gyandev, Ekanath and Tukaram and others believed in absolute devotion and simplicity in religious life. Personally, many of these gurus were free from caste prejudices but they did not launch any socio-religious movement as did their counterparts in North India.

Bengal, Assam and Orissa were basically the strongholds of Shaivism and Tantra. Jagannath of Puri was originally a tribal god although he is now in Vaishnav garb but his rituals indicate tribal influence.[11]

Nathism in Bengal, Assam and Orissa is also known as yogi pantha due to the influence of the medieval reform movement.

From our appraisal of the guru phenomenon in the Upanishads and the subsequent period, it becomes somewhat evident that the classical type of the Vedic guru imparting training in Vedic texts with all their complexities in terms of its oral transmission with exclusive stress on their proper pronunciations, style of recital and memorization of these texts, with long duration of the stay of pupils in the gurukul, often located in forests areas, away from community, gradually loses significance and almost withers away till the Mauryan and post-Mauryan period, until bold attempts for its revival with some alterations by Shankaracharya in eight and ninth centuries A.D..

Since the advent of the Mauryan period and the emergence of the centralized state power inaugurated by a series of changes in social, political and economic structure, with rise and spread of Buddhism, Jainism, Ajivikas, Lokayats and a host of other religious and philosophical sects, one witnesses a variety of religious teachers challenging the old Brahminic, Vedic style of gurus in Indian society. This period also witnesses the emergence and spread of different religio-mystical cults sponsored largely by the lower social orders with their primitive legacy. The influence of the variety of Tantric sects with their preoccupation with yogic practices or kaya sadhana on all major religions and sects ranging from Buddhism, Jainism and Vedic sects apart from other sects like Nath, Kapalika, Siddhacharya and others, is quite evident.

Advent of the British rule and the Guru phenomenon

With the advent of the British rule, the guru phenomenon based on earlier Nath, Siddha and other Tantric sects and subsequently evident in the medieval Bhakti movement lost its earlier prominence. There are numerous social, political and cultural factors responsible for the guru phenomenon receding into the background in Indian society. It is not possible to examine these factors at length at this juncture. We will attempt to briefly mention some of the more significant factors which we think contributed in sidelining the guru phenomenon.

The first major factor that vitally influenced this development was the approach of the British administration and scholars in assuming and accepting the dominant social and cultural ethos of the traditional Indian society. They favored the version given to them by the Brahmin scholars about the religious and social traditions of Indian society. Thus the Brahminical and Vedic perception and interpretation based on such presumptions were accepted as the appropriate perspective for understanding Indian society.

Secondly, even the Indian scholars and social reformers who were exposed to Western ideals, development and values based on the liberal and democratic framework of European and particularly the British society also projected classical Vedic ideals and the social order as having all the ingredients of such a liberal outlook and society. Here the slogan advocated by Raja Ram Mohan Roy and his supporters was restoration of old Vedic ideals. Indian society had experienced social and cultural decay because of the impact of the alien systems of the Mughals and others. They advocated social reforms in Indian society evoking an imaginary ideal social order that prevailed during the Vedic period. They welcomed with zest the Western liberal values and spread of the Western educational system and social order for the progress of Indian society and polity.

Swami Dayanand Saraswati who founded the Arya Samaj went to the other extreme of rejecting outright Western values and liberal order by advocating that we had a much better society and cultural and social order based on Vedic ideals and that we have hardly anything new to learn from the western world.

The nationalist movement and a large number of our national leaders from the Indian National Congress subscribed to such an outlook. They also found it convenient to popularize the demand for self rule and political independence on the basis of such premises. The British advocacy of India as a backward country and justification of the British rule for the emancipation of Indian population from such primitive, barbaric legacy also found an effective rejoinder from such glorification of the Indian past heritage by Indian leaders. The nationalist leaders who also by and large came from higher castes and better off sections of Indian society also found it quite convenient to adopt and advocate such a Brahminic version of Indian society. Such a backdrop hardly left any space for the rival religious or cultural groups as was the case in the medieval and earlier phases of Indian society to project and propagate their alternative religious and social positions and practices. The guru phenomena thrived in this cultural and religious interface.

The Post-Independence Period

In the post-independence period, especially the first decade of independence, when India could attain a comparatively new threshold of economic, political and social development, one hardly notices any significant spread of the guru phenomena. It is essentially during the last three or four decades that one witnesses an extensive spread of the guru phenomena all over the country. The wide spread growth of the guru phenomena is largely linked with the rapid spread and growing influence of the Hindutva forces in India. Several other factors have also contributed to the rapid and amazing spread of the guru cults in recent years. We can only enumerate some the significant factors which we think have played a more vital role in this direction.

It won't be an exaggeration to say that factors which explain the fast growing influence of the Hindutva forces in all probability account for the extensive spread of the guru phenomena. Of course, it is not our contention that these factors are identical but the correspondence between the two cannot be overstressed.

It is not possible in this brief appraisal to highlight all the factors instrumental in the growth of the Hindutva forces. Nor we are competent enough to tackle such a task. Since th eighties the B.J.P. and its associate organizations such as VHP, Bajrang Dal, Durga Vahini, Sant Sammelan, and several others under the banner of the R.S.S. have witnessed a rapid rise on account of several political, economic and social factors. We can briefly mention some of the prominent factors responsible for this development. Since the seventies the Indian economy witnessed a deepening energy crisis, a paradox to the Indian path of "independent, self-reliant development" culminating in a severe crisis of foreign exchange along with the growing structural crisis of global capitalism. The late Mrs. Indira Gandhi coming into power in the eighties shifting from her earlier thrust of Garibi Hatao, nationalization of financial institutions and independent foreign policy opted for or had to opt for the policy of neo-liberalization as advocated by institutions like the I.M.F. and World Bank under the pressure of American imperialism. The Indian economy and polity had experienced a severe jolt since the mid-sixties and this got articulated in the political upsurge in West Bengal, Andhra Pradesh, Bihar and other parts of the country in the form of the Naxalbari revolt, peasant agitations and workers struggles culminating in recurring state and Bharat bandhs. This growing discontent got articulated in the growing influence of communists and socialists along with the rightist political parties like Jan Sangh and similar formations in different parts of the country and their posing a serious challenge to the congress's monopoly of power. The Indian National Congress could not continue to retain its political hold over the electorates on the basis of its earlier umbrella character based on an alliance of upper caste, Muslim and other minority votes and dalit castes, especially at regional levels. The emergence of new social classes with their expanding economic base and also numerical strength posed a serious challenge to the Congress rule. The new social class largely recruited from the middle and backward castes also benefited from the expanding industrial base in rural and urban areas. In order to retain its political hold, the Congress openly started playing the communal card in the 1980 general elections. This became blatantly evident in the Jammu and Kashmir elections.

This sharp turn in the congress policy also provided a golden opportunity to the BJP to use the communal card more effectively and also skillfully. Since the 1980s, the rathyatra and Ram Mandir politics with the support of the newly emerged entrepreneurial classes and other middle castes who had not found any space in the congress rule enabled the BJP and allied forces to rapidly expand their influence in the country.

The electronic media, its extensive spread since the eighties with the relay of The mahabharat and Ramayana serials also significantly boosted the appeal of communal forces to gain a larger foothold in Indian society. Along with the use of the television, other devices such as manufacturing audio and video cassettes based on religious mythology, devotional songs based entirely on Hindus scriptures and god heads were also used effectively to spread the influence of the Hindu communal propaganda. Such religious propaganda with its blatant communal overtones helped not only communal forces but also contributed in a big way in providing a social base for the growing flocks of gurus in many parts of the country.

The rise and extensive spread and popularity of the guru and gurumai phenomenon in the last over three decades all over India could be attributed to this favorable environment. The extensive patronage they received from the corporate sector and the ruling strata has facilitated the popularity and influence of the cult of gurudom in no small manner.

Apart from this, the forces unleashed by neo-liberalism with its exclusive stress on the unregulated market mechanism have facilitated the spread and popularity of the guru phenomenon. The world of gurus with its infinite variety of appeals cultivated by its seasoned operators has become a big attraction cutting across caste and class borders and thereby has successfully created a huge entertainment market. The sale of audio and video cassettes alone fetches over Rs.1400 crores annually in the Indian entertainment market. If one takes into account the huge amount of money generated through T.V. serials based on the infinite variety of mythological figures, the total financial market and profit generated from such programs would probably exceed the total capital generated from all other entertainment markets put together.[1]

As Prof. Panikar has aptly argued, since independence the extensive spread of religiosity and the commoditization of religion largely account for the rapid rise of the guru phenomenon in the last over three decades in this country.[12]

The state patronage, open admiration and presence of prominent state as well as central political leaders, irrespective of their allegiance to any particular political party is also largely responsible for the rise and institutionalization of the guru cults in India. The corporate sector has also extended large scale support by the presence and sponsorship of industrial magnates and business tycoons of ramkathas, bhagwat sapthas, shiv parayans, radha krishna celebrations, gayatri yagnas, and similar religious discourses and festivals initiated by modern gurus all over the country. Apart from this, other major factors instrumental in the rapid rise and popularity of the modern guru phenomenon are increasing insecurity, alienation and despair experienced by practically all sections of the Indian population cutting across caste and class lines as a result of cut-throat competition and the inflated consumerism let loose by the global policy of neo-liberalism based on the unregulated market mechanism. Modern godmen cater to these needs. Most of the modern gurus' success and increasing popularity could be attributed to their art of oratory and skill in manipulating their audience's mind-sets and providing an effective escape mechanism from their routine world of sorrows and anxieties.

References

1. Mangalwadi: World of Gurus. P 76, 1974
2. Peter Brent: Godmen in India. P 287
3. Ibid, Mangalwadi
4. Peter Brent, Ibid
5. William Carkner: A Tradition of Teachers-Shankara and the Jagadgurus Today. PP 3-4, Motilal Banarsidass, Delhi 1983
6. Ibid, PP 8-27
7. N. N. Bhattarcharya: History of the Tantirc Religion, PP 148-149, Manohar, New Delhi 1984
8. Ibid, P 283
9. Ibid, P 284
10. Ibid, P 303
11. Ibid, P 307
12. K N Pannikar: Ungodly Men, Unholy Activities.

5

Rajneesh - The Background

Rajneesh Chandra Mohan, one of the most controversial among the modern godmen, was born in the district of Raisen, Madhya Pradesh, on 11th December 1931. His father Babulal, a Jain businessman, had to shift to Gurudwara, Narsimhapur in 1954 on account of financial problems. Rajneesh had his early education at Narsimhapur. From 1944 to 1951, he studied in Jabalpur and obtained a Bachelor of Arts degree. In 1957, he completed his post graduation in philosophy securing the top position. According to his biographer, Dr. Ramchandra Prasad, he was an exquisite painter, a voracious reader, a poet and an amateur photographer. It appears that due to adverse circumstances he had to discontinue his studies for a while and work as an assistant editor in the daily newspaper Nav Bharat.

From 1957-1967, Rajneesh taught philosophy in two colleges. Subsequently, according to Dr. Prasad's version, he gave up his teaching assignment to devote his life to "the spiritual regeneration of humanity, to spread practical spirituality for every man."

In a more recent, exhaustive and critical appraisal with a deeper psycho-analytical perception, James S. Gordon remarks: "Rajneesh's late teens were a time of turmoil and contradictions. He fell in love and his girlfriend Shashi died. He advocated socialism and became disillusioned with it, denounced Gandhi and deeply mourned his death. He mocked religion as he looked for answers in the Jain, Buddhist and Christian scriptures. He read esoteric books, practiced magic, yogic breath control and self hypnosis, and hypnotized his friends and family. He spent time with the eccentric babas who had taken him under their wing and met a variety of people - musicians, politicians, sages and sadhus."

During his college career he had acquired a reputation as a small town rebel and the prankster of Jabalpur. Initially he resembled the western Bohemians who were his contemporaries. He used to run 16 miles a day, reportedly "just to feel him."

In 1960, he began to travel around India, lecturing to students, religious groups and others, "attacking the country's most cherished institutions and beliefs, spreading a gospel of doubts and discontent." In 1965, some of Bombay's Jain businessmen formed a radical organization named Jeevan Jagriti Kendra and extended material and moral support to Rajneesh to propagate his teachings. The founders of this body briefly cherished the hope that Rajneesh would become a tirthankara, a saintly teacher of Jainism. They soon got disillusioned as by the late sixties, Rajneesh came to the view that Jainism was in no way different from other traditional religious - parochial and now irrelevant in its beliefs and practices. He ridiculed Jain asceticism as masochism, and mocked its elaborate dietary prohibitions and strict non-violence.

Simultaneously, Rajneesh extended his offensive against all orthodoxies. India's ancient religions, he argued, were now dead: their priests a pack of hypocrites and petty tyrants, lulling the minds of their followers with empty rituals, oppressing them with fears of domination and assurances of bliss in this and the next life. He also condemned socialism to which all major political parties pay at least lip service. He said that India's whole attitude towards sex, from arranged marriages to the suppression of sexuality in adolescence, to the clandestine affairs of adulterous men, was life-denying and perverted.

During 1968-1969, Mahatma Gandhi's birth centenary year, Rajneesh focused his attack on the Mahatma. He claimed that Gandhi, whom in many ways otherwise he respected, had been a Hindu chauvinist, and not really ecumenical. He dubbed him a masochist who loved to manipulate others by starving himself, a pervert who refused to make love to his wife, and an old man who brought naked young girls to his bed. Further, he described Gandhi's Experiments with Truth as experiments with food and sex.

After a few years Rajneesh was to state: "With or without reason, I was creating controversies, creating criticism." In fact, as described by several other critics and his ex-disciples, Rajneesh consciously adopted an offensive stance against established religions and prominent figures as an effective strategy for continuously stealing the limelight and drawing large crowds. Obviously, western as well as eastern religious teachers found his arrogance unbearable. Rajneesh, unlike other god men in India who establish their authenticity on the basis of their connection with their renowned gurus and to a lineage that might go back before written history, stated that he had no guru, did not acknowledge his debts even to obvious sources like Gurdjieff and Ouspensky, or even J. Krishnamurthy, whose influence is so evident in his writings.

Rajneesh's radical presentations, the freshness of his style, especially his outrageous messages, attracted the curious, the adventurous, liberals and radicals, young and old, men and women. A section of Indians with their heterodox opinions and questioning minds were getting disillusioned with conventional religious practices as well as the political leadership. They saw in Rajneesh a modern man, critical, sexually liberated, a person of a different sensibility, and also an anti-establishment figure. He thus attracted a wide range of people, cosmopolitan's speculators, bureaucrats, artists, unemployed graduates, neo-rich urbanites and also a large number of upper class women.

Accuracy and consistency were often wanting in Rajneesh's speeches, and as pointed out by Gordon and several others, the more erudite could easily pick out distortions, exaggerations and inaccuracies. However, they also did find in him a germ of truth or the taste of authenticity.

Influences on Rajneesh

As pointed out by his biographer and great admirer, Dr. Prasad, although Rajneesh possessed a brilliant intellect, no one could have been more militantly anti-intellectual than him. With his superb oratory, penetrating parables and courageous critique of our cultural and religious traditions, it is suggested, he began to hold a commanding historical significance in India today.

His daring denunciations of the traditional philosophy, religion, scripture, morality, values and ideas, his outspoken criticisms of men like Gandhi and Vinoba Bhave, and his bold advocacy of sex as a legitimate means of salvation, won him many enemies, yet thousands admired him as Bhagwan. "Bhagwan Rajneesh is an enlightened one, who has become one with infinity. Infinity breathes through him. He is not a person but the Divinity personified. Transcendental truth shines every moment through him. He lives beyond cosmos, beyond being, in nothingness, in the great void, Nirvana".

Further, it is suggested that through discourses, books, meditation camps etc, Rajneesh was seeking to awaken people to "freedom" and authentic "individuality." To the ascetic who has excessive attachment to detachment, his invitation was for fulfillment, naturalness and spontaneity. The passion of his soul was, Dr. Prasad suggested, making people free and genuine. It is also claimed that Rajneesh resigned his job to concentrate on the spiritual regeneration of humanity. He also was quite optimistic about the realization of his cherished goal: "I see a spiritual regeneration in the whole world is in the offing, and a new man is about to be born. We are passing through the birth pangs."

His followers, as stated by Dr. Prasad, are largely drawn from the richer strata and Rajneesh also openly advocated that only the rich could become spiritual, and "that the materially poor can ever be spiritual is out-and-out absurd".

Even though born a Jain, Rajneesh refused to be called either a Jain or Hindu. He also rejected intellect as a valid source of knowledge. His acceptance of mysticism and silence was projected as an indication of influence of both contemporary Western philosophy and that of Buddhism in his teachings.

Tracing the other sources of influence on his mind, the same biographer mentions Rajneesh's assumption, that ultimately reality is only one and that diversity is illusion, draws from the Upanishads. His contention that the average man is ignorant or unenlightened was probably borrowed from Gurdjieff's view of man as machine.

His doctrines of inner void, shunyavada, and sudden enlightenment as brought out by Dr. Prasad were derived from his familiarity with Zen Buddhism, particularly from the writings of D T Suzuki. Several of his stories and parables, it seems, were also drawn from Zen

Buddhism. Dr. Prasad also maintains that the influence of J. Krishnamurthy is very much evident in Rajneesh's hatred for conventionalism and orthodoxy and his passionate plea for spontaneity and freedom.

Rajneesh's view of sex and mysticism was a queen amalgam of Buddhist tantricism and modern psychology. P.D. Ouspensky's stress on the kinship between sexual and mystical states had a far-reaching influence on Rajneesh. Apart from that, the influence of Colin Wilson, Kenneth Water, D. H. Lawrence, Nietzsche and others was also quite apparent in his preaching's. Rajneesh's critique of the contemporary politico-economic situation in India, it appears, was largely based on the writings of Arther Koestler.

Besides the above, it is further indicated that there was much that Rajneesh borrowed from religious leaders like Mahavir, Buddha and Christ. He was familiar with their teachings and freely quoted and misquoted them. At times he appears to have even placed his ideas into their months to exploit their authority!

Rajneesh's philosophy was also in a sense an anti-philosophy due to his pronounced anti-intellectualism. Dr. Prasad prefers to address him as a 'mystic of feeling'. He was categorical about his refusal to accept reason as the basis of truth or knowledge and also held that words could not express it. Dharma, according to Rajneesh, has nothing to do with thinking or thoughts. Thinking does give results but not satisfaction.

Similarly, Rajneesh also held that 'Truth' or 'God' is 'unknowable'. No one knows anything. Neither does the wife know her husband, nor beauty, or truth. Neither reason nor the words of the scriptures or the gurus can tell us know what Truth is. All those who have known so far have known only through silence, not knowledge. Thus it can be said that Rajneesh shows ways of killing the mind. Truth emerges only, according to him, in a state of thoughtlessness. Intellect is the 'chief villain'.

Behind all the multiplicity in the world, Rajneesh advocates, there is only one reality - void, emptiness. He also calls this God or Brahman. He also rejects the idea of duality of creator and creation and holds that by reason or intellect, 'voidness' cannot be proved. This he accepted on the authority of the scriptures. Also like other Indian thinkers,

Rajneesh agrees with the abstraction that man's soul or self, void, begins to think of itself as an individual man. Man finds himself in bondage, but this is, Rajneesh contends, illusory.

He also shares other Indian religious preachers' beliefs in Hindu concepts such as the transmigration of the soul, rebirth, and the theory of karma. He also says, like others, that once God somehow becomes individualized, it remains an individual soul until it attains self-realization. Prabhupada of ISKCON also argued on the same plane.

During coitus, according to Rajneesh, "husband and wife create circumstances in which a soul can descend into a body". Does this mean he is talking of a duality of soul and body, which otherwise he rejects? But, as one critic points out, he is not bothered about such confusion and contradiction in his teachings.

In his well-known work, Sex to Super-Consciousness, Rajneesh asserts that religion so far has condemned sex as sin and made man more sexual. The children born out of this sexuality, according to Rajneesh, obviously are sick and weak, frustrated and degraded. Rajneesh, hence advocates that children born out of 'free love' would be supermen, as contemplated by Nietzsche, and all the problems of the world would be solved!

Rajneesh also suggests that man's problems are also due to ignorance about his true nature. "Man," he says, "imagines that he acts and thinks. In reality, like a machine, he only reacts." Somebody insults you and you become angry, which according to Rajneesh is a mechanical reaction. The root cause of man's problems is his ignorance of his freedom. The solution to all problems, he advocates, lies in self-realization. Because, according to Rajneesh, our true self is void, self-realization is the same as God-realization, which in turn implies attainment of a mind devoid of all thoughts.

For thousands of years, religions, the scriptures and gurus, Rajneesh argues, have been cruel to man. They led him to search in temples, scriptures, morality, contemplation or concentration at the saints' feet. The search, however, should be within us. This is meditation. Man's problem, Rajneesh finds, is that he lives at the level of intellect, and so ignorantly take reality to be dual – self and non-self – good and bad, body and soul, as opposite categories. Salvation lies beyond the mind.

Shorn of all the verbal jugglery, one wonders where Rajneesh really differs in the above formulation from traditional Hindu religious philosophy.

Referring to the ideological basis of Rajneesh's preachings, Dr. Prasad argues that some of the great Upanishadic ideas are also found in Zen Buddhism, and Rajneesh is quite familiar with them. However, according to Dr. Prasad, the Upanishads form only the theoretical side of his teachings. To understand Rajneesh's philosophy and mysticism, it is important to trace its link with Zen Buddhism. Typical of the spirit of Zen which also finds reflection in Rajneesh's teachings are the following doctrines:

1. All work is useful in so far as it is really creative and this it cannot be if it submits to forms, pious practices, and the guru and so on.
2. Buddhahood is attained by looking inside one's own mind.
3. Work out your own solution with diligence.
4. A special transmission outside the scriptures, no dependence upon words.
5. Zen lives in facts and hates all abstractions and concepts, which are like so many cages, in which the flow of life is foolishly confined.
6. The approach to Zen is total, encompassing the whole man. No man, according to Zen, can be wholehearted unless he has come into his own wholeness. Zen brings man into union with life and with himself, and proposes to make him realize that the world is not something other than his own very self.

Zen Buddhism, according to D.T. Suzuki, is one of the Mahayana schools of Buddhism. Without their Indian garb, Rajneesh's references to 'void' in his well-known work The Kranti Beej, remind one of the Zen doctrine of emptiness. In his book Antaryatra, he suggests that the reason why science (or religions) has not been able to destroy ignorance and why our history is full of wars, crimes, hatred, conflicts and social struggles, is that so far we have only cultivated our head and ignored the region around the navel, which is the root of our existence.

It is also interesting in this connection to note that when the world was getting into the grip of a 'yoga wave', Rajneesh revived tantra.

Both yoga and tantra aim at union with the divine, he says, but yoga is a struggle, tantra is a path of surrender. Yoga produces pride. Tantra makes us humble, gentle and loving. According to tantra, as interpreted by Rajneesh, "If a seeker is not interested in sex, he is not a seeker at all." Further, it is argued that tantra is not concerned with philosophic quests but with life. Sex is the very "pre-supposition" of life. Hence, according to Rajneesh, sexuality and spirituality are two aspects of one energy.

Rajneesh's contention that sex is a source of divine energy and advocacy of a longer duration of coitus with creation of a permanent state of bliss won him many enemies as well as friends. He was cynically dubbed the 'sex guru'. Rajneesh compared the sex act with meditation, explaining this in terms of surrender. "Anything becomes a God," he said, "if you can surrender. Surrender to your wife and she becomes divine." Tantra, he claimed, is amoral. He hated morality because he felt that it creates hypocrisy. He had also no hesitation in advocating that "being inconsistent is a virtue, a sign of being progressive".

Political and Social Theory

Rajneesh's views on political economy are also equally unconventional. For instance, he argued, "We are poor because we have accepted poverty." He also held that capitalism and socialism are not two contradictory systems. "Socialism is the goal, the end, and capitalism the means to achieve it." That is why, he argued, he was in favour of socialism and yet not against capitalism. He also thought that it was not necessary to have had a revolution to establish socialism in Russia and China, nor was it necessary in India.

He said (in the seventies before he left India), "What we need today in India is an atmosphere congenial to the development of capitalism. India should take a decision that for fifty years it will allow capitalism's full growth." In fact, he contended that capitalism is just taking roots but we are smothering its growth. "First," he said, "let the industrial revolution be ushered in. Let the entire country be filled with industries. Let there be million of Tatas - big and small."

According to him, whatever industry the government took into its hands began running at a loss. Investment in the public sector was nearly double of that in the private sector, but all investment in public sector was yielding no returns or profits. Yet the government wanted to nationalize the rest of industry. This over-simplified view reveals either Rajneesh's ignorance about the basis of political economy or is a deliberate distortion of facts, or are theoretical formulations to suit his own ideological framework.

Rajneesh's views shocked and repelled many people but they particularly attracted groups of wealthy businessmen in Bombay. In 1964 he had begun to hold meditation camps for these men and their families in mountain resorts. Ma Yoga Laxmi, coming from a wealthy Kutchi business family, was his first real disciple. Her father had had close ties with several political leaders including Gandhi, Nehru and Morarji Desai. Laxmi had gone into social work and politics and was the secretary of the Bombay branch of the All-India

Women's Conference when she met Rajneesh in the mid-sixties. After attending two of his meditation camps she accepted Rajneesh as her master and began to travel with him. In 1970, she became his secretary and raised the money that permitted him to stop his travels and settle into a Bombay apartment. From 1971 to 1981, till Rajneesh left for the USA, Laxmi managed all the practical affairs of the guru, such as raising money, later administering the ashram etc.

Until 1970, Rajneesh had been a philosopher, lecturing on politics, sex and society. Subsequently he was projected as a religious man teaching disciples. But in India, as pointed out by Frances Fitzgerald, whose work we will later refer to, such distinctions are not absolute.

In his early camps conducted in Bombay and Mount Abu, which later earned him notoriety, Rajneesh announced, "I am here to wake you up." The earliest camps, it seems, were fairly sedate: talks twice a day to the several hundred who came from all over India for quiet meditation (on the breath and the navel), and self-hypnotic exercises. Meditation, Rajneesh insisted, would not happen until people undid the 'knots of negativity' in their bodies, minds and emotions. Agitation and catharsis were regarded as conditions to loosen the physical constrictions due to chronic stress, a common occurrence in modern life, and the fixed patterns of thought and feeling imposed by family and society.

Innovative Techniques

In the late 1960s, Rajneesh, as indicated by Gordon and others, had begun to combine traditional techniques with the expressive devices he borrowed from Western psychology and particularly from the human potential movement. Bio-energetic exercises derived from the work of Wilheim Reich and his pupils such as screaming, crying, rolling eyes and shaking were performed in a sequence with Indian mantras, Tibetan humming and Sufi dances.

Over the years, Rajneesh designed dozens of meditation techniques for different temperaments and occasions. These included active techniques for the morning and quieter ones for evening meditation, with mirrors, pillows and infant pacifiers, indoor and outdoor meditation, meditation in automobiles and aeroplanes, relaxation meditation done in the afternoon, meditation that could be done singly, in pairs or in groups, in the early morning or late at night. He refined them, at times developed them into stages, and gave them different names such as Kundalini, four-stage shaking, dancing, awareness, Nadabrahma. a Tibetan humming technique, and Gaurishankar, a candle-gazing technique, so called because according to Rajneesh, it could get you as high as Gaurishankar.

The best known and most dramatic technique was the chaotic, which later was called 'dynamic meditation'. Dynamic meditation is in many ways, as pointed out by Gordon, a microcosm of Rajneesh's methods and his outlook. It was supposed to a synthesis of eastern and western techniques, a shock to habitual patterns of thought and behaviour. It was, at least on the surface, antithetical to the conventional Indian religious practices of prayer and meditation. For this, Rajneesh said, no holy place or elaborate ritual was necessary, no wordshipful attitude, no priests and no austerities were required. One could simply put on a tape and do it.

As a matter of fact, Rajneesh devised and modified his multifold meditation techniques in response to his rapidly rising number of young western disciples, closely watching their background and their peculiar temperaments and needs. Rajneesh in this sense was not only a very shrewd observer of others' responses and experiences but also had a remarkable ability of innovating and adapting ways and techniques that would suit their temperament.

Genesis of the Organization

In the 1970s, Rajneesh founded what he called the Neo-Sanyas International Movement, and initiated six disciples as the first step in creating a spiritual awakening around the world. He gave his disciples new names and, at the request of Laxmi, as he said, a mala, or a bead string, with a photograph of him on it. It was also at Laxmi's suggestion, it seems, that disciples were instructed to wear the traditional orange robes of holy men. The next year, Rajneesh changed his own name as well. Until then, his supporters had called him acharya, or teacher: Acharya Rajneesh. Now he look the title 'Bhagwan' (from a list drawn up by a disciple who knew Sanskrit) and called himself Bhagwan Sri Rajneesh.

In Bombay, Rajneesh began to attract some of the westerners along the spiritual tourist routes. His unorthodox views had become a major attraction. As suggested by Fitzgerald, in her excellent study of four Utopian communes, Rajneeshpuram in Oregon being the principal one, "Here was a guru unencumbered by tradition, an Enlightened Master, who could quote Heidegger and Sartre, and who furthermore believed in technology, capitalism and sex. Rajneesh was unique also on the ashram routes."

Rajneesh also liked westerners, paid special attention to them, taking interest in their personal problems and aspirations. Though his disciples never realized it, Rajneesh, as brought out by Fitzgerald, learned a great deal from the westerners he met in Bombay and Pune. Teertha, one of his early American disciples, brought him his entire library, Rajneesh, as noted by others also, was a voracious reader and quite a good listener as well. When he explained his 'dynamic meditation' to Indians, he spoke of waking the goddess Kundalini, the so-called female scrpent, as described in Hindu mythology, that lies at the lowest chakra, the base of the spine, and releasing her energies to rise to the highest chakra, the thousand petaled lotus of the mind. While explaining the 'dynamic' to westerners, he would speak of removing the psychological block lodged in the body as physical blocks and releasing this body energy to the brain. The conception was still Tantric, but in English it sounded like Withelm Reich. Richard Price, the ex-director of the Esalen Institute, a Gestalt therapist, and an early admirer turned critic of Rajneesh, referring to Rajneesh's Book of the Secrets, said that "it fitted very well into the Gestalt framework". The guru reminded him a lot of Alan Watts, but it did seem occur to Price that the guru might not have read Watts.

According to Teertha, Rajneesh showed keen interest in what the western Esalen therapists were doing, and promised to incorporate some of their therapies into his own work. Teertha did not take the guru's words seriously. But three years later Rajneesh did just that. The westerners in his ashram first were taugh primal scream and encounter group therapies, and later, when they were more in number, he branched out into Gestalt, bio-energetics, rolling and so on.

As Fitzgerald suggests, what the guru made of these therapies is a mystery even now. At times, he related them to Tantric tradition. Stating that they have been tried by seekers of Tantra for centuries, the mystic beings Sarahapa and Tilopa and Kanohpa had tried them. He said that for the first time he was trying to give these experiments a scientific basis. They were conducted in secrecy for a long time. At other times he explained them simply as a means to meditation: "They will help you to unburden the garbage that you have repressed within yourself." At still other times, he would explain them in purely secular terms as cures for western nuroses.

The Pune Ashram

In 1974, Laxmi moved Rajneesh from Bombay to Pune. His health had already deteriorated by this time; he had developed diabetes, asthma and several allergies. The climate was better in Pune and now he had enough disciples to establish an ashram - the Rajneesh Foundation.

Laxmi bought a villa with six acres of land and several outhouses in an affluent suburb of the city. The guru, who had formerly spent a good deal of time talking with individual disciples, in Pune saw his flock only twice a day. In the morning he lectured, and in the evening he held darshan, answering questions submitted to him and showing the path of sanyas.

Rajneesh began with speaking about the world's sacred scriptures, about the Upanishads and Vedanta. His lectures have culminated into a huge body of literature - ten volumes on the Bhagvad Gita, several books on Buddha's sutras and on Bodhidharma and the Zen masters, lectures on the songs of the Baul mystics and the poems of the Sufis,

Kabir and Rumi, two volumes on the fragments of Pythagoras and two more on Heraclitus, books on Lao-Tzu, Chuang-Tzu and Lien Tzu, the Taoist masters, several volumes on Yoga, Mitra, Tibetan and Indian Tantra, and volumes on sex as a source of divinity.

He lectured in alternate months in Hindi and English. He could speak for hours without any notes. His essential message, as summed up by Fitzgerald, was the central one of the Hindu-Buddhist tradition: that God is in all things, a living current of energy flowing through the temporary and illusory world of forms, and that the Buddhas were those who saw through the illusion of self and of time to the great Oneness of existence.

Like Krishnamurthy, he admitted Christ, Lao-Tzu and the great mystics of other traditions into the galaxy of Enlightened Beings. His early lectures were more or less theoretical. He would do a series on the Upanishads or Tantra or on the New Testament. Later his style degenerated into a more personal, eclectic one, telling Zen parables, jokes, stories from the life of Buddha or the Sufi sages, and citing for instance, Gurdjieff, Socrates and Bob Hope in a single lecture.

Major Attraction

By 1976, Rajneesh Ashram had become a major attraction along the guru route, especially for western tourists. In Seeking the Master - a kind of guide to spiritual India published in 1980, it rated the longest entry and the equivalent of at least three stars. Thousands of westerners poured in – so many that even the huge Pune ashram could not accommodate them. Many proably came only out of curiosity, because Rajneesh's advocacy of sex as a means to divine transcendence made him the most controversial of the Indian gurus. Many stayed, not necessarily for Rajneesh's lectures but also for the liberal atmosphere, the free sex and other activities going on in the ashram.

Under Laxmi's direction, the permanent workers and residents in the ashram, around 600 of them, created an arts-crafts centre that turned out clothing, jewellery, ceramics and organic cosmetics, all for sale, and staged music, theatre and mime performances. The visitors were offered at least nine types of meditation – dynamic to Zen, apart from classes in yoga, karate, Tai Chi, acupuncture, Sufi dancing and Shiatsu massage. In 1975, the ashram offered two kinds of western therapies;

by 1979 it offered some 60 of them including several invented all the ashram. As Fitzgerald describes it: "Like an octopus, the ashram reached out and embraced everything that came its way; eventually, it included almost every booth in the entire holistic New Age marketplace."

With regard to life in the Pune ashram, accounts of those who took sanyas and those who did not differ sharply in certain respects but they are consistent in describing a madhouse-cum-carnival atmosphere. Each day, hundreds, at times thousands, of westerners in ochre robes flooded into the ashram for dynamic meditation, where hundreds of people screamed, sang or moaned as they shook their bodies and together yelled "Hoo! Hoo! Hoo!" at the top of their voices. Rajneesh had said, "I am going to bring your insanity out, unless you become consciously insane, you can never become sane."

There were therapy groups and meditations, but the distinctions between them were not always clear. In one meditation, as Fitzgerald recounts, "You had to sit and answer the question "Who am I?' for two days." In some therapies people were experimenting a lot with so called

'Tantric Sex' in the hope of some experience of the divine. As Fitzgerald says, just who anyone was sleeping with seemed to be of less importance as there were all kinds of love and energy going around. Rajneesh advocated losing one's mind and being completely spontancous and living in the present, not the past or the future. He believed that chaos helped.

The ashram was not a place for Hindu purists, nor was it for people who worried too much about what disciplehood and surrender might impty. Rajneesh said, "The ego has to drop. The mind has to disappear, for God to be, you have to disappear." An American bio-energeties therapist, as revealed by Fitzgerald, who spent three months with the guru in Bombay, thought this unhelpful. "Rajneesh encouraged the letting go of one's own responsibility," he said, and that is where he left it. It was one thing to ask people to drop the obstructive chatter going on in their heads and another to ask them to drop the process of discrimination. Bhagwan made no distinction between the two.

The same therapist also participated in dynamic meditation, and was disillusioned. What he saw from the Esalen perspective was a series of cathartic techniques to which he had become inured by then. When he saw three or four hundred people doing the 'dynamic' meditation, he felt it was nothing but mass auto suggestion. There were people all around him in a state of regression. They had become infantile and were relating to a father figure. People were attached to Rajneesh as to a God. It was in no way different than a simpleminded devotion to a God, the kind of devotion that Rajneesh had earlier come out strongly against. The therapist viewed this as not something peculiar to Rajneesh but a problem inherent in Hinduism.

As against this, some old disciples like Ma Satya Bharati were all praise for the way things were happening. A divorcee from the US in her early forties, she wrote two books about her experience in the Pune Ashram. In one book she described taking sanayas as "a return to innocence and a liberation". According to her, "to surrender to a Master" isn't to surrender anything that is real. On the contrary, "it is to surrender, to give up all the dreams, all the peripheral accumulations that the ego is made up of. We can't surrender anything that's real, Bhagwan says, because as we are we don't have anything that's real. Everything about us is false, borrowed and inauthentic."

Satya Bharati said that she took up dynamic meditation in order to get rid of the madness that Rajneesh spoke about. Thus western disciples who identified completely with their guru's teachings could continue to live in that make-believe world for years.

In Pune, Rajneesh had often said that he would 'go into silence' and that he was waiting only for something to happen to his disciples by just being in his presence. In India, it is customary for holy men to go into silence at some point in their lives. But in an ashram full of growth movement therapists, this was a bit ironical; by going silent, Fitzgerald says, "Rajneesh became the guru equivalent of an orthodox Freudian analyst.

Spiritual Laboratory

Where Rajneesh differed, it seems, from most other gurus was in his pragmatic approach to the question of spiritual disciplines and practices. He advocated that traditional techniques of meditation which worked during Buddha's time are no more effective for the modern man. For 20th century people, he said, new techniques had to be developed. With this logic, he turned the Pune ashram into a kind of spiritual garage, into a laboratory for all sorts of experimentation. For him the only test of legitimacy was what worked, or what seemed to work.

The western therapists at the ashram introduced the growth movement techniques they had learnt and from there on, experimented, adapting their techniques to the particular purpose of the ashram. Some of the therapies they invented, it is said, played a direct role in establishing the master-disciple transference. In these therapies, unlike those of the encounter movement, there was, as some disciples reported, "an almost tangible sense of Bhagwan's presence". Teertha, who had come from the Esalen Institute, was a guide in various meditation techniques in the Pune Ashram. When he felt that someone was open and vulnerable, he would tell him/her to sit and look at a picture of Bhagwan. That was enough to transform one's being.

The ashram therapies differed from the growth movement techniques also in other respects. There was a sense of total acceptance in the groups in Rajneesh ashram. Nothing was condemned. There were no limitations, no restrictions: one could take things to the extreme. Group leaders in the West placed limits on what happened in their groups because of their own fears and sense of accountability. Their image would be at stake. Here, it was felt, the responsibility was Bhagwan's, so the therapists could allow almost anything to happen; they could afford to take risks.

Irresponsible Risks

This freedom (or absolute dependency, viewed in another light), as pointed out by Fitzgerald, was apparently what many of the therapists had been looking for all along. Thus a number of them took tremendous risks with peoples' mental well-being, particularly for those whose mental health had not been tested. The film Ashram made by the German film maker Wolfgang Dobrowolny in 1978 documents the risks that they took. Among the boundaries some of the therapist 'transcended' both on screen and off were the usual strictures against sexual aggression and physical violence. This was also supposedly logical, as the theory behind dynamic meditation was that participants should give physical expression to their repressions and frustrations in order to get rid of their 'emotional blocks'. Rajneesh thought of these therapies as advertisements for the ashram.

Teertha and Somendra, group leaders, were merely extrapolating this notion in their groups by encouraging participants to act out all the emotions they felt for each other, including the desire to inflict grievous bodily harm. No one was actually reported to be killed in these encounters, but a number of people, naked and weaponless, spent a good deal of time and energy in taking out their aggression. There were several cases of rape in the sessions, several cases of fractured limbs and various other injuries.

In 1977, as widely reported, Richard Price, the Esalen director and Gestalt therapist visited the ashram. Observing one of Teerth's groups, he wrote a letter of protest to Rajneesh stating: "My experience in my first two weeks at the ashram in the meditation camp was excellent. I felt a deepening, an enrichment, and attachment. During the last two weeks, my experience was quite the opposite. I had softened and opened only to be confronted with Teertha's autocratic, coercive, life-negating style of 'leadership', a style reinforcing violence and sexual acting out of the most unfeeling kind; a style negating soft emotions and emerging sensitivity and manipulating group pressure to force conformity. Is this what Bhagwan is about?"

Price, who died in an accident in 1985, initially had a serious interest in the ashram's therapies because Teertha was from the Esalen Institute and he himself had sent many people to the Pune ashram and had become a 'mail order sanyasi' himself. Thus he was personally and professionally involved.

With his long experience as the Esalen director, Price was aware that any decent and responsible leader would protect participants against any injury, and that could be done without suppressing any genuine expression of anger, sexuality or aggression. Talking about Teerth's ways, he said, "It is as if the worst mistakes of some inexperienced Esalen group leaders of many years ago have been systematized and given the stamp of God." Rajneesh's reply to Price's letter was amazing. He wrote to him that among other things, it was only 'objective compassion' to allow those obsessed by violence to get it out of their system.

In this connection, it is interesting to refer to Gita Mehta, who in her book Karma Cola quotes Ma Yoga Laxmi's reactions to these therapies: "We have a meditation in the ashram where the disciples beat each other. Hai Ram! What simple pleasure they get from hitting and thrashing, I tell you only yesterday one boy had his wrist smashed but he is happy and it is very beautiful. Today, poor chap, is in the massage meditation, he is having oil rubbed over the broken parts."

Violence in the ashram therapies ended only in January of 1979, a short while after the notorious case of the Jonestown mass suicide. Therapy groups subsequently were discontinued altogether. Rajneesh had a neat explanation, of course, saying that psychotherapies were needed only during the initial stage because the thousands of people coming to his ashram from the West were not yet enlightened enough to heal their own psychological wounds.

Such whimsical, arbitrary, and dictatorial attitudes had become pronounced in Rajneesh's ashram in Pune. It was manifested in other programmes and the approach of the ashram. For instance, the guru was a great advocate of birth control for India. According to Laxmi, he had once met the late Prime Minister Mrs. Indira Gandhi, and conveyed to her that she should assume dictatorial powers to enforce the sterilization programme so that no family of India had more than one child. Bhagwan also advised his disciples not to have children because they had come to the Pune Ashram to "work on their own growth". The result was a great many abortions and sterilizations. This was also encouraged because Sheela and her associates wanted a work crew and not a lot of pregnant women and babies around.

Western Bias

By January 1979, it seems, the Pune ashram had changed decisively in character. In the first two or three years, it had an Indian flavour. A lot of people who came were middle aged and eminently respectable citizens of Pune. In time, more and more westerners came to the ashram and fewer Indians. Ultimately, by the time Rajneesh left for the US, there were four to six thousand westerners in his audience every day and only a few hundred Indians.

Rajneesh himself was responsible for this radical transformation, as not only did he give special attention to westerners but also appointed them to all the top positions on the ashram staff. He also instituted western therapies, filed the ashram schedule with them for 21 days every month and barred Indians from these therapies.

It is interesting to note that as the ashram's complexion changed, Rajneesh also seemed to change with it. His lecture style altered. His lectures became less focused, less thought provoking. By 1979, they were often little more than a collection of quotations, jokes and aneedotes combined with bitter attacks on political and religious leaders. The jokes also were generally ethnic and vulgar. His sanyasis, as pointed out by Fitzgerald howled with laughter when he uttered various vulgarities – like little boys hearing their first dirty joke.

After the violent therapies came 'energy darshan', in which Rajneesh, touching the forchead of a young woman, would make her and the next six or eight people next to her jump and twitch like galvanized frogs while the disciples rejoiced and applauded.

Public Relations Problems

By this time the ashram was having public relations problems in India. The people of Pune city objected to the crowds of young people hugging and kissing in the streets. This was not the only complaint. Among the westerners who came to the ashram, there were, it seems, some borderline psychotics and since the ashram had no screening procedures, some of them went over the edge and ended in Pune hospitals.

Moreover, some of the young westerners were financing their stay at the ashram in unconventional ways. A fair number were smuggling opium, hashish and marijuana to Europe and a few young women were found to be working as prostitutes in Bombay. While ashram authorities feigned ignorance of these activities, the drug-smuggling, at least, was fairly common knowledge in Pune. There were also all sorts of rumours about the nature of the therapies. Finally, Bhagwan himself had become a public relations problem. Rajneesh's foul language and style of functioning, the exhibitionism of ashram inmates, the rumours about sexual orgies in therapies, and other activities disturbed the people of Pune. The ashram began receiving threatening letters, and several sanyasis were assaulted in the streets. In May 1980, a young Hindu, in the middle of a discourse, abused Rajneesh and threw a knife at him.

Apart from this, the ashram faced other difficulties with the Indian government as well. Laxmi had introduced large sums for Mrs. Gandhi's election campaign. But after 1977, when Mrs. Gandhi lost the elections, the new government under Morarji Desai disapproved of the ashram's activities. Income tax officials ruled that the ashram did not qualify as an educational institution or as a charitable or religious organization and would have to pay taxes on all donations received. Ashram authorities were asked to pay taxes with penalties.

The Oregon Commune

Rajneesh found the situation in Pune growing more and more tense and unmanageable. On 31 May 1981 he left abruptly for the United States with only 18 of his large band of disciples. Only a handful of the thousands of people in the ashram had known about his departure in advance. He had stopped delivering lectures from March under the pretext of an outbreak of chicken pox in the ashram. In April, Ma Anand Sheela had announced that Bhagwan had entered the ultimate stage of his work, and that he had gone into silence. He would lecture no more.

With his select band of disciples, Rajneesh entered the US on health grounds and on a tourist visa. Ma Anand Sheela, Rajneesh's new secretary, accompanied him to the US, completely displacing Ma Yoga Laxmi. Sheela, was the youngest daughter of a Baroda-based industrial family. In the US for studies, she had married an American, who later died. On a trip home she had been taken by her father to see Rajneesh. A month later, in early 1973, she became a sanyasin. She grew close to Rajneesh and rose to positions of power in the Pune ashram. She was to later become Rajneesh's right arm and play a key role in the way things went at Oregon.

Before Rajneesh went into silence in Pune, he spoke on a number of occasions about the 'new commune' he would create. Man, he argued, had outgrown the family. The family had served its purpose, but had exacted a heavy price in neurosis. The institution of marriage had been founded, he said, out of a desire for security. Love could not be legalized. Most marriages, he said, were held together merely by guilt or fear or a sense of dependency. People grew up obsessed by love and hate for their parents. Families demanded obedience from children, which in turn breeds mediocrity. Families taught children to accept religious dogmas blindly, also encouraged aggression, competitiveness, and possessiveness. Rajneesh also subscribed to the view that private property and its concomitant ills of jealousy and confliet were the creation of the patriarchal family.

He visualized the 'new commune' as a 'liquid family' where men and women would stay together only as long as they loved each other and where children would belong to everyone. Children would have mothers, but they need not know who their fathers were. Women would run this commune, according to Rajneesh, as they were more intuitive and down-to-earth than men, and less involved in their own egos. This commune would be free from churches, orthodoxies and rituals. People could discuss all forms of religion and philosophy. The commune, in short, would give birth to a 'new man', who would not be bothered about social status or wealth, but would live joyfully, playfully, knowing how to sing and dance. He would be an 'authentic being', with a commitment to the 'scripture of nature'. He would love others and be honest and trusting. There would be no ambition and no politics in this commune.

Bhagwan's perspective plans were widely circulated in central Oregon, USA. These proposals were discarded by local religious authorities as manipulations of a "foreign cult out to destroy the American family". But as Fitzgerald argues, the source of these proposal was hardly Indian. In Buddhist philosophy, man must live with insitutitions: to 'transcend' them is not to do without them but see them for what they are. Rajneesh's new commune, as she points out, was in fact one of those mirrors Rajneesh hung up before his western disciples for it reflected exclusively the ideals of the American counter-culture and human potential movement. Rajneesh's idea of the commune seems to have been inspired by his western disciples themselves.

The sanyasis actually came to Oregon in the summer of 1981. The site was selected by Sheela and her second husband Swami Prem Jayananda. The ranch was, as Rajneesh had wanted it, large and isolated, 19 miles from the nearest tiny town Antelope. The price fixed was US$ 5.75 million for the huge 64,229 areas of wild land and 17,000 acres leased from the Federal Bureau of Land Management. The land was rocky, unkempt, and eroded by flood. In fact it was known as Big Muddy Ranch.

'Realising the Vision'

The sanyasis came to Big Muddy with enthusiasm and large sums of money, to make Bhagwan's vision real, "to give full scope to his 'Buddha field'", to serve as the birth place for the 'new man'. On the six acres of the Rajneesh Ashram in Pune, the emphasis was on transforming people through therapeutic techniques and meditation. In Oregon, on the 64,000 acres of 'Rancho Rajneesh', sanyasis were expected to reclaim and transform the earth itself. Relentless work was projected as their meditation. In their commune, sanyasis were expected to live productively, in harmony with their own nature and the natural world surrounding them.

In the first year itself, their achievements in meeting their physical targets were quite impressive. They made mobile homes for themselves, planted trees to control erosion, installed new irrigation systems, dug wells, cleared land, built a dairy barn, cultivated crops and fruit trees. The plan obviously was for a city of several thousands, not a small commune. From the autumn of 1981, it is reported, disciples from other places sent a sizcable portion of their earnings

– almost 15-30 per cent

– to the ranch.

In Oregon, Sheela replaced Laxmi and took over the entire administration of the ranch. Here, unlike in Pune, therapy groups were no longer the focus of all activities. Here working on oneself was interpreted as doing work to build a community.

The western disciples initially struggled with the problems of how to do away with all dogmas and rituals. The struggle, it seems, turned out to be comical, because the more they talked about 'spontaenity', 'playfulness', and 'authenticity', the more these slogans degenerated into dogmas which their guru had opposed all along. The height of absurdity can be seen in the fact that in September 1982 the Rajneeshpuram city council passed an ordiance prescribing that a joke must be told at the start of every meeting. The ordinance, as suggested, might have been conceived in a spirit of playfulness but the joke eventually became a ritual formula and the laughter became expected behaviour. So the basic contradiction between a commune and 'spontancity' could not be resolved. The commune could not do without rules. The only was out of this dilemma was self-deception – a state that many sanyasis seemed to have achieved.

In Pune, sanyasis had been at least free to involve themselves to whatever degree they desired. They could drop in and out of Pune, live on the fringe of the ashram. It was by and large understood that they were there for themselves, and the guru's sole purpose was to work on them. In Oregon there was a subtle shift. There was pressure on everyone to direct all their energies, all their resources, to the ranch, to make 'Bhagwan's vision real'. Their development, their flowering, was secondary.

Some of those who settled in the commune had experience in construction and agriculture. Swami Anand Nair, Ph.D. in philosophy, who coordinated agricultural projects on the Ranch, was a dryland farmer in Australia. Swami Deva Wadud, the city planner, was trained at the Harvard Graduate School of Design. Most of the sanyasis were highly educated, city born, Pune Ashram-trained amateurs. A survey conducted by Nirman Sundberg revealed that 64 per cent of the ranch's members had bachelor's degrees, 36 per cent had advanced degrees, including 12 per cent who had doctorates; 22 per cent of the disciples had graduate or undergraduate degree in psychology or psychiatry. Sanyasis were made aware of the urgent need to create a new man and a conscious community as soon as possible because Bhagwan could foresee that humanity was at crossroads and there was imminent danger of its destruction.

Gordon also gives quite an interesting account of the daily darshan of Bhagwan on 'Rancho Rajneesh' for his disciples: "At two o'clock all work on the ranch stops. It is time for the daily darshan with Rajneesh. Only here in Oregon, it is called a drive by, not a darshan. Sanyasins do not talk to him but sit in silence with him. They stand on the side of the dirt road, in their red and orange and purple work clothes and their boots, silent in namaste, or swaying, dancing to some other thythm! Their Master wrapped in a long gown, and sparkle cap, diamond watch on the wrist that rests on the steering wheel, drives slowly past them in one of the Rolls Royces." Further, the same author observes, "On my first day I found the performance ridiculous and vulgar. This is the kind of display I would expect from an Indian maharaja or an obtuse Catholic prelate in an underdeveloped country, not from Master who mocks pretension. What kind of intimate relationship is this?"

Unquestioned Authority

With regard to Sheela too, Gordon's observations deserve consideration. He writes: "She is a small woman whose large dark eyes are her most striking feature. Even on the ranch she, like her Master, favours unexpectedly luxurious clothes – silk and satin in the midst of sanyasi denim. There is a brittleness and an edge of sarcasm in her voice, a tendency to pontificate that almost never leaves her, except when she speaks to Rajneesh. Then her voice grows young and breathy and she sounds like an adoring daughter. She seduces and wheedles and bullies, sometimes all of them at once."

Sheela was the president of Rajneesh Foundation International, the tax-exempt American counterpart of India's Rajneesh Foundation Ltd., and the religious teaching arm of the expanding intenational sanyasi empire. She was also Rajneesh's personal secretary. The dual roles, as Gordon says were comparable in the sanyasi world with the premier and the first secretary of the Communist Party in the Soviet Union. It gave her virtually total control over the policies and plans not only over the sanyasis in Rajneeshpuram but over other centres around the world.

Rajneesh, of course, was the unquestioned source of Sheela's power. Though he maintained silence, as Sheela revealed, he was the guiding force behind all the decisions and directions that she gave. Bhagwan was telling her to "be more assertive" and she was the only one who had direct and regular access to him.

Huge Network

By the spring of 1985, a small place of 2,500 residents was converted into a part frontier town, partly hip fantasy and partly bureaucratic concoction, along with a wide network of institutional structures such as Rajneesh Legal Services, the Rajneesh Investment Corporation, the weekly Rajneesh Times and the Rajneesh Modern Car Trust, along with other commercial ventures like the Zorba the Buddha restaurant which served vegetarian food, as well as beer, wine and liquor, the Noah's Ark Boutique which sold jeans and shirts, socks, sweaters, silk dresses etc. There was a religious book store that offered only Rajneesh's books and tapes, a stereo store, a beauty parlour, and a deli. There was also the Hotel Rajneesh, situated at a little distance from the town, meant for visitors, primarily wealthy sanyasis, and also Rajneesh Mandir, spread over 2.2 acres, where several hundred sanyasis did dynamic meditation and 15,000 people gathered during the annual summer festival for darshan of their master.

There were dozens of buses for inmates and visitors for transportation. Some 2,000 acres outside the city were under dry land cultivation, 60 acres under organic vegetables, an 1,800 sq.ft. green house full of flowers, plants and sprouts, a vineyard, 2,800 chickens, 100 beehives, and 550 head of grazing beef cattle.

The sanyasins also constructed a huge earthen dam called Gurdijieff Dam and 140 check dams, reshaped streambeds, and planted thousands of trees to help stop flooding and erosion and to irrigate their crops. All their farming was organic, sewage was biologically treated and purified for irrigation, and 70 per cent of everything they used was recycled.

As the ranch grew, it received a good deal of publicity, particularly in Oregon. Its program for water conservation, its recyling projects, its mass transit system, its organic farming methods, and the energy and intelligence of the sanyasis who created all this were favorably reported for quite some time. But these achievements were slowly eclipsed by the growing fleet of Rolls-Royces. In India, Gordon remarks, Rajneesh was known as the sex guru, in America he was known as Rolls-Royce Guru! But Rajneesh was not really bothered about such a reputation, because he enjoyed even notoriety, as long as it kept him in the limelight.

Flaunting of Wealth

In displaying his wealth so conspicuously, in ignoring accusations of selfishness, Rajneesh was actually ridiculing the presuppositions of his New World audience, particularly the Christians who are inclined to associate spirituality with poverty, modesty and charity. He wanted to impress upon them that wealth was immensely spiritual, a pre-condition for spirituality. Poverty was worse than useless and voluntary poverty is an inverted form of pride. He also took pride in calling himself "the rich man's guru" and condemned charity as a tool for enslaving the poor.

According to Gordon, Rajneesh's "display of wealth was a lampoon of the far greater wealth and power of the Pope and many of America's

TV evangelists. They acted humble, kissing the earth and praising the impoverished. They were hypocrites and Rajneesh was at least honest, as he praised the wealth he enjoyed and condemned the poverty he avoided."

Gordon also has an interesting psychological explanation for Rajneesh's passion for collecting Rolls Royces, which numbered over 93 before he left the ranch. As he points out, collecting was a symptom that had existed with Rajneesh right from childhood. As a boy his mother had seven extra pockets in his pants so that he could collect more stones from a nearby beach; he had filled his room with them. Later, he collected books, then fountain pens, then hats and towels, then watches, each more expensive and ornate then the last, and finally cars. Always the best and most expensive. Hence, it was a fixation of sorts.

By 1985, Rancho Rajneesh was the largest and by far the most heavily capitalized, best known and most closely observed commune experiment in USA. The 2,500 permanent inmates were entrusted with various administrative assignments and all shared their devotion to Rajneesh. About 1,500 were members of the Rajneesh Neo-Sanyas International Commune, a religious body whose members paid taxes on a prorated share of the commune's income. Some commune members 'worshipped', as the sanyasis had come to call 'work', as therapists or teachers at the Rajneesh International Meditation University. Others prepared food in the cafeteria and restaurants, cleaned rooms, maintained roads etc. They recovered free food and lodging, clothes, laundry service, and a small allowance for incidental expenses.

Most of the other 1,000 residents worked in one or another tax paying corporation that did business on the ranch, i.e. Rajneesh Travel International, Rajneesh Medical Corporation, Rajneesh Legal Services etc. Apart from that there were other organizations like Rajneesh Rebalancing (an eclectic therapeutic message) and Rajneesh Counseling. Siddha, a psychiatrist who worked at the Rajneesh medical centre, was also the university's vice-chancellor. There was also the Rajneesh Humanities Trust.

Assets Donated

By 1985, over US $ 130 million and an extraordinary amount of free labour had gone into the ranch. Some wealthy disciples had given hundreds of thousands, even millions, in cash and securities or Rolls-

Royces and jewelery. They had also lent money to the commune, the corporations, the car and jewelery trusts, probably as much as US $ 35 million all together. Working sanyasis were almost compelled to part with their income and assets. Devices used for collection were anxiety-provoking announcements about Rajneesh's frail health, the threat of imminent nuclear war, urgency of building a commune and creation of new man.

In Pune too giving had been strongly encouraged. Laxmi and her associates insisted that parting with ones wealth was a sign of 'commitment to Bhagwan' and of non-attachment to material things. Wealthy disciples were also given favoured treatment – private darshans with Bhagwan, living space in the ashram. At Oregon, however, fund-raising, under Sheela's direction, was a highly organized, high-pressure affair. Pune had been a much smaller operation comparatively.

The ranch at first produced no money and required enormous investments. Ma Yoga Sushila who was one of the chief fund raisers at the ranch, and in Europe, promised important positions 'close to Bhagwan' to large donors. Pleas for the urgency of the cause were liberally spiced with guilt-inducing warnings of disastrous consequences should money not be forthcoming. Bhagwan's health might suffer, the ranch might go under, the new man would have no place to be born. Some sanyasis were reportedly asked to sign over their inheritance, their homes, and their jewelery or to contact parents from who they had been estranged to ask for money for 'emergencies'.

After the first year, it appears, the commune itself began to generate money. The largest source of collection were the four yearly festivals. There were also three smaller festivals celebrating Rajneesh's enlightenment day in March, his birthday in December, and the enlightenment day of his father (and of all disciples) in September. Each of these attracted several thousand sanyasis to the ranch. The largest celebration, on Master's Day/Guru Poornima, in July, was called the Annual World Festival.

For sanyasis everywhere, the Annual World Festival had actually acquired too much awe, that like pilgrims heading for Mecca - disciples saved their money to reach the ranch and for their contribution for this day. It was estimated that in 1984, 15,000 people came and spent over US $ 10 million.

The sale of Rajneesh's books

- there are over 350 to 500 published collections of his discourses and personal conversations during darshan with his disciples in English and Hindi
- brought, in all probability, US $ 1 million a year.

By 1985, the commune authorities claimed that some 30,000 people in a year were paying for courses and training programs at Rajneesh International Meditational University, some of which cost as much as several thousand dollars a month.

Making Enemies

The ranch was growing and prospering materially. But by early 1984, one could easily see the increasing coercion of sanyasis and fear as well as hospitality towards the outside world. Ranch leaders Sheela, Vidya, Puja, Karuna, and K. D. were getting more and more isolated and defensive.

Earlier, when the sanyasis came around 1981, Antelope, the neighboring town, had only 39 people, mostly retired and committed to Christianity. They were nervous as they thought Bhagwan with his followers and group orgies would be a source of disturbance in their quiet locality. When the disciples arrived, they wore ordinary clothes, without their malas, to allay these fears. They gave a party and invited all the local people. Those who stayed late got uneasy. According to Fred Christenian, a nearby rancher, "the sanyasis got so drunk and so free that Sheela sat on my lap… guys were dancing with guys… one girl took off her blouse…" He could not imagine "what kind of religious groups" would throw a party like that. Sheela initially told reporters and townspeople, "All we want to do on the ranch is to create a lovely farm. We have no therapy programs and meditation center here. There will be forty people or so on the ranch."

By 1981, the townspeople were becoming increasingly skeptical. These people clearly were not farmers. Why did doctors, lawyers, and businessmen want to farm? Why were so many of them settling on the ranch?

Within months of the sanyasis' arrival, 1000 Friends of Oregon, a public interest group concerned with land use issues got involved. 1000

Friends was founded in 1975 with the backing of the late governor Tom McCall. Its purpose was restricting and regulating development, setting aside large portions of the Oregon countryside for recreational use and preserving the state's natural beauty. 1000 Friends opposed the development of the ranch so vigorously that the conflict brewing between the sanyasis and the Antelopians was precipitated.

In September 1981, the ranch had purchased a total of nine lots in Antelope and asked for permission from the Antelope city council to build a printing plant and office complex in town. This escalated the Antelopian's anxieties – what connection could there be between a printing plant and "a lovely farm", they asked. The townspeople and the ranchers felt threatened by the sanyasis' money and power and the phalanx of lawyers they could deploy. Consensus was that the sanyasis had lied.

They did not bother about anyone excepting themselves and were seen as dangerous. They treated the sanyasis as unscrupulous and untrustworthy. "In the past three years," as pointed out by Fred Christensen, a local resident, "every time they talked, it turned out to be a lie. They did not want Antelope and now they run it. They said they wanted a farm and now they have a city."

In October 1983, the Oregon attorney general Dave Frohmoyer issued an 'advisory opinion' at the request of the legislature with regard to the 'religious nature' of Rajneeshpuram. The city, he asserted, violated both the state and federal constitutions' guarantee of the separation of church and state. There was a "total fusion of government and religious functions". He recommended withholding revenue sharing funds from Rajneeshpuram and several other strictures.

While the state was tense about 'the pervasive and unavoidable' influence of religion on Rajneeshpuram, the US Immigration and Nationalization Service (INS) was against extending preferential status as a religious worker to Rajneesh. The INS also refused to change his status from the visitor's visa (that he had initially been granted for medical reasons) to permanent resident status.

In 1984, under the pressure of hundreds of letters of recommendations, many from prominent non-sanyasis, the INS granted Rajneesh preferential status as a religious worker. But it did give the verdict on his residence application. According to one authoritative source, the agency had doubts about whether Rajneesh's medical condition actually justified his initial visa.

Since 1981, the INS, it seems, had also been investigating the status of foreign sanyasis and the marriages – as many as 600, that had taken place between sanyasis who were US citizens and those who were not. INS was all the more skeptical because of what appeared to be a large number of convenient marriages by followers of a teacher who had otherwise reportedly condemned marriage.

Seeds of Discontent

Although Rajneesh observed silence for three and half years in Oregon, he was the center of life on the ranch. His drive-by darshans were as important as the morning and evening discourses had been in Pune. Disciples from all over the world came for silent communion with him.

Rajneesh did communicate even verbally during this period. He used to have his daily conferences with Sheela. There were conversations with Ma Vivek, his long-suffering caretaker-cum-lover, and with Devaraj and Devageet, his physician and dentist. There were also meetings and talks with other disciples, most often, according to many sanyasis, with women with whom he had a sexual relationship, and with wealthy donors, and some selected journalists for publicity.

For all important decisions on the ranch, Rajneesh was, in most cases, the final arbiter. On at least three occasions, it is reported, Rajneesh instructed Sheela to make public statements on his behalf, and all the three declarations proved too dramatic and disturbing for the movement.

The first of these declarations came late in 1981, when Rajneesh, through Sheela, announced the formation of the 'religion of Rajneeshism', based on fragments of the guru's discourses and interviews. It worked out details of the tenets of the new religion and its structure. The new religion was to be administered through three categories of office-holders: acharyas, arihantas and siddhas. It also prescribed a mantra to be recited at the beginning and end of each day. Sanyasins henceforth were to be called Rajneeshees.

Many of the sanyasins felt baffled and betrayed, because all along their guru had fought against dogmas, rituals, priesthood and the hypocrisy of all organized religions. Earlier Rajneesh had contrasted 'religiousness' with 'religion'. The former, he had said, happened only when a Buddha or a Krishna or a Mahavir or a Christ is alive. It was a love affair, liberating, shattering and transformative. "Religion," according to Rajneesh, "was born when religiousness dies."

"Rajneeshism," Bhagwan elaborated in an August 1985 interview that was included in An Introduction to Rajneeshism, "would be a kind of religiousness, not a dogma, a cult or a creed but only a quality of love, silence, meditation and playfulness. It was a 'religionless religion". He had, he added, an advantage over the other great spiritual teachers, Jessus, Buddha, Lao-tzu, Krishna. He had a perspective they lacked, as they were unaware of each other. As he came afterwards, he learned from their mistakes. His religion, rooted in an understanding of history, would for the first time unite the meditativeness of the eastern traditions with the activism of the West. It would be available to everyone. All other religions, he declared, "will disappear into Rajneeshism as all the rivers disappear into the occan."

In September 1983, Rajneesh, through Sheela, spoke again. This time it was on a more a prophetic note. He predicted that 1984-89 would be a period of crisis. There will be every kind of destruction on earth including natural catastrophes and man-made auto-suicidal efforts. The holocaust is going to be global, he said. There will be floods which have never been known since the time of Noah. The only refuge, Rajneesh asserted, would be within a "Noah's ark of consciousness". Even if people survived physically, only those with meditative minds would be able to endure the chaos that would follow a nuclear war. Each week for months, the warning was printed in Rajneesh Times.

Sanyasis, as a consequence, worked to turn the ranch into a literal Noah's Ark. They accelerated their efforts for self-sufficiency, prepared shelters and caves in the hills, where they could preserve their Master, his books and themselves in the event of nuclear war. Sanyasis in California closed their centres. Of course, the prediction never materialised.

On 5 March, Sheela again issued a statement on Rajneesh's behalf about AIDS. It was, Rajneesh said, the "disease with no name" that Nostradamus had predicted. Before the end of the century, it was predicted that it would wipe out two-thirds of the world's population.

"If a person is ready and can drop sex altogether through understanding and without repression, that is the safest protection from the disease," he said.

Instructions immediately were issued by Rajneesh Medical Corporation that even those who were monogamous should use rubber surgical gloves for foreplay and condoms for intercourse. AIDS became an obsession with the ranch for quite some time. All kinds of precautions and prohibitions on food were imposed on and off.

Sheela used Rajneesh's apprehensions as tools to justify the tactics she had adopted to establish and enlarge the ranch, the extraordinary devices employed to protect it from illegal attacks and legal challenges from outside and dissent and doubt from within. If the ranch and the other communes were presumed to be the womb of the new man, the Nietzschean superman on whom the future of humanity depended, for whom Rajneesh was supposed to be the mid-wife, then any and all measures to ensure his and their survival and well-being were justified.

Siege Mentality

The atmosphere of self-proctectiveness and secrecy thickened each month. The demands for physical and ideological purity became more intense. In time, as Gordon points out, the ranch became an armed camp with a siege mentality, the 'religionless religion' as totalitarian and suppressive as any cult that he had visited.

Initially, Rajneesh had been protected in his house by a few unarmed sanyasis. In October 1982, the incorporated city of Rajneeshpuram created an armed police force called the Peace Force. An explosion occurred at the Rajneesh Investment Corporation owned hotel, causing US $ 180,000 in damage. By 1982, vehicles on their way to the ranch were observed from several guardposts on the road. Visitors' cars and clothes were sniffed by dogs trained to detect drugs.

The Rajneeshpuram Peace Force became a visible and oppressive presence on the ranch. There were 16 regular officers ad 30 reserves, well-trained and equipped with pistols, rifles, shotgungs, and at least 28 semi-automatic weapons.

By 1984, Sheela and the others in positions of leadership had started operating as if the dangers they perceived from the outside world were also threatening from within. The devotees close to Sheela were treated with indulgence. Others, who had happily devoted their lives – working 12 hours a day – to make Rajneesh's vision come true, were treated as potential traitors, subjected to psychological intimidation and verbal assaults. Sanyasis who requested a change of work were routinely accused of 'negativity' and often assigned to tasks they liked even less. Those who questioned arbitrary policies in the commune or the aggressiveness toward the Oreganians were accused of disloyalty to Bhagwan. Everyone on the ranch was now required to line up for Rajneesh's daily drive-by and to be smiling and happy while there. Sanyasis were expected to report anyone they heard being 'negative' or critical of the ranch's policies to Sheela.

Rajneesh Times was subjected to continuous, at times bizarre, censorship from Sheela and her confidante Shanti Bhadra. The paper's motto was "positive journalism direct from the source". But what it offered was constant comparison of the blissfulness and perfection of ranch life with the banality and degradation of the world outside. Its editorial cartoons depicted the sinister forces organized against sanyasis. Nothing critical about the ranch could be printed, only smiling faces were allowed in photographs.

The ranch language was also altered into a kind of doublespeak to make oppression seem like spiritual discipline, coercion a form of caring, and discipleship a kind of permanent second childhood; work had become 'worship' and departments 'temples'. Coordinators metamorphosed to 'moms' who made all decisions for those they supervised. Sheela was called 'Big Mom'. In Guyana, Jim Jones was, not surprisingly, called Dad and his wife was Mom.

Under the pretext of promoting unity, but really to discourage potentially critical thinking, sanyasins were told not to speak of others, particularly, of decision-makers, in the third person. It was always "we" – as "when we saw the need to arm ourselves". Gordon's remarks are quite pertinent, he was reminded of psychiatrist Robert Liffon's description of the 'loading of language' in Chinese thought reform, and of the party slogans from Orwell's 1984: "War is Peace", "Freedom is Slavery", "Ignorance is Strength".

Crazed with Power

Sheela, in the meanwhile it seems, was falling apart and at a school board meeting in 1983 at Rajneeshpuram, was out of control. She began by attacking Margaret Hill, the former mayor of Antelope. "Margaret Hill was a teacher;" she said, "look at her face now. She looks retarded." Then she turned, as reported, like a gunner looking for a new target, and spotted Marcia Whichlman, whose husband had recently died in a hunting accident. Sheela commented "He (Mr. Whichlman) shot himself because she was screwing around with another man".

Sheela could not keep up her paranoiac, suspicious, witch-hunting, aggressive postures for a long time. As crisis deepended and the commune's problems multiplied, her bravado could not be maintained. This becomes evident from Gordon's description of Sheela as he found her during his visit in 1984, an ailing, obviously drugged person who he felt should have been in bed, if not in the hospital, but who was dragging herself around. He came to know from her that she just had a bout of thrombophlebitis, a recurring affliction. She was too tired for a formal interview.

Gordon's diagnosis of Sheela is worth reproducing: "I found myself taking on the role of a physician, feeling compassion for her, beginning in my mind to formulate a kind of 'differential diagnosis'. Had she been taking drugs? I wondered. Amphetamines could have been responsible for the aggressiveness of the Marcia Wichlman episode, and tranquilizers or painkillers might produce a psychosomatic cycle. I could easily imagine that after long periods of intense control on the Ranch and unremitting hostility to those outside it, she would go into a state of psycho-physiological exhaustion in which she would be vulnerable to depression

– aggression turned inward
– and physical illness. Or perhaps it was some combination of drugs and character, the pressures of being a dictatorial leader, and the conflict with the outside world".

Bhagwan broke his three-an-a-half-years silence in October 1984. Initially, during his discourses, Rajneesh repeatedly reiterated that he was "an ordinary man", and "ordinariness is blessed". The only difference between him and his listeners was that of knowing. He claimed that he knew himself and they did not know themselves.

Dissecting Relegion

"All religions," Rajneesh asserted, "are based on fear. They are anti-life. No religion has accepted a sense of humour as a quality of religiousness. My religion is the first religion which accepts man as a whole, as he is." Further, "There is no God." In the past, he said, he had used Buddha, Krishna and Christ as 'jumping boards' to reach people, but they were not Gods. The people who believe in God are really the people who cannot trust in themselves. They need a father figure, a 'big-daddy'. The extreme asceticism of the Jains he dubbed "ugly". Krishna was a "male chauvinist" and Buddha anti-life, Jesus who believed he was "the only begotten son of God" was "neurotic", the victim of hallucination. Pope John was "the Polack". Mother Teresa a "criminal".

In contrast to them, Rajneesh believed, he was scientific and flexible. He claimed he had not given his disciples any beliefs, but only methods, 112 methods of meditation. The Judeo-Christian Bible was a closed system, a collection of violent and pornographic tales. The Rajneesh Bible, as he called this series of lectures, "is an open system". His was really the first and the last religion. As Gordon argues, Rajneesh skillfully dissected religious pretension and hypocrisy, lampooned rigid and authoritarian political structures, but was all the while permitting what he attacked.

He said, "To be rebellious is to be religious," but the routine life of those attached to him was becoming more and more conformist, increasingly constricted by rituals and ceremonies, dogmas, rules and regulations. His nominees, Sheela and others, smothered doubt and stifled the slightest signs of independence. His commune was protected by guard posts and semi-automatic weapons. People on the ranch learnt not only to shut up but also to shut down their critical faculties and turn off their awareness.

Sheela Leaves

On Monday, 16 September 1985, Rajneesh called a press conference to make a shocking announcement. Sheela and a dozen other commune leaders, including Puja (next in rank to Sheela on the ranch) had left the commune over the weekend and gone to Europe. Calling these a "gang of fascists", he accused them of poisoning his doctor, Ma Yoga Vivek, and also the Jefferson county district attorney and the water system. He also alleged that Sheela had misappropriated commune funds and left the commune US $ 55 million dollars in debt.

Later he added a number of charges of theft and arson. He alleged that they had harassed the people of Antelope and created a Stalinist regime on the ranch, bugging rooms and telephones and communicating with one another in secret codes. The most treacherous act alleged was an attempt to bug his bedroom and to incapacitate or kill him by poisoning him.

Sheela and her associates had in June 1985 itself sensed that they could not hold out to the authorities for long, and that the authorities would soon be coming to arrest her for various frauds perpetrated with her connivance. Rajneesh's lawyers had been confident of at least fighting charges of immigration fraud. But Sheela and her associates, as reported, were not up to a battle in court as they had long passed the point of rationality. They were exhausted, crazy with tension, and in a state of paranoia. Vidya had fallen ill under the pressure, and all the drugs that Sheela took did not help her sanity. She stopped trusting anyone, including Rajneesh himself. She had been bugging his bedroom for several months and he had run out of patience with her.

Rajneesh however claimed he knew nothing of any of these crimes until Sheela and her gang had left and other sanyasis came and informed him. He also insisted that things would change now as the 'fascists' had left the ranch. Sanyasins would dance and sing again, they would talk to their families and outside friends again, they would make peace with their neighbours and give Antelope back to its rightful owners, he promised.

Sheela's departure created a sensation. Journalists poured into the ranch, closely followed by personnel from several law enforcement agencies. The Federal Bureau of Investigation, waiting to swoop on the commune, had been looking for 'a stool pigeon'. They got the Bhagwan himself. Rajneesh showed them an enormous number of sophisticated wiretapping devices installed in the phone system, in the hotel rooms and in other places, including a secret underground tunnel with entry into Sheela's house.

The sanyasins greeted the revelations with a mixed feeling of horror and relief. Along with Sheela, several other kingpins had left the ranch, including Ma Yoga Vidya, her close associate, Ma Prem Savita, the chief accountant, Ma Anand Su, the president of Rajneesh Investment

Corporation, Shanti Bhadra, the treasurer of the Rajneesh Foundation International and several others holding key positions.

Rajneesh's contention that he was unaware of their crimes till other sanyasis reported them to him after their departure could not be even remotely possible. To believe it, as Fitzgerald points out, amounts to believing that the entire top echelon of the organization had carried out a coup against itself and then driven itself into exile for no reason. And also that the Rajneesh and all his sanyasis had not noticed that all the leaders, including all the chief finance officers, had gone. The story became even less believable in some days. Within a week, it came to light that Rajneesh had replaced all the departing office bearers even before their departure, and had installed at the center of power a group of wealthy American sanyasis that Sheela had called "the Hollywood gang".

Rajneesh's new secretary and the president of Rajneesh International Foundation was Ma Prem Hasya, a former Hollywood movie producer. She had come to the ranch in 1982 with three friends. They had together bought a few of the guru's Rolls Royces for him and contributed a good deal of money. They were treated as privileged guests at the ranch. The new leaders quickly reassured commune members that despite what Bhagwan had said, Sheela and her companions had not taken money from the ranch accounts and that the Rajneesh organizations were financially not in bad shape.

Looking for a Scapegoat

Initially, Rajneesh had agreed to co-operate with the Federal Bureau of Investigation. But soon he began to complain that instead of arresting Sheela and others the investigators were trying to collect evidence to destroy his commune.

Rajneesh also declared that the concept of 'Rajneeshism' had been entirely Sheela's invention: he himself had never claimed to be a religious leader. He called upon his disciples to destroy all traces of the religion and said there was no necessity for them to wear malas and sunset colored clothes. (But when his disciples made a bonfire of their red robes and appeared without malas and in plain clothes, he rebuked them for so easily giving up the symbols of their attachment to him). He also announced in September 1985 that the commune lawyers would withdraw their cases against state and country officials and change the name of the city of Rajneesh back to Antelope. It was also suggested that Oregonians might now drop some of their law suits against the commune.

The strategy was quite clear. He thought that he would be able to restrict the investigations and would get away by placing the blame for everything on Sheela and others who had fled, extricate the commune from a number of expensive law suits, and normalize its political relations. Sheela, for her part, was selling interviews to the German press in which she blamed Rajneesh for ruining the commune with his incessant demands for more diamond watches and more Rolls-Royces and his absurd idea that they should build an AIDS treatment centre in Antelope.

The investigators, according to Oregonian reporters, did not find much in the way of documentary evidence as probably Sheela and her successors had destroyed a good many files. Still, they were accumulating evidence on the basis of information given by many ordinary sanyasis. Also, three persons who had gone with Sheela had also returned and given evidence. By mid-October the Portland hotel and three aeroplanes were put up for sale by the commune leaders. Rajneesh had begun to feel threatened. A federal grand jury convened by the local attorney issued a 35-count indictment charging Rajneesh, Sheela and six others with a conspiracy to evade immigration laws. Bhagwan, through his lawyers, could not strike a deal with the Portland INS office. He attempted to escape from the US by hiring two chartered jets. But federal customs agents foiled the plan.

Rajneesh was arrested, sent to jail, and stripped of his robes. After his lawyers struck a deal with the attorney's office, Rajneesh pleaded guilty to two felonies, i.e., making false statements to the immigration authorities in 1981, and concealing his intent to reside in the United States. He got a ten-year suspended prison sentence, and agreed to pay US $ 400,000 in fines and prosecution costs and to leave the country within five days and not come back for at least five years. The same day, he boarded a plane for New Delhi.

On 28 October 1985, the day Rajneesh was arrested in North Carolina, the West German police had arrested Sheela, Puja and Shanti Bhadra in their Black Forests resort hotel.

Closing Down

After Rajneesh's departure from the ranch, Dhyan John assured the remaining sanyasis that the commune would continue to exist and suggested ways of making it profitable. But a week later it was announced that the commune was closing down and the sanyasis should make arrangements to leave.

By the end of December 1985, most of the sanyasis had departed from the ranch. 85 of the Rolls-Royces and the ranch itself were put up for sale to pay off the debts. By February 1986, only a 100 people remained on the ranch. The rest were taking up their lives in the world again. Quite a few of them had resources – like Isabel and Niren, who simply sailed off to Europe or South America for vacations. Others, as reported, went back to working in the outside world just as hard as they had on the ranch, working as waitresses or house cleaners, and going to school at night. At the age of 35-40, they had to rebuild their lives from scratch.

None of the ordinary sanyasis, according to Fitzgerald, actually knew that Sheela was drugging and poisoning people and not many had known about wire tapping. The astonishing thing was that despite a variety of clues and other indications, most of the sanyasis did not even suspect that something terrible was happening at the ranch.

It is difficult to make a correct estimate of Rajneesh's influence in terms of the total number of disciples who took sanayas and received a mala and a new name from Rajneesh. Official records appear to be inaccurate as in the late seventies the figures were periodically increased by increments of 50,000. Sheela cited totals of 3,00,000, 350,000 and 4,00,000 at different times. In 1984, Bhagwan himself claimed that he had half a million disciples, and in 1985 he claimed they were one million.

According to several sanyasis who had access to mailing lists, there were in all probability never more than 40,000 initiated sanyasis the world over, of whom over 10,000 to 15,000 had probably dropped sanayas by the time the Oregon commune ws established.

Many sanyasins, convinced of Rajneesh's wisdom, of his great mission, and of the urgent need to create the new man now, before the expected holocaust, acceded to the choice of Sheela as chief spokesperson of their guru. But this was not the case with others. For them adjusting to the changes was more difficult. They were scared of Sheela. The jobs she gave them did not recognize them or make use of their talents; it subdued them, excluded and demeaned them.

Misgivings

Deeksha, who was a radical feminist prior to joining the Rajneesh cult, also got disillusioned soon after the commune was established in Oregon. In retrospect, Deeksha felt that the characteristics she had regarded as harmless, even endearing foibles in a man she loved, now seemed evidence of vanity and deceit. Rajneesh, she said, was proud that Brahmin women cooked for him. He read only a few books from his library, and that too, only selected chapters and passages. He ordered photographs to be taken from angles that minimized the size of his nose and used a cream so that the sun would not darken his skin. He had his gowns designed to emphasize his height and the width of his shoulders.

Deeksha had become skeptical about her role even whilst in Pune when she was asked to promote sterilization. However, she still thought that Bhagwan would help bring about a spiritual revolution, "that we would become enlightened, transcend greed and jealousy." But she had apprehensions that "the balance between the just things and the ugly things" in the ashram was shifting. She realized that Rajneesh was becoming increasingly violent, cocreive, and deceitful.

She admitted that even in Pune, Rajneesh permitted and encouraged "everything" including prostitution and even drug dealing, as long as it brought him money. Deeksha claimed she had seen Rajneesh beat Ma Vivek badly. She also knew that the ashram hierarchy had instigated the fires at the warehouse and clinic and said she had strange dreams in late 1979. In one such dream she saw the ashram was empty and decaying, the gardens overgrown.

In the US, she was horrified by the glimpses of her guru during her twice daily private meetings with Rajneesh. She saw his real face, and found it frightening and dangerous. Often, she said, "he was high on valium and incoherent. At times, he seemed to be praising Hitler, whom he called a 'genius' and Goebbels, whom he declared the "greatest practitioner of mass persuasion".

When he was lucid, reportedly, he taught her and Sheela to maneuver people, to create "buffers, little Sheelas, little Deekshas". She felt that they were being tied more closely to him by knowledge of criminal activity.

Despite this disillusionment, Deeksha continued to stay at the ranch. The decision to drop the guru and the commune was quite difficult and equally painful as she had invested over ten precious years of her life and donated large sums of her money to Rajneesh and his commune. All her friends were there, even her mother was a sanyasin. In Pune she had hoped that things would be 'better' in Oregon, and perhaps she might be of help in improving the situation.

Within a short time, Deeksha realized that Rajneesh was 'bored' with helping people to live the spiritual life. She felt things would never change. "The door to meditation had closed and the door to competition open," she was to say later. She felt it was time for her to leave. Sheela warned her on her departure "Remember that if you create trouble, I can take care of you in twenty four hours".

After she left, rumours reached her that she was accused of stealing hundreds of thousands of dollars from Sheela's Swiss bank accounts. In her distress she had gone to J. Krishnamurthy for help. Krishnamurthy, it seems, told her that "what (Rajneesh) is doing in the name of spirituality is criminal – you have made a great mistake in giving him power over your life".

Gordon also provides a very vivid account of other prominent disciples of Rajneesh who got disillusioned with him over a period of time. Pramod, the former British diplomat, who had lived in the Pune Ashram and was head of the 'translation department', said that on Bhagwan's first drive-by darshan in Oregon, he experienced nothing except flatness and sadness. Nandan, who had quickly moved into a position of authority, soon began to resent the lies and corrosiveness which had become the characteristic style of the ranch. She felt that although Rajneesh had taught them to be spiritual rebels who could find their own truths, it was precisely for this that they were being punished now.

Hugh Milne, who for eight long years was personal bodyguard to Bhagwan, left the movement in 1982, less than two years after it had moved to Oregon. He was publicly denounced by Bhagwan himself and harassed and haunted by Bhagwan's followers. When it became clear to him that people were about to leave his cult, Bhagwan had said, "Wherever you go, I shall haunt you," and that they would have no peace.

Hugh Milne had a severe mental breakdown and had to spend some time in a psychiatric hospital. His book 'Bhagwan, the God that Failed' describes the whole process of his involvement with the guru, his rise to a position of eminence within the movement, and then the realization of how corrupt and deceitful the organization had become.

While narrating his experience, he mentions that when he first met Rajneesh in Bombay there were only about 25 westerners gathered around him. Seven years later, he had a worldwide following which he estimates was around 5,00,000 and thriving centres in almost every major city in the world. According to Hugh, the emphasis was on 'spiritual sexuality', and the physical release of inhibitions was a major factor in attracting so many people from the West. The fact that this doctrine of free love was being preached by an Eastern mystic gave it an even more compelling, exotic attraction.

Instant Enlightenment

Milne further writes, "We dressed in orange robes, which in India signifies a celibate and recluse, one who has renounced the world. But we were encouraged to have as much sex with other people as we could, with many different partners. Meanwhile many disciples lived in the fanciest hotels in Bombay and Pune. Normally it takes many hard years to attain enlightenment, but here was somebody who told us it could happen instantly. Not for his followers the long wait and the cold asceticism usually associated with a religious quest."

In Bombay and later in Pune, young western girls, as Milne states, walked around in their orange diaphanous robes, revealing that they wore no underclothes. At one of Bhagwan's centers, on a dirt farm, people walked 20 miles or more to gaze at these strange foreigners who were meditating completely naked. Bhagwan also attracted a very large number of voluptuous female disciples who made a mockery of the decorum associated with eastern religious philosophy.

Milne further reveals, "When he first arrived in India in 1973, stories already were in circulation that Bhagwan slept with his female disciples. This happened so often and with such an exotic selection of partners, that it shocked many Indians." Bhagwan's love of publicity and his belief that any publicity, good or bad, was to be sought, also was contrary to the traditionally accepted code of eastern religious mystics.

In Pune, and later in Oregon, Milne points out, there was a dream, a promise of a new way of life, of a free enlightened and loving community, to be held up as an example to the world of what was possible. But what did it become? Totally regimented, alarmingly conformist in its own ranks, militaristic, a mini-empire ruled by a recluse with a penchant for every expensive toy. The main activities of the commune in Oregon degenerated into fighting law suits, making money, spying, conspiring and scheming.

Radha, another close disciple of Rajneesh, also got disillusioned on the ranch. She worked as a spiritual therapist in Oregon until early 1985. Although, as Gordon points-out, she was one of the few sanyasins with direct access to Rajneesh, she felt uneasy and unsatisfied, "The energy, the light were gone. There was no teaching to be recovered. He was just an ordinary, sweet, jolly, sometimes brilliant and often tedious Indian." Bhagwan's commune now repelled and frightened her.

During this period, several other disciples who lived outside the ranch also dropped sanyas. This was largely the reaction to the increasingly arbitrary control the ranch was exercising over them and their centres. For instance, a nurse who lived in California found she had to continually resist her local centre leader's pressure to marry a foreigner and move into the centre and send more of her pay cheque to Oregon.

An earlier set of disciples had produced exciting ventures, large discos and restaurants, successful business in the nine European and three Australian communes, but with rigid standardization and control with regard to prices, these ventures declined in popularity. Even some of the closest, oldest and most loyal disciples like Poonam became alienated. When Gordon spoke to her in 1986 in London, she traced her disafferction in a way that a patient might recall the toll that a chronic illness had taken of a previously healthy and happy life.

Bitter Ending

The alliance between Rajneesh and his 'once-trusted' Sheela was over. Sheela in an interview given in Germany alleged that Bhagwan was a 'super fraud' who freely used laughine gas and a mood elevator called Ecstasy to hypnotize his audience. Rajneesh, is reported to have, in a fit of divine rage, called Sheela a 'bitch' and said that all she wanted was "to get into his bed", but "I don't make love to secretaries".

When Sheela left the movement, she was accused by Bhagwan of almost every imaginable crime, including murder, poisoning, bombings, radiation poisoning, scheming to kill Rajneesh with a radiation bomb, bigamy, treason, building concentration camps at the commune, drug abuse, widespread bugging, conducting experiments in laboratories with animals, using spy cameras and hidden tape recorders. In short, deceit, deception and distrust finally became an integral part of the movement.

After returning to India, Rajneesh lived in Manali and Kathmandu for some time, and then left for Greece. (Incidentally, Rajneesh left Manali without bothering to clear a huge bill incurred by him and his small band of disciples booked in a posh hotel!) In Manali, Rajneesh toned down allegations leveled against Sheela that she had misappropriated the commune money to the tune of Rs. 66 crore. He stated: "Nothing is missing in our books but there is a possibility that the people who were raising funds in Europe had put some money away in a Swiss bank."

After leaving India, Rajneesh was denied visas to Greece, Switzerland, Great Britain. Holland, Jamaica and Nepal. The frustrated guru and his disciples had to return to Bombay in June 1986, and finally to Koregaon Park in early 1987.

Back to Pune

Back home in Pune too, Rajneesh received a very cool reception. Posters were put up by the Hindu Ekta movement demanding his explusion from the city. Public meetings were organized in Pune in protest against his arrival in the city.

Within 24 hours of his arrival, Rajneesh had been asked to leave town. In desperation, senior disciples moved heaven and earth to convince the police commissioner that there would be no law and order problem. The police ultimately set down several conditions that the Rajneeshees would have to agree to. As late Swami Anand Maitreya pointed out, they were forced to sign the agreement - the option was for Bhagwan to leave the city.

The ten conditions agreed to were: (i) Daily discourses of only two hours and five meditations of one hour each, (ii) Discourses to be open to police officers and men accompanying them, (iii) The discourses must not be 'provocative' and against any other religion, (iv) The number of foreigners residing in the ashram to be restricted to 100 and their names to be informed to the police, as and when asked, (v) The number of foreigners visiting the ashram not to exceed 1,000, (vi) No member of the ashram or visitor to be allowed to carry fire arms, (vii) Consumption of drugs and liquor prohibited on the ashram premises, (viii) Smoking of cigarettes during the discourses to be banned, (ix) Visitors and members of the ashram prohibited from indulging in any 'obscene' behavior in or outside the ashram, (x) Police officers to have the right to visit the ashram any time of the day and night.

Rajneesh referred to these ten norms as the 'ten police commandments'. Despite this bravado, however, as one regular visitor to the ashram pointed out, the fear of being pushed out of Pune took its toll on the Bhagwan who became just a shadow of his old self. There was little wit and dry humour in his discourses, also gone were the sex thearapies and sharp digs at other religions.

The ashram had reportedly to still clear taxes amounting to Rs. 4 crore. The ashram disputed the order stating that there was no need for the ashram to pay any taxes since it was a religious and charitable institution. But tax experts argued, "Charitable to whom? They are charitable only to themselves. And religion, what religion do they practice?" Similar objections were raised against the ashramites' contention that it was an educational institution. It is surprising to note that according to Anand Svabhav, the ashram did enjoy tax exemption between 1973 and 1983, but it was subsequently suddenly withdrawn.

Raising Objections

Despite the toning down of the ashram's activities, retired Air Chief Marshal H. Mulgoankar who lived in the vicinity of the ashram raised objection against Bhagwan's arrival on two different grounds: (i) On grounds of national security and (ii) Irritating neighborhood encroachment. According to him. "In times like ours, when alien powers are forever ready to destabilize a political set-up unfavourable to them, a place like the Rajneesh Ashram can prove a boon … a person comes here, loses his identity for all practical purposes, assumes a name

- Swami something or the other
- and is free to do what he will. It is an excellent placement for conduits."

Ulhas Dhole Patil, ex-mayor of Pune and owner of Hotel Kapila at Koregaon Park which did roaring business thanks to the large number of visitors to Rajneesh Ashram, was instrumental in preventing the demolition of unauthorized constructions at the ashram site. According to him, the disciples seemed more subdued now and their number had reduced to about 25 per cent of the previous strength. Rickshaw and taxi drivers, vegetable vendors, hoteliers and other small business folk were happy about the return of Bhagwan as the business turnover in this area was around Rs. 3 to 4 lakhs a day.

However, an opinion poll conducted by marketing and market research consultants among middle class and upper middle class residents of Pune's Deccan Gymkhana area revealed that 76 per cent of the people asked felt that financial gains from Rajneesh's return would not compensate for the disadvantages. 89 per cent felt that the Bhagwan's return would add to the drug problem and 64 per cent felt that it was 'proper' on the part of the authorities to ask Rajneesh to leave Pune.

Nevertheless, as per the report that appeared in the September 1987 issue of Gentleman magazine, "Most people in the Koregaon Park area are of the view that the ashramites and visitors to the ashram are 'qualitatively better' than those who frequented the place earlier. A resident of the area who gives rooms out to the disciples and who did so even earlier says,

'They used to be dirty, many were drug addicts, and one long haired specimen used to stand the whole day and beg for money."

The Role of Women

It is interesting to note that women played an important role in running the Rajneesh Ashram in Pune and also the commune at Oregon. All personal secretaries and companions of Rajneesh were attractive women with strikingly different traits and mental make up.

Ma Yoga Laxmi, his first secretary, was a soft-spoken middle aged woman and long time associate, who was mainly responsible for establishing the Pune Ashram and raising the money for the guru's comfortable living and the running of the ashram. She was rudely ousted from her post, probably in full connivance with Rajneesh, by Sheela, an attractive 35 year-old disciple, familiar with the American set-up. Known for her arrogance, pride, vanity, decadent lifestyle and scheming ways, she was similar to her guru in various ways because it was Rajneesh who encouraged her and advised her to act in a high-handed autocratic style. Ma Laxmi was neglected for long in the US. Probably because of the humiliation she suffered in Oregon, Laxmi left the commune, became very sick in the US and returned to Bombay. However, in keeping with her character, she continued to visit the ashram.

Ma Sheela was the aggressive go-getter. It was she who fixed up the site for the commune in Oregon. Once Sheela disappeared, the void created was promptly filled up by 48 year-old Ma Prem Hasya (Franscise Meredill), a wealthy American Jew and ex-wife of big-time Hollywood producer Al Ruddy (The Godfather). Sheela had earlier accused her of being part of the "Hollywood mafia" that was engaged in drug-peddling in Oregon but Ma Hasya had denied it and in turn accused Sheela of attempting to poison Devraj whom she married in 1983.

The 36 year-old Ma Neelam, the wife of a prosperous businessman of Ludhiana, from whom she was separated, and whose school-going daughter also became a sanyasin, was the last secretary of the guru. Neelam seemed to symbolise the new Rajneesh image in Pune - quiet, mature and seeking no personal publicity.

Break with the Past

In 1988, Rajneesh dropped the suffix Bhagwan and instead opted for the ancient Japanese word 'Osho'in which 'O' implied great respect, love and gratitude and 'sho' meant 'multidimensional expansion of consciousness and existence showering from all directons'. In 1989, he dropped the name Rajneesh altogether, signifying his complete break with the past.

Despite the series of scandals, ranging from drug-peddling, prostitution to even allegations of murder leveled against his followers, reinforcing his image as a gigantic impostor and his followers as a group of brainwashed cultists, Rajneesh, as reported, emerged from all these attacks with his reputation among a large member of his followers virtually untouched. None of his critics could adequately explain why he continued to attract such large numbers of disciples from among professionals and the intelligentsia, and how his books and cassettes containing his eclectic philosophy continued to find a ready market. The master showman in him, it seemed, came forth every time one thought that the man had exhausted himself. From the day he emerged on the national scene, till the end, even in death, he was surrounded by controversy.

Controversial Death

Rajneesh died on 19 January 1990 in his Pune Ashram. Only two of his disciples, Swami Amrit and Swami Jayesh, were present when he breathed his last. His family and the mass of devotees had no option to accept this duo's version about Osho's last moments.

Both of them contended that Osho had told them to keep his body only for ten minutes in the Buddha auditorium soon after his death for darshan for his devotees, and that immediately after that to have it cremated at the Tulsiram Ghat close to the ashram. Ma Yoga Laxmi, as his first secretary and one of the earliest devotees, too was shocked to learn that the cremation was over when she reached on 19 January itself. Thousands of Osho's devotees were similarly disappointed. When Swami Amrito was asked why he did not summon any of the family members (who were also devotees) when he knew that Osho was dying, his only excuse was that he was following the well-established practice that only those whom Osho wished to see could be admitted. But a contradiction was that the family was involved in funeral rituals although Osho had left behind no such instructions.

The only person who had a look at the body before other disciples was Dr. Gokul Gokani, consulting ENT surgeon and a devotee who issued the death certificate. Amrito had no convincing reply even as to why an ENT surgeon was summoned. Swami Jayesh too was evasive. At the time, an Illustrated Weekly of India reporter was also denied a meeting with the family members.

It was this well-orchestrated strategy to keep the whole affair under wraps that gave rise to suspicions. Rajneesh's devotees and anybody wanting to investigate the circumstance around the death had to be satisfied with Swami Amrito's claim that the last words of Osho were uttered by him while looking at Swami Jayesh: "I leave you my dream."

Another interesting incident was the issue of a press release by the commune on the evening of 19 January. Even though Osho was on his death bed and was supposed to have been in great pain for over 20 hours, the commune thought it fit to distribute among the Pune press copies of a statement reportedly issued by Osho on Shirley MacLaine! The statement, supposedly by Osho, warned the West about the harmful effect of the 'inner workout' exercise being propagated by the famous Hollywood actress. It went on to quote Osho as advising Shirley Maclaine that she should put a statutory warning on her video tapes.

Later, Swami Amrito firmly held that it was thallium poisoning and irradiation which ultimately took Osho's life.

"The powerful conservative Christian establishment of America with which the big corporations have close links had never taken kindly to Osho because they were threatened by his radical teachings. They wanted to harass and even eliminate him so that their pet beliefs and their dominance may continue," he said. "Osho was the worst nightmare for the conservative US administration. It could not reconcile itself to the fact that a non-white, non-Catholic, Third World citizen was storming the strongest and mightiest Christian establishment in the world. In four years Osho's teachings blasted the central tenets of that society. In four years Osho achieved something that would have taken four centuries for others."

A few days before Osho's demise, another death took place in the Pune ashram in suspicious circumstances, that of Ma Vivek. According to Ma Neelam, a member of the inner circle, Ma Vivek had died of an overdose of sleeping pills. The mystery of her death is still not cleared.

There was also talk of a secret group of devotees performing black magic on Osho. According to one version, Osho himself had expressed his fears that somebody was practicing black magic on him. The thallium and irradiation also, as reported, could have weakened his nervous system, but was not such as to cause sudden death. The immediate cause of the death, it was alleged, was something else. The conduct of the coteric managing the affairs of the ashram caused even more suspicions and rumours.

Whatever might be the real cause of Osho's death, a clique in which foreigners are in an overwhelming majority has steadily gained control of the Osho empire. Swami Jayesh and Swami Amrito formed the nucleus even when Rajneesh's health had started declining. Out of 21 members of this inner core only five were Indians while the rest were all foreigners. The chairman Swami Jayesh, vice-chairman Swami Amrito and the secretary Ma Anando were all foreigners. The coteric side-stepped any questions about the financial and legal aspects of the ashram.

It is claimed the Osho had given instructions for the setting up of a committee to be called

'The Inner Circle'. The purpose for the formation of the committee, it is suggested, was to reach unanimous decisions about the continued functioning and expansion of the commune as the guru was tired and wanted to retire. It is not at all clear to whom Osho gave these instructions. The family of Rajneesh found no representation in this inner circle.

Osho's death resulted in a financial windfall for his empire. According to a statement issued by Swami Chaitanya Keerti three days after the death, sales of his books, audio and video tapes sky-rocketed all over the world. Thousands of advance orders were received for tapes of his last journey and thousands poured in for a darshan of his marble samadhi.

With regard to the future of Osho's movement, the central question raised is that the 21-member inner circle may ensure the smooth functioning of the routine activities (which also is a doubtful proposition), but who will have the spiritual authority to introduce new techniques of self-realization and convince sanyasis that they would work, as Rajneesh often did, to sustain the movement?

Rajneesh in Perspective

We have provided a brief account of the origin, growth, decline and resurgence of Rajneesh's movement, till the death of this most controversial godman of post-Independent India.

As we have seen, despite the scandals and accusations surrounding him, Rajneesh continued to attract large crowds and managed to retain an impressive number of disciples till he passed away in January 1990.

How does one explain this? For this we have to go back a little and look at the spiritual and psychological enquiries and quests that had been taking place at and around this time.

Drawing from East and West

It is interesting to note that the basis of Rajneesh's appeal to his western disciples lay in his social experiments establishing the philosophical connection between the eastern guru tradition and the western growth movement. There was Yogic 'energy' and growth movement 'energy'; the two notions were vague to begin with and Rajneesh seems to have fused them expertly in his philosophy.

The two main instructors of Rajneesh's movement, Teertha and Siddha, were drawn from the human potential movement which had acquired a wide following in the West. Teertha (Paul Lowie), an Englishman and the guru's right hand in Pune, drawing inspiration from the Esalen Institute in the U.S. had set up his own growth centre at London. His centre had flourished but after a while his therapists were at a dead-end. They had tried meditation but found most of the eastern techniques unsuitable as people could not sit still for long periods. While he was looking for a new acupuncturist, he came across an Indian who told him about the 'dynamic meditation' taught by Bhagwan Rajneesh. He found that dynamic meditation which involved a great deal of physical activity was well suited to his purposes.

In Rajneesh, he also found an enlightened master. Because of Teerth's connection with Esalen, a lot of Californians came, and from Esalen spread to various other movement circles, to the Reichians, to the group around R.D. Laing and others. Eventually, as reported, hundreds of therapists and other growth movement participants came, some stayed permanently with Rajneesh, others went home on his instructions.

This rush of therapists to Rajneesh was not difficult to account for, as pointed out by Fitzgerald. In the 1970s, Esalen and other big growth movement centers were periodically swept by enthusiasm for one or another exotic religion or technique. One year if it was Sufi dance, another it was Soviet experiments in para-psychology, a mind-control system evolved in Chile, or Tibetan Buddhism. Then one year why not Bhagwan Shri Rajneesh? Also, the gurus had a particular appeal for these therapists. The growth movement therapists had inherited the spiritual ferment which formed an integral part of the Esalen movement right from its inception.

In Search of Something New

In the 1940s and 1950s, a number of psychologists in the US broke with both Freudian and behavioural psychology, to form what they called humanistic psychology. They were, as reported, rather a mixed group of professionals, ranging from Gestalt psychologists to 'sensitivity trainers', to neo-Reichians with contradictory leanings. But, as suggested, the name human potential movement did identify the belief they held in common, the belief that psychology had the potential not just for curing the sick but also for improving mankind. Freud, they felt, saw all human beings as neurotic, an outcome also of a neurotic civilization. Such pessimism about human nature was not acceptable to these psychologists. They held that by letting off his repressions, man would come to his full flowering, something in to the state of nature.

They were, in the main, practitioners, uninterested in thcory. They evolved a chain of powerful techniques that had immediate results. The books by Arthur Janov (father of primal scream therapy) or Alexander Lowmen (creator of bio-energetics) owing allegiance to this school were more or less pop psychology marked by lack of concern for the scientific method. This lack of concern was inherent in their view that 'humanist psychology' stood in opposition to 'scientific psychology'.

Abraham Maslow was the only one who made a sustained attempt to define humanist psychology. What interested him was not mental illness but mental health. He studied people who made the full use of their talents, capacities, and potentialities. He made a list of people whom he thought were self-actualized, such as Jefferson, Spinoza, Goethe, and Washington. According to his theory, the human being had to satisfy each level of need before graduating to the next one, i.e., one had to fulfil, for instance, 'belongingness needs' before one could graduate to 'esteem needs' and above that, 'growth needs'. This theory, now much quoted in business management texts, rules out the possibility that some one could be a fine mathematician, or for that matter, an interior decorator, without a healthy love relationship and high self-esteem. As pointed out by Fitzgerald, Rajneesh's statement that only the rich could be truly religious was actually pure Maslow.

The academic psychologists found these growth movements much below their intellectual dignity to criticize. The outcome was that practice went so far ahead of theory as to become quite independent of it. Another consequence was, as the movement grew, it split and went in different directions. Some of its practitioners moved into mainstream psychotherapy, others went into business management, some went into pop psychology, evolving the language and the therapies that enterprencurs like Werner Erhard could package and mass market.

Those around Esalen and the newer growth centers joined the movement not to learn more sophisticated forms of life adjustment but to seek higher forms of consciousness. They were radicals, but as suggested, radicals of a different kind. While the political radicals denounced 'elitism', distrusted all forms of authority and were committed to genuine democratic organization, the so called growthmovement radicals in contrast looked for teachers and sought an elite of 'the self-actualising'. They sat at the feet of Fritz Perls, Carl Rogers, Ida Rolf and other star therapists. They became disciples, but in the end, it seems, they were always disappointed. Hence they were looking not for therapists "but for personifications of whatever they meant by 'authenticity' and 'awareness'; they were aspiring to get high on 'peak experience' and stay there".

Even at Esalen, it is reported, the growth movement solutions proved inadequate. Richard Price, one of the directors of Esalen, said, "Alan Watts introduced us to Buddhism in the mid-sixties and it seemed to put what we were doing into a more inclusive framework. After that Esalen was a mix of therapy and interest in Buddhism."

In fact, it was Watts who constructed an intellectual bridge between the therapists and Bhagwan. Alan Watts said, "If we look deeply into such a way of life as Buddhism and Taoism, Vedants and yoga, we do not find either philosophy or religion as are understood in the West. We find something nearly resembling psychotherapy". Therapists traveled from ashram to ashram in the hope of finding what Watts had seen. But they were disappointed most of the time because apart from meditation, the ashrams and monasteries taught religion and philosophy much the same way as these are understood in the West, and on top of that, claborate systems of rites and rituals and social morality which did not suit the therapists at all.

Easier Option

The Tibetan Buddhists, for instance, required Sanskrit and memorization of five thesis and the 34 thoughts. The Vedants priests were no less rigorous in their demands. Apart from that, the therapists felt they were male chauvinists and insisted on celibacy. Bhagwan Rajneesh turned out to be the exception. His English was faultiess and he demanded nothing except surrender and trust in him. Like Krishnamurti, he was a modernizer and an iconoclast and yet he was, so he said, an enlightened master, willing to take responsibility for the surrender of his disciples. In India, he was something of a paradox. He was, as one Anglo-Indian writer later christened him. "the progressive guru".

Apart from this, Rajneesh had certain unique abilities and he used them eleverly for gaining popularity and gaining a hold over others. He was a keen obsever and had a deep insight into human nature. He was a master hypnotist and was also a voracious reader. With his post-graduation in philosophy, he was exposed to both western and oriental schools of philosophy. His command over Hindi was exceptionally good. He was a good listener and a man of fertile imagination with brilliant innovative power. This could also be seen from the hundred-odd techniques of meditation that he evolved in the Pune Ashram within a short span of six to eight years.

Rajneesh had a rare sense of humor but could be extremely ruthless in executing his plans. He took special delight in manipulating people. He cleverly learnt from his western disciples about various techniques and therapies used by them in their growth movements and modified and integrated them within traditional Indian meditation systems and projected them as his own. Most of them were invented keeping in view the needs of his western followers.

In order to gain proper insights into the set of meditation techniques adopted by Rajneesh, it would be imperative to examine the theoretical framework of his perspective and the central core of his teachings. First we shall present the basic tenets of his teachings and subsequently examine how his perspective differs from the perceptions and approaches of other godmen in this country, and the contradictions inherent in his framework. We have already briefly summed up his ideas earlier. Now we shall examine some aspects of his teachings at greater length.

Zen Influence

Zen Buddhism is the inexhaustible source, as pointed out by his biographer Dr. Prasad, from which Rajneesh drew not only stories and parables but also his conception of Nirvana. According to Zen, the mind must be emptied of all its substance, all contents of self-identification as a prerequisite for enlightenment. To those who want to realize truth, Rajneesh recommends the Zen way. Instead of describing an object or talking about it, one should enter right into the object itself. See it from inside, feel it inwardly. Intellectualisation does not help.

Rajneesh and all Zen adherents contend that the sciences are uniformly centrifugal, extroverted and they look 'objectively' towards the thing they pick up for study. The position they subscribe is to keep the thing away from them and never to identify themselves with the object of their study. They are utterly scared of being 'subjective'. Rajneesh said that one must remember that as long as one stands outside, he remains an outsider; for that very reason one can never know the thing itself. Rajneesh regards intellect as a superficial center of activity.

The entire teachings of Rajneesh show his apprehension of the dangers of objectivity. As we develop intellectually, he argues, our sense domain is invaded by intellect and the naivete of sense experience is lost. Simple biological needs are contaminated by egocentric intellect.

Rajneesh, as brought out by Dr. Prasad, alludes to the Zen concept of 'no-mind', to the doctrine of void, and quotes, in the Kranti Beej, Buddhidharamas's well-known reply to the first emperor of the Liang dynasty who was eager to know the ultimate principle of Buddhism. The sage is reported to have answered, "vast emptiness and nothing holy in it". The Mahayana Sutra says, "Everything is emptiness, all things having the nature of emptiness have no beginning and no end. They are neither faultless nor not faultless, they are neither perfect nor imperfect. In emptiness there is no sensation, no perception, no discrimination, no consciousness. There is no decay and no death. There is no knowledge of Nirvana, there is no obtaining of Nirvana, there is no not obtaining of Nirvana".

As D.T. Suzuki points out, "All the sutras belonging to the prana class of Mahayana liternature are imbued thoroughly with the idea of sunyat. This sutra, considered the most concise and comprehensive of all the parjana sutras is daily recited at the Zen monastery.

According to Rajneesh, God, soul or truth are not the central elements in an individual's life. Everyone in the world, every living organism, is engaged in the act of regeneration, in giving new form and structures to life.

Rajneesh suggests that man's initial experience of samadhi, of super consciousness, must have been derived from his experience of the sex act. "The lightning that flashes during the sexual act is self-transcendence." The coital union, according o Rajneesh, enables one to transcend all duality and to become one. The union of man and woman is "the symbol of the union of Purusha and Prakriti, of Creator and Creation, of God and Soul, Shiva and Shakti".

Tantric Links

Rajneesh's closest links in philosophy, according to Dr.Prasad. are with the Tantric Budhists who believed that sukha or bliss is not possible at all without the body, that it is the quintessence of Brahman. Rajneesh, under Tantric inspiration, stresses the significance of Sadhna, the path towards upliftment of your soul, which, he suggests, could transform even gross self-pleasure into the boundless serenity of perfect bliss.

Serenity of Perfect Bliss

The Tantric attitude to sex is summed up as follows: "In our ordinary life we have the experience of the most intense pleasure in our sex experiences. Wide is the difference between this sex pleasure and perfect bliss which is the ultimate nature of the self and non-self; yet the distinction can be wholly removed by a total change of perspective and process. The sex-yogic sadhna of the Tantriks is a sadhna of transforming this sex pleasure into a realization of infinite bliss in which the self and the world around are lost in all providing oneness conceived also as Nirvana."

Rajnesh too regards the body as the abode of all truth. In his books 'Wings of Love' and 'Journey Inwards', he glorifies the body and love of one's life. He actually states,

'In my view, a virtuous life is entirely different. It is not a life of internal conflict but that of internal peace, melody and harmony. It is not a life of self hostility but that of unity and awareness. The supreme soul is perfect harmony. If I wish to merge into divine harmony, it is essential that I should have a note of harmony within me. How can this note of harmony be produced? Never by treating the self with contempt nor through self-reproach and self-hostility."

According to Dr. Prasad, both Buddha and Rajneesh reject the two extremes of sensuality and self mortification. In almost every collection of Rajneesh, one encounters a spirited defence of the body, of spontancity and freedom and advocacy of the Middle Path.

Unlike the other religious teachers in India, Rajneesh speaks of the navel as the most important region in the humon body, According to Rajneesh, the present education system and social structure help the individual only towards mental development.

He traces the roots of widespread mental imbalance in modern Indian society in the present educational system. He even explains the prevalence of wars, crimes, hatred, conflicts and social struggles in terms of an unbalanced educational framework. Hence Rajneesh advocates turning away from the education of the intellect to the cultivation of the navel region.

One of the false beliefs and deceptive illusions of the modern age, according to Rajneesh, it is that the head is the central region of the body. Actually, he says the navel is the 'root'of our existence. The seeker hence should travel downwards, toward his roots, descending from his mind to the heart and from the heart down to his navel and then finally to his atman, his soul. According to Rajneesh, the half witted yogi who passed upwards and the misguided guru who wants to lead the seeker to the atman by ignoring the navel reach nowhere. The seeker should realize that the navel and not the head is the centre of contact between the body and the atman and that when he was in his mother's womb, it was through his navel that he received his nourishment, Rajneesh points out.

Religion for Rajneesh, as Dr. Prasad observes, "is an inward revolution, a wholesale psychological transmutation, a re-born-ness". The religious aspirant and seer withdraw into himself." Rajneesh does not believe in a personal God. Since all life is one, there is neither God and man nor a universe and God.

According to Rajneesh, to know truth is an uphill task and its price is life itself. Seeking satisfaction in the scriptures implies imprisoning oneself in a set of doctrines of man's own making. Rajneesh insists that that which has been formed in the human mind cannot be divine. Similarly, what is recorded in the so-called sacred books mirrors the author's own aspirations and feelings, not truth, because truth, according to Rajneesh, is beyond all verbal communication, birthless and beginningless. "When man's consciousness is liberated from the prison house of coded religions and theological doctrines, truth, self-begotten and self-created, reveals itself."

We have briefly summed up the major tenets of Rajneesh's preachings. We shall now attempt to briefly anylyze the significance of his world view, its practial implications, its relevance, its internal coherence and the basis of its appeal. It would be fruitful to examine his teachings at two different levels, one in terms of his theoretical framework, and two, its practical application.

Budhism and its Derivatives

Although Rajneesh denounced all established religions, as we have seen, two major currents of thought which decisively influenced his perspective are Buddhist philosophy and Tantric practices. But his teachings have very little in common with the original preachings of Buddha, although he swore by Buddha and never tired of repeating his name, parables connected with Buddha, and advocated the Middle Path like Buddha.

Rajneesh was much more influenced by Zen Buddhism which draws inspiration from Mahayana Buddhism, the idealist, distorted version of original Buddhism. Shunyawad or the doctrine of void, a state of emptiness, was propounded by Nagarjuna, which also became an integral part of Mahayana teachings.

In order to appreciate the distinction between Buddha's perception and subsequent distortions of his ideas in the form of Mahayana and other sects, it is essential to briefly refer to the historical context or Buddha's emergence, the central core of his teachings, their relevance to modern society and also their interpretation in Mahayana texts.

The age of the Buddha was the time, as brought out by the Late Prof. Kosambi and Deviprasad Chattopadhaya, when the organization of the state had begun to develop within the womb of tribal structures. Magadh and Koshal had already emerged as state powers on the ruins of the tribal societies. In this sense the age of the Buddha witnessed the most momentous social upheavals in the Gangetic valley. Buddha himself came from the Shakyas who, though tribals, were at a higher stage of development. The Shakyas had no king. Theirs was a republican form of government where the administrative and judicial business was conducted through public assembly by collective deliberations.

Buddha was full of reverence for tribal institutions, a prominent feature of which was tribal democracy and this was threatened by the emerging state powers.

The other feature of this period, vital in the understanding of the role of early Buddhism, was the creation of the new administrative machinery within the orbits of state power which encouraged the king to be a tyrant who oppressed his subjects by punishment, taxes, torture and robbery. The change in society, as Prof. Kosambi points out, was also marked by a new set of practices like mortgage, interest and usury. Along with the state powers, there emerged during the period a strong and influential merchant class.

The control of the state mechanism by violence led to suppression of tribal elected assemblies and the need for their sanction for administration. In fact, as suggested by Prof. Kosambi, these kingdoms could not have expanded under tribal conditions. A whole new class of people engaged in trade and the production of commodities needed immunity from tribal obstruction. To them it was most important to have a king who could ensure safety and new heights of prosperity.

The Magadh state willingly performed this function as the royal house itself was engaged in extensive trade in grains and commodities. The king further claimed all the privileges of former tribal chiefs but hardly any of their obligations.

Budhism, as Chattopadhaya observes, proved to be a tremendous success because it offered a substitute for the lost tribal values. Buddha, with his heritage of tribal morality, was appalled by the new realities he witnessed. He saw his own people, including women and children, cruelly exterminated. He saw the emergence of base greed and insatiable desire which resulted in patricide, as in the cases of Pasenadi who was killed by Virudhaka, and Bimbisara who was slain by Ajatashatru who in turn was killed by his son. As a matter of fact, patricide for the sake of the throne was the outcome of the emergence of new feudal values.

Confronted with this new dominant force, Buddha naturally sought peace in the 'quietude of the heart', by withdrawing himself from reality. After prolonged and intense meditation he at last realized the peace and quietude he longed for.

The monastries or sanghas that Buddha established had an ultra democratic constitution based on the conventions of tribal democracies. There was complete equality within the collectivity. The monks were drawn from all walks of life irrespective of caste and religion. From the lowest Chandala to the highest Brahmin all were equal.

The members of the sangha were not supposed to possess any private property. They had to live a simple life wearing coarse clothes and begging for their food. The minimum items of clothing, a needle, a razor, a water jug and beggar's bowl were all that a monk could keep for himself as his personal belongings. The monks were obliged not only to study and meditate within the sangha but were also expected to go out and beg for their food, impart the knowledge of dharma to the people, and instruct them on self discipline and self-purification. These made the monastic order respectable and attracted large numbers of people to it.

The basic doctrine taught by Buddha is popularly known as the Four Noble Truths. They are :

(i) All living beings suffer.

(ii) The cause of suffering is desire, possessiveness, greed, craving and egocentrism.

(iii) Whatever is caused can be removed by removing the cause.

(iv) Hence, suffering can be eliminated by following the eight-fold path. The eight-fold path consists of:

- Right views
- or the understanding that the conquering of desire and greed is the path to happiness and that the eight-fold path is the means to this end.

- Right purpose or aspiration
- not to indulge in sensuous luxuries. To work for the happiness of others.
- Right speech
- one must be truthful and always speak in such a way that mutual understanding and friendship are enhanced.
- Right action
- abstaining from theft, adultery, killing, etc. and only conducting activities that are conducive to the welfare of others.
- Right conduct
- one's way of living must not harm others.
- Right effort
- which includes mental discipline to remove evil thoughts and development of good thoughts.
- Right mindedness
- one must be aware of the evils generated by attachment to bodily pleasures and must take steps to remove them.
- Right meditation
- which involves mental discipline and concentration.

Life, according to Buddha, was a ceaseless flow from one state to another. The continuous process of life, death and rebirth is determined by karma. According to the law of karma, good deeds would always beget good results. The Buddha said, "The beginning of wisdom is from good must come good and from evil must come evil. This is the first law, and all things that live are ruled by this law."

Buddha also held that the struggle for enlightenment, perfection and Nirvana had to be waged within man. One must look within and conquer one's cravings and desires by conquering one's own ego.

It is true that, as argued by Damodaran, in self-aggrandizement, the egoistic and selfish drive to own and possess private property, not only obstructs man's self realization but also creates disorders and strife in society. But the crucial question which remains unanswered is, what is the cause that generales greed and the passion for possession?

It appears that Buddha, with the historical limitations in which he found himself, in his analysis could not take note of the intensity of exploitation and class contradiction of the varna vyavastha, the caste system. It was the expanding varna vyavastha under the monarchical state that played havoe with tribal virtues, encouraged the spirit of possession and provided a fertile ground for greed and hatred.

Used and Abused

The new ruling classes of the expanding empire, realizing the growing popularity of Buddhism, found it profitable to utilize it as an ideology to hold society together and to regulate human conduct by social and religious norms instead of by coercion and violence. Ashoka the Great made Buddhism his state religion. He sent Buddhist missionaries to distant lands, established friendly relations with many countries and thus consolidated his empire.

The traders followed the missionaries under the banner of Buddhism and in a favourable climate of peace expanded their trade and became prosperous. These wealthy traders became the pillars of the monastic order. They willingly donated a part of their ever increasing wealth to the sanghas.

With the support of this wealth, Buddhist monasteries and vihars sprang up in different places and the monks became more and more 'respectable' and affluent. This also led to recruitment of many unift, unworthy and self-seeking persons. Idleness and lust and other vices began to corrode the inner life of the monasteries.

The degeneration of the sanghas was also reflected in the dilution and distortions of the original preachings of Buddha, in the form of the emergence of Mahayana and other sects within the fold of Buddhism. As noted by Prof. Chattopadhaya, the emergence of the Mahayana was a drastic departure from the creed as originally preached by the Buddha. The Mahayana introduced metaphysical and Upanishadic idealism in Buddhism which is very much alien from the spirit of the original teachings of Buddha.

Within a few centuries after the death of Buddha, there was the most dramatic transformation of the creed. One manifestation of this process was the conscious cultivation of superstitions which ultimately transformed Buddhism beyond recognition. As suggested by Prof. Chattopadhaya, Mahayana is one such distorted version of Buddhism.

Mahayana incorporated the essential features of Upanishadic idealism within the Buddhist framework. However, the Neo-Buddhists could not reconcile the Upanishadic world-denying theology with the Buddha's realistic and rationalistic attitude. Hence, they felt the need to tamper with the memory of the historical founder of the creed. This they did with the formulation of an elaborate theory called "Buddhalogy".

Instead of Buddha they started talking of many Buddhas called the Boddhisattvas. These Buddhas have nothing in common with the material world. According to Mahayana interpretation, their form or rupa which appears as body to our mortal eyes is reality created by the mind alone (manomaya). Thus, as Prof. Chattopa-dhaya suggests, with this theological trick, the historical Budha is made to vanish. Like everything else about the Mahayana, the theory of the Buddhas and Boddhisattvas acquired mystical form. The most noteworthy aspet of this is the distinction between dharma kaya, nirmana kaya, and rupa kaya.

The dharma kaya assumes more importance for the purpose of our discussion because Rajneesh's formulation about the Buddhist philosophy appears to be largely derived from this concept. This concept is also interpreted as that of the 'cosmical body of the Buddha'. As Prof. Chattopadhaya explains, "The key to it is the Mahayana concept of dharmata, which means the ultimate reality or the absolute. This absolute is supposed to be beyond the reach of our ordinary knowledge and indescribable by our ordinary language, beyond asserting the bare fact of its existence which the Mahayanists call tathata or 'bare suchness'. From its point of view, all objects normally known are sheer nothingness

- a circumstance that leads the Mahayanists to identify dharmata with sunyata, the latter meaning nothingness of the world of experience. Only the perfect saint in his state of final salvation or nirvana is supposed to realize this highly mystical absolute
- a state of realization in which nothing remains but the absolute itself. Hence the other word for dharmata is nirvana."

The paintings and statues of a Mahayana monastery reveal the superimposition of a mixed and monstrous pantheon on the simple atheism of the Buddha. Prof. Chattopadhaya explains this degeneration of the original Buddhist teachings to the parasitic existence of the monks who lived luxuriously on the lavish gifts of the merchants and kings. Absence of the worries of their own material existence created conditions suitable for philosophical speculation. With their exclusive concern with learning and thinking, the Mahayanists could add to the mode of philosophical discussions. This was their great contribution to Indian philosophy.

Rajneesh, with his advocacy of shunyavada or the state of void as a perfect state of bliss, actually followed in the footsteps of the Mahayanist school. Thus Rajneesh's calling himself 'Osho' at the final phase of his existence was nothing but a crude mockery of all that Buddha stood for.

Rajneesh's simultaenous advocacy of Zen Buddhism and Tantricism raises some interesting questions and sounds paradoxical, as it is a herculean task to reconcile these two contradictory view points. However, again, it is essential to understand Rajneesh's own interpretation of Tantra and subsequently explore the origin of Tantra and to examine some more authentic interpretations of the tantric schools.

As we noted earlier, Rajneesh's closest links, according to his biographer, Dr. Prasad, are with the 'Tantric Buddhists' who believed that sukha is not possible at all without the body. In our ordinary experiences of pleasure based on basic physical impulses, Rajneesh finds the possibility of perfect bliss. Tantric sadhana, Rajneesh says, could transform even gross sense pleasure into the boundless serenity of perfect bliss. His entire thesis on sex to super-consciousness also rests on this foundation. As Rajneesh insists, "If you wish to go beyond the body, if you wish to be liberated, be ever devoted to it".

Roots of Tantra

Now we shall briefly refer to the other viewpoints on the origin of Tantrism and in the light of these interpretations we shall examine the relevance and significance of Rajneesh's interpretation of Tantrism.

Scholars have claimed a hoary antiquity for Tantrism on the following grounds :

(i) The earliest trace of animal sacrifice which forms an important part of Tantric worship is found to have been prevalent as early as the Indus culture period;

(ii) The Narayanitantra says that the Vedas have originated from the Tantras, proving thereby that the Tantras were prevalent before the Vedas were composed;

(iii) Many of the semi-magical elements found in the Tantras bear close resemblance to those found in the Atharvaveda;

(iv) Many of the deities like Shiva, Shakti, Vishnu, Sunya, Ganapati and others who find a prominent place in the Tantras are also mentioned in the earlier texts.

Professor Chattopadhaya who thinks that the Tantras developed from the agricultural rituals of the primitive people dates them as far back as the Indus valley civilization.

The basis of the Tantric philosophy, as widely acknowledged, is the doctrine of Prakriti and Purush as propounded by the Sankhya school of thought. The Purusha can work only through Prakriti, implying that Purush is inactive while Prakriti is active. Hence Prakriti is presumed to be more important than the Purush.

A close perusal of the Tantric texts reveals the fact that the majority of the Tantras centre around the mother cult and are heterodox in nature. This is probably due to the fact that the cult of the mother goddess developed greater affinity with Shaivism which flourished mainly outside the orthodox Brahmanical fold.

D. Chattopadhaya traces the origin of the Tantras to obscure cults and agricultural rituals. Of the five Ms of Tantra, madya or wine, mansa or meal, matsya or fish, mudra or parched kidney beans and maithuna or intercourse with a Chandala woman, he specially refers to madya and maithuna. He provides extensive sociological evidence to indicate how primitive tribes made use of wine for the purpose of promoting agriculture and increasing fertility of the soil. The belief in the magical power of wine was also common among the Vedic people which could be seen from the extensive use of soma in the sacrifice. Fertility of the soil and sexual intercourse are interconnected among many tribals.

As Rajneesh shows affinity to the Buddhist Tantrism, it would be pertinent to briefly refer to some important sects of Tantrism. Prof. Chattopadhaya while referring to various seets of Tantrism aptly remarks, "With vast literature on the subject, Tantrism still remains an enigma to our academic world."

Tantric Sects

To begin with, the vast literature on Tantrism, paradoxically enough, is itself a hindrance to its proper understanding. This does not certainly mean that such texts do not contain any elements of genuine Tantrism whatsoever. They do. But they also contain many other things. From various quarters and in various ways, alien and hostile thoughts were continually grafted on original Tantrism, making it difficult to recover its genuine form from the texts on it. We may examine some examples of these superimpositions. In one type of the texts, efforts were being made to expound Tantra within the general structure of Buddhist philosophy, more specifically of Mahayana Buddhism. Tantrism is explained as an outgrowth of Mahayana Buddhism, in fact, its descendant form.

The basic outlook in all these texts is derived from sexual imageries and the texts are permeated with strong elements of magic. The central theme revolves round the union of the male and female, though expressed in such terminologies as shunyata and karuna, pragya and upaya, vajra and padma

- all arbitrarily taken from Buddhism. The ritual aspect of these texts is overtly based on the practice of sexual union.

M.M. Bose, an eminent authority on Tantrism also brings out the hollowness of the contention of the connection between Buddhism and Tantrism. He argues, "In the Buddhist Tantras we come across descriptions similar to what we have just discussed about the Hindu Tantras, they are simply transcribed in the Buddhist Tantras. It seems that the names Shiva, Durga etc. of the Hindu Tantras are simply transcribed in the Buddhist Tantras as names of Vajrasatva, Vajradakini etc. In the Buddhist Tantras too, the worship of Chandi, Tara, Varati etc is prevalent. As in the Tantras revealed by Shiva, bizarre deities are imagined, so in the Buddhist Tantras we come across deities like Heruka and others. In the Buddhist scriptures expounding the view of the Buddha (i.e., genuine Buddhism), the five 'M's are strongly denounced.

Buddhist Tantrics, however, behave differently. The practice of the five 'M's constitutes a basic feature of the Buddhist Tantras. The indulgence in wine and meal, so severely denounced in the Buddhist scriptures, is extolled in the Buddhist Tantras."

Buddhist Tantrism, as suggested by Lldela Valle, is practically Hinduism or Shaivism in Buddhist garb. Rajneesh, while advocating Buddhist Tantrism, very conveniently ignores the basic fact that like Mahayana Buddhism, Buddhist Tantrism too violates the fundamental postulates of the Buddha. Moreover, in original Tantra, there is no reference to either soul, God or liberation, heaven, prayer or sacrifice, features which are associated with essentially developed religions. In this ancient belief, the human body and nature are viewed as two aspects of the same basic reality. Whatever exists in the human body also exists in the universe. This is the conclusion of all Tantra. The wisdom of Tantrism is explained by all on the basis of this theory. The Purans and the other shastras have accepted this theory.

There are, thus, two aspects of Tantric theory and practice. One of these is the external aspect and is concerned with the universe. The other is the internal aspect and is concerned with the human body. There are two forms in which the success of the Tantric practice manifests itself. One is the aspect of external nature, of earth, the other is the aspect of the internal nature, i.e., nature as human body. You can attain success by developing the forces latent in you, or again, by controlling external or natural forces, you can move towards an expression of your own internal forces.

Cult of the Body

The relationship between the forces lying dormant in nature and in the human body is indeed astomshing. The practices of the basis of which this intimate relationship is known, established and brought under control, constitute Tantra sadhna. Its basis is deha tatva, the cult of the body. That is why Tantra is all along so deeply concerned with the questions concerning the body.

We have very briefly touched on some aspects of Tantra. There are several other vital facets such as different dimensions of its sadhna, its mantras, tantras or chakras, its various schools, conflicting interpretations, controversy connected with its origin and revival of the Tantric practices in the medieval period, Tantra and Taoism and similar proto-materialist trends in other countries, its geographical spread, etc. which we cannot explore here satisfactorily.

Rajneesh, projected as a sex guru and a great exponent of Tantra, hardly found it necessary to examine any of these aspects closely connected with the emergence of Tantra in this country. He was either blissfully unaware of such vital aspects of the school of thought which is supposed to have influenced his perspective so deeply or he found it inconvenient to deal with all these important facets of Tantra because they may have challenged his own teachings.

Rajneesh's Own Brand

Rajneesh, it seems to us, must have been aware of the problems involved in upholding Tantra. In spite of these constraints, Rajneesh strongly advocated Tantra because as it appears, he could conveniently use some of its elements as an integral part of the new theoretical edifice he tried to construct for his disciples.

This contention can also be substantiated from Sudhir Kakar's interesting interpretations of Tantra as a part of the healing traditions of Indian society (in 'Shamans, Mystics and Doctors' to which we will refer in greater detail in the concluding chapter of this book). He argues, "Tantra is said to have appeared in India at the beginning of this era. Assimilated, though uneasily, in all the great Indian religions, Tantra had become a pan-Indian phenomenon by the sixth century and remains one to this day."

Revived, disapproved of or barely tolerated, Tantra's relationship with the dominant religious orthodoxy has never been easy. When Rajneesh offered his own particular brand of Tantra to the thousands who flocked to his Pune Ashram, he was in the best tantric tradition, also making fun of the scandalized Hindu establishment. The contemporary official Hindu culture, essentially formulated by Vivekananda, Gandhi and other 'reformists', is decidedly anti-Tantric and keeps Tantra well outside the ken of permissible interest.

The observations of Sudhir Kakar succinctly convey the reasons which must have prompted Rajneesh to adopt Tantra as an integral part of his teachings, as this was convenient to boost his image as a 'rebel' against Hindu religious orthodoxy. Morcover, it also helped establish his advocacy of sex as a source of divinity. Tantra could also fit into the conceptual framework he evolved to attract his western disciples. In the process, he contradicted the basic tenets of his own preachings but that hardly bothered him. His concept of Nirvana, void, or a state of perfect bliss, borrowed from the Zen or Mahayana sect of Buddhism, flatly contradicts dehavada, the proto-materialist basis of Tantric philosophy.

Camouflaged Inconsistencies

It is not surprising to find that Rajneesh could get away with several gross contradictions and inconsistencies in his teachings. This was possible for the simple reason that an average Indian (or for that matter even western) listener knows so little about religious scriptures or various schools of thought that it hardly requires much effort to exploit his ignorance and gullibility.

Rajneesh in this respect is not the only one, Most of the godmen in India as well as other countries have managed to thrive by taking advantage of the innocence of their average followers and playing upon their psychological needs of dependence, and the emotional insecurity and sense of alienation, frustration and anxicties, all of which are becoming so widespread in modern society.

Socio-Economic Context

It is our contention that the emergence, growth and decline of modern godmen and their cults, though they fall within the religious domain, can be properly grasped only as a sociological phenomenon. For the adequate comprehension of the significance, internal dynamics and contradictions inherent in these cults, it is imperative to examine them in the particular socio-economic and historical context in which they manifest.

Any attempt to evaluate these cults in abstraction or in isolation from the given context would only provide a partial and lopsided understanding. Such a dialectical approach has considerably facilitated our understanding of these modern godmen and their cults in terms of the basis of their appeal, their rise and decline, the type of following they attract, their significance and the contradictions in their practice and preachings.

Rajneesh emerged on the Indian scene in the mid-sixties when the country was passing through a period of political disillusionment and economic depression, at a juncture when the ruling Congress as well as Left parties were passing through a phase of internal crises and splits.

In the West too, this period coincided with the increasing disillusionment of hippies and other counter-culture groups with their style of living, the growing recessionary trends in the world capitalist economy, rising unemployment and growing inflationary pressures. The emergence of Rajneesh as a critic of the established religions, political set-up, socialist phrase mongering, Gandhism and set conventions and rituals based on hypocrisy, all appealed to the neo-rich, professionals and youngsters. It appealed even to some sections of radicals who were getting disillusioned with the set norms and the prevailing code of ethics and morality, and were looking forward to an alternative which could justify their comfortable living, sexual promiscuity, self-indulgence, and their arrogance and could permit them to have the satisfaction of following a higher, spiritual path of self-realisation devoid of any sense of guilt.

Fitzgerald's observations are quite pertinent in this context. She says that Rajneesh, after all, had made a career of outrageousness. As an assistant professor at an obscure university from 1960-1966, he had drawn crowds in cities across India by attacking Gandhi, socialism, and orthodox Hinduism. Later, he had became the outrageous guru who attacked Pope John II, Mother Teresa, and Morarji Desai. Later westerners had poured in and laughed at his anti-Catholic and anti-Hindu jokes. He made his listeners feel that they belonged to an elite of true free thinkers, who saw beyond the superstitions and pathetic social props of everyone else's existence.

The same writer also cites several instances of glaring contradictions between the ideals of 'new man' and celebration of spontaenity, sexual abandon, openness, individuality and authentic existence in his commune and the autocratic functioning, dehumanization, suppression of individuality, dogmatic adherence to routine and other suffocating modes of existence in the Oregon commune as experienced by a majority of Rajneesh's disciples.

Ideals Violated

The commune was to give birth to a 'new man' who would not be not a 'fixed character' but an 'authentic being' with a commitment to 'the scripture of nature'. He would love others and hence be honest and trusting. There would be no ambition and no politics in this commune.

How these ideals were flagrantly violated in practice can be illustrated by a look at the publication of a booklet called Rajneeshism, attempting to establish his religion with the same rigidity of all other established religions. The booklet set down four religious holidays in the year and described ceremonies to be used on the occasions of birth, death, marriage and caring for the sick. Of course, he subsequently denounced this booklet as Sheela's creation when the tide was turning against him in Oregon.

In Pune too, as we have seen, things were not very different. If something appeared to be wrong or unjust or foolish, that was only the disciple's myopia, it was otherwise in the guru's encompassing vision. As Jocelyn Roberts observed, Rajneesh had created a traditional Oriental despotism and this form of government inevitably gave rise to resentments, rivalries, cliques, and factions, the very things that Rajneesh had said they were learning to do without.

Likewise, with regard to life in the Oregon commune, it is stated that the concern against pollution in Oregon almost amounted to obsession. There were also the clearly excessive security measures and restrictions, and the attempts by Sheela and the others to control and regulate the European communes. The impulse in each case was to control and the concern in each case was purity. This was in sharp contras to the ideals of spontaenity, authenticity, individuality and sexual freedom advocated by the guru umpteen number of times in his discourses.

Another tendency that developed in the commune was the elaboration of ceremony, costume and hierarchy. The degrees and titles that were awarded to the leaders had, for instance, increased four fold. Sheela came to be formally known as Bodhisatva Ma Anand Sheela, M. M., D. Phil, M., D. Litt. M. (RIMU). Acharya, one of the editors of the guru's lectures was called Sambodhi Ma Prem Maneesha, S.R.N., R.M., R.M.N., M.M., D. Phil. M. (RIMU) Acharya. These titles and degrees of course were from Rajneesh International Meditation University.

Even in the way they dressed, an exhibitionist element had become dominant. In Oregon, Ma Sheela had dressed for special occasions, such as a press conference, in long red robes with the Rajneesh symbol embroidered on the front, a mala with pearl or diamond beads, and an embroidered scarf on her head. Rajneesh himself for some time dressed up like a Christmas tree, in glittering robes and diamond watches. In Pune, he had worn plain white. He had always had a fancy for the theatrical, but in Oregon, as Fitzgerald pointed out, he went in for pageantry. When he drove the few hundred yards from his house to the lecture hall, or the half mile to Sheela's compound for a press interview, his Rolls-Royce would be accompanied not only by pilot cars, but also by two helicopters with a rocket. His performance was briefly summed up as "a cross between Oscar night and a Latin-American dictator's evening out."

Thus, power struggles, scheming, spying, lies, secrecy, hierarchical structure, corruption, nepotism, favouritism, cliques, double standards, and other such deformations became a part of the cult. And yet, aided by the prevailing social and psychological conditions and his clever incorporation of a medley of therapies, Rajneesh succeeded not only in attracting large numbers of disciples who paid an exorbitant price for spiritual advancement but also managed to hold them in thrall even through his various international capers.

Reference

Gordon, James Golden Guru. Pp. 23-24.

Acharya Rajneesh, Path to Self Realization, Bombay, Jeevan Jagriti Kendra, 1971.

Prasad, Ramachandra The Mystic of Feelings, Motilal Banarasidass, Delhi, p. 197.

Fitzgerald, Frances Cities on a Hill, Picador, USA. 1986, pp.289-90.

Gordon, Ibid., p. 109.

Gordon p. 163.

Fitzgerald, p.377.

Milne, Hugh Bhagwan The God That Failed. Sphere Books Ltd. London, 1986, p.7.

Fitzgerald, Ibid.

India Today, December 15, 1985, p.38.

Lele, Vijay, Gentleman, September, 1987, p.73.

Sunday Observer, February 15, 1987.

Lele, Ibid., p.78.

S. Balakrishnan "Was Rajneesh Murdered". The Illusrated Weekly of India, February 11, 1990, p. 12.

Fitzgerald, Ibid., p.284.

Prasad, Ibid., p.88.

Damodaran K. Man and Society in Indian Philosophy. P.58.

Chattopadhya D. Living and Dead in Indian Philosophy.p.154.

Prasad, Ibid., p.141.

Chakravarty, Chintaharan. Tantras – Studies on their Religion and Literature, pp.7-18.

Chattopadhya, Sudhir Reflection on Tantra. Pp.8-9.

Chattopadhya D., Lokayat, pp.324-25, PPH.

Bose Post-Chaitanya Sahajiya Cults of Bengal. Calcutta, 1930. p.547.

Chattopadhya D., Lokayat, pp.332-33.

Kakar, Sudhir Shamans, Mystics and Doctors – A Psychological Inquiry into India and Its Healing Traditions.

Oxford University Press, 1982, p. 152.

Fitzgerald, Ibid. pp.341.

6

Morari Bapu

Introduction

The focus of this appraisal on Morari Bapu has been guided by various considerations. Morari Bapu is unique in many ways. He is a modern guru and claims no following in terms of disciples. Unlike several other gurus of his stature, he is easily accessible and doesn't claim any special power for miracles. He also suggests that he doesn't believe in superstitions. He has also no pretention of tracing his legacy from any distinct guru parampara (tradition) or any well established lineage. His past, in terms of his childhood, family background, social and financial status, his performance in education etc are easily accessible and verifiable. There is also hardly any pretention of his lifestyle, good habits, family life and his routine activities.

He is widely admired as a unique exponent of Tulsi Ramcharitmanas. His presentation is simple and lucid. Nevertheless, it is important to note that there is close correspondence between his rising curve of popularity for katha recital and the extensive campaign for Ram Janmbhoomi and the construction of the Ram temple in Ayodhya, culminating in the destruction of the Babri Masjid in the early 1990s. Thus, it also reflects on the convergence of the Hinduism Revivalist upsurge with the increasing popularity of the discourses on the Ramcharitmanas in the last over four decades.

The gross contradiction between Morari Bapu's preaching of the cherished ideals of truth, love, compassion and non-violence as the core of the Tulsi Ramcharitmanas and the practice of the connivance with the state in Gujrat, under Narendra Modi's regime, of unleashing an unprecedented communal carnage in 2002, which resulted in a massive massacre of Muslims, destruction of their properties, their uprooting from residential areas and brutal atrocities and raping of their women. Even after almost a decade of communal holocaust, Muslims are still exposed to all kinds of insecurity and hostility in many parts of the state. We have focused on Morari Bapu especially because he has acquired a reputation as a promoter of communal harmony and is sympathetic towards the cause of minorities.

The second chapter exclusively deals with the archaeological findings about the society, material culture, geographical locations of towns, Sri Lanka, and other vital data of that period. This appraisal seems essential to us as our presumptions and popular myths of this period deserve serious examination.

The third chapter deals with the riddle of ramayan. There are not only hundreds but thousands of versions of ramayan which are popular not only in different regions of this country, but also in many parts of Asia. Hence a brief perusal of this wide variety of versions of ramayan deserve consideration.

The fourth chapter provides a profile of Morari Bapu. We have attempted to provide a faithful account of Morari Bapu's distinct achievements, unique traits as a modern guru, his life sketch, and other details as made available from the website on Bapu and from his biographies.

The fifth chapter deals with the gross contradiction between the preachings and practices of Morari Bapu. Morari Bapu's public image and contention about commitment to the Gandhian values of non-violence, truth, love and compassion (which he also claims are the values upheld by Tulsi Ramcharitmanas) and the gross distortions and violations in his application of these ideals. Tulsi's Brahminic bias and his adherence to the Hindu dharma shastra's code of maintaining the degrading position of women and lower social strata of India and upholding of chaturvarna and karma principles based on the hierarchical caste system are quite visible in his works. Morari Bapu also doesn't show any hesitation in identifying with the BJP and VHP's communal agenda on the erection of the Ram Mandir in Ayodhya where the Babri

Masjid is demolished and similar demands like the abolition of article 370 on Kashmir from the Indian Constitution.

Distinct Features of Morari Bapu as a Modern Guru

Morari Bapu : A Case Study of a Corporate Guru in the Age of Globalisation. Bapu has acquired fame as a unique exponent of Tulsi Ramayan. There is a debate about Tulsi versus Valmiki Ramayan as the salient features of both are quite distinct. Apart from this debate, there is equally relevant in-depth research going on the multiple versions of ramayan. There are a variety of versions in India itself. For instance, the Southern version is totally different from the Northern version. Similarly, the other versions of ramayan in countries like Indonesia, Japan and also some of the European countries are not comparable. Ramayan is presumed to be an earlier epic than The mahabharat in terms of historical chronology. The social, material and cultural aspects of human society during the period of ramayan as brought to light by the Archaeological Survey of India also deserve serious consideration as it provides significant information on Indian society, its culture, institutions and material aspects at that early historical juncture. One should also take note of the controversy around the historical validity of Ram's existence and the myths around ramayan.

Ramayan's first printed version has been found in Nepali language and this was made available only around 1130 A.D.. The Tulsi Ramayan is a popular version explaining the society and culture of that period. Morari Bapu's version also is unique because apart from being based on the content of Tulsi Ramayan, one finds a lot of improvisation in terms of his understanding of contemporary Indian society and its problems.

Bapu hails from a small distinct village called Talgajarda in Bhavnagar district of Gujrat. He comes from a humble family background and has a family association with the village temple with a history of oral katha recital. His educational background is poor given that his household had a limited income. He is influenced by his grandfather whom he regards as his real guru. Bapu has had a difficult passage of upward mobility and popularity.

His empire consists of numerous activities with distinct and amazing dimensions of his interests, ranging from literature to music, folk culture, national and global religious congregations, cultural festivals and literary conferences.

Bapu with his limited literacy is a genius in terms of his command over language, graphic memory, rare confidence, and ability to win over enemies. He would be at home with academics, literary giants, religious scholars, artists, poets, writers and of course, ordinary laymen in both rural and urban India. He is equally at home with NRIs, corporate leaders and political personalities and even exponents of rationalism.

He has conducted sermons at varied locations such as Mansarovar, Kailash and Bhutan, frequenting both urban and rural areas. There is a terrific demand for his Kathas. People book much in advance, often for over a year, and that too without much assurance. These sermons are extremely expensive affairs although he doesn't charge any fees or donations for himself since long. However, the minimal arrangements required for a sermon with a huge attendance as well as provision of food, prasad etc for a period of upto nine days, usually from 9:30 am to 1 pm, rakes up high expenses.

Bapu has a profound variety of admirers. His physical fitness and energy are remarkable. One hardly finds him fatigued.

Bapu also differs from other gurus because he is not in favor of institutionalization of multiple activites. He actually dissolved several trusts which were earlier established and now conducts his activity only through one Sitaram Trust. There is no institution established in his name.

He is not a sanayasi but a family man observing all family rituals and customs in terms of arranging his children's marriages in traditional ways and observing other rituals.

Bapu now operates almost like a cultural ambassador of the country. There is no verbal or explicit proclamation in this context. One gathers his feeling from his visit to other countries like US, Bhutan, UAE where his presence invites state officials, political leaders etc to bless the occasion. It becomes a cultural, semi-political get-together .

In his discourses to NRI audiences, especially in USA, one can easily notice his advocacy of Hindu resurgence. In his recent discourse in New Jersey, he also released a volume of an encylopedia of Hinduism prepared on the basis of the writings of religious callers from different sects of Hinduism across two decades.

Historical Backdrop of Ramayan

Ramayan is a well known epic poem. It is widely believed that Valmiki's Ramayan is a thousand years old and was written before the Mahabharat. Unlike the Mahabharat which, apart from the tale of the Pandav-Kaurav war, provides a variety of references and depictions of other events and incidents reflecting Indian culture, traditions, customs and rituals and is regarded as an unparallel treasure of Indian civilization. As against this, ramayan is entirely based on the portrayal of one major narration. This was the widely held belief till 1870, before the findings of German scholar Max Weber on Indian history and culture. Subsequently, several other western and Indian scholars have contributed a series of articles and books on this subject.

Almost all western scholars on the basis of deeper studies have brought out that Valmiki's Ramayan could not have been written earlier than 700 B.C. because there is no reference to Buddha or Pataliputra. Prof. Keith quotes the view that this Ramayana could not be older than 300 B.C..

Prof. Sankalia, on the basis of archaeological evidence and exploration, divides the epic into 4 or 6 cantoes as follows:[1]

1. During the earlier phase there must have been accounts of Ayodhya, Kishkindha and Lanka based on folk songs and relevant legends.
2. Poet Valmiki must have assembled this material and prepared this epic poem which might have been based on 12,000 shlokas.
3. This epic was divided into 6 cantoes and subsequently new shlokas were added.
4. In the original epic poem, a variety of other depicitions of nature and magical spells were added and three traditional geographic recitations emerged.
5. Towards the final version, Balkhands with numerous geographical depictions and Uttarakhands with a new chronology and Valmiki's divine inspiration and other incidents were included.

Valmiki must have designed this epic poem around 300 B.C as Pannini makes no reference to Ramayana and any other character or incidents associated with this epic. Sankalia is also of the view that ramayana would have been written approximately a 100 years before the Mahabharat as one doesn't find any reference to Krishna.[1]

Exaggerated Projections of Towns in ramayan

The descriptions of Ayodhya, Kishkindha and Lanka are based on exaggeration and with time, more and more inflated accounts of these towns were incorporated. The description of the palace in Ayodhya, where for instance Kaushalya was residing, could not have been made of brick, stone or marble. Houses were made only of clay, hence when Kaushalya became unconscious on hearing the sad news of Rama's expulsion to the forest, a reference is made of clay flowing from the ground.

In all likelihood, the reference to Gopur could be applicable to temples in South India of a much later period.

Such references place ramayan as late as 8th or 10th century A.D.. In any case, this would not be very surprising as the oldest edition of Ramayan we have is in old Nepali language printed in 1028 A.D.. Hence it is evident that till the 11th century A.D. and also subsequently, there is a continuity of new editions in ramayan and Mahabharat.

Lanka

With regard to the location of Lanka, several scholars have explored the various possibilities of its locations and have inferred that :

1. Lanka was located in Madhya Pradesh.
2. Parmeshwar Iyer, after examining all existing references in ramayan, concluded that Lanka was situated near Jabalpur.

Supashraya, son of Supati, who first spotted Ravan eloping with Sita, describes him as a dark man with shining skin, with a bright lady who very politely requested him to make way from the narrow passage of the rocky track that he was occupying, and he could not disrespect such humble request. As other knowledgable persons subsequently informed him that this black man was a king of demons, Sanakalia suggests that this incident brings out three crucial elements of ramayan:

1. Ravan was non-Aryan and had a dark complexion.

2. Sita was very fair as was typical of an Aryan lady.
3. Ravan while eloping with Sita was passing only through a forest track.
4. The road he travelled was so narrow that only a single person could pass through it.
5. Ravan must be of ordinary appearance and must not be looking extraordinarily powerful, otherwise he would not have spoken to Suparsha with such modesty.
6. Ravan's Lanka must be close-by whiche he could reach by foot from Dandakaranya and Panchvati from where the abduction took place.
7. One has to cross the sea to reach Lanka and this sea must have been located near a mountain. This could also be inferred from the report that Hanuman had climbed the Mahendra mountain to cross the sea. This seems to be the original version as Hanuman vividly gives this description to Sita when he meets her in Lanka.

This is further corroborated by Hanuman in Sunderkand where he narrates that all his monkey colleagues had lost their way in the Vindhya mountain and as there was no time to return safely, they were almost on the verge of starvation and death. In the meanwhile, they came across Sampati who informed them about Ravan eloping with Sita from that track. Hence they came down from the Vindhya mountain and after swimming for about 100 yards (Yojans) entered Lanka at night.

This incident also proves independently that Lanka was located only near the Vindhya mountain and the ocean which Hanuman crossed was not so vast that one can't easily cross. Hence the early edition of Ramayan notes that Hanuman swam across the ocean while both coming and returning from Lanka.

According to Iyer, ordinarily one Yojan could cover around four and half miles. Apart from this, there were small rocks in this ocean where a swimmer could take rest while crossing. Hence for a person like Hanuman, it should not have been difficult to cross such an ocean. In such an ocean, monkeys prepared a bridge using stones and trees and could cross around 100 Yojans within five days.

Parameshwar Iyer, with the expertise of a geographer and geologist, has prepared a map indicating the smallest geographical details which provide an accurate account of the description given in the Yudhakanda of ramayan. Even the other descriptions of the mountains and the Trikut hills which are supposed to be located near Ravan's Lanka is ideally applicable to the Indrani hills near Jabalpur.

The eastern region of Madhya Pradesh close to the upper part of Chhota Nagpur adivasi area, which is surrounded by sal forests must be the location of Bali and Sugriva and also the site of the Ram-Ravan war as there are frequent references to monkeys throwing sal trees against the enemies and demons who also indulge in similar techniques. The word "Lanka" seems to have originated from Munda dialect and implies 'long distance' or 'island'.

Hanuman was tied in Lanka with chir, valkal and kshoma threads and these plants are grown around Chota Nagpur and Bengal.

Hence Prof. Sankalia, on the basis of such evidence, concludes that Lanka of Ramayan must have been located near Jabalpur in Madhya Pradesh.

In Balkand, Ram is being projected as an incarnation of Vishnu which is an indication of its subsequent addition. Ram's image, mannerisms and behaviour as projected in Ayodhya and other kands almost confirm that by the time of the prevelance of the present Ramayan, Ram was assumed to be of divine incarnation and the seeds of such a belief system were already sown.

Although Ram was a mortal, this assumption or belief about his divinity must have been prevalent right from the very early period. It may also be possible that when Ram and Laxman, with their simple bow and arrow and sword could defeat demons (adivasis), this element of divinity might have been attributed to him. Whatever was not openly pronounced or was implicit in other recitations (kands) found concrete and vivid expression in Balkand.

Ravan

The manner in which Ravan is projected with his multiple heads and hands also provides a key to the period during which Ramayana could have come into existence.

The first appearance of Ravan comes in Aryanakand. After witnessing the destruction of Khar, Dushana and around 14,000 demons, Shurpnakha goes back to Lanka. This description doesn't provide any clue about the location of Lanka. Ravan, for the first time here is projected with ten heads and twenty hands seated on a throne of the great height of a viman (airplane). There is no doubt that this description is full of exaggeration but it raises the basic question of understanding how or historically when such mode of analogy of man with multiple heads and hands must have originated. According to Sankalia, such descriptions of individuals of such great prowess and amazing super human qualities must have originated, in all likelihood, before 4th or 5th century B.C..

It is also equally important to keep in mind that in ramayan, we come across a description of Ravan as an ordinary being, having a single head and two hands and two legs. Eminent scholars like Ramdasa drew our attention to this about 70-80 years ago when while carefully probing through the narrations of Kishkindha and Suderkand, he also brought out that Kumbhkarna, Shurpnakha and others were actually tribals and they were found in the forests of Amarkanta and Chhota Nagpur. In Aranyakand Ravan while addressing Sita comments, 'I will carry you with my two hands.

Similarly, in Ashok Vatika, he tells her that Ravan's head would not bow before any woman. Hanuman, in Sunderkand, when he enters Ravan's palace describes Ravan sitting on his throne as a person with single head and two hands. Even after his death in the battlefield, there is description of a woman crying only with a single head of Ravan.

Ramdasa and Dr. Hiralal have also pointed out that Ravan had only two hands and all his kins came from the Gond tribe and were residing in the vast forests of Amarkantaka. Even now, Ravan commands respect and awe as one of their kings and by Lanka, the implication is that he was residing in a lonely tall house. There are folk songs with such a description.

Hence, it can be safely assumed that the original Lanka must have been located somewhere in this vicinity. Prof. Sankalia also substantiates his contention by sighting recent evidence in the form of an old map which mentions old Lanka's location in the Amarkantaka area and this view has prevailed from the early period.

Dress and Ornaments

Whatever evidence we have based on the archaeological findings of this period and even in the early literature on ramayan, women and men were shown wearing only two dresses, one short dhoti or mini saree and other upper garments like shawl which covered chest and shoulder.

Dresses were made not from silk but linen. Even the upper garments worn by Sita during their exile could not cover her breasts.

Daily Diet

Five items are usually mentioned as part of their daily menu: Rice, til, gram, kulath, and meat.

Rice and different preparations of rice were the staple diet of this period. In Valmiki's Ramayan, there are several references of meat preparation, even beef. Along with meat, even fermented drinks were commonly used. According to Prof. Sankalia, in all probability, liquor prepared from the mahua flower was also common. Even now we come across mahua trees in tribal areas.

Concluding Observations

On the basis of the exhaustive archaeological appraisal of the period of ramayan and available material evidence, Prof Sankalia draws following conclusions:

1. Ramayan undoubtedly is an epic poem as it doesn't provide historical, geographical and other vivid accounts as one finds in the Mahabharat.
2. Despite these basic limitations, it is possible to do an archaeological study of ramayan.
3. The study reveals that on the basis of the evaluation of the entire narration of ramayan, this epic could be divided into minimum 3 and maximum 5-6 periods.
4. It is possible to fix the period of each historical phase chronologically with the help of archaeological findings.
5. The Adi Ramayan or the original Ramayan which is designated as Ur Ramayan in English or German must have occurred in the region known as Koshal and Mithila in eastern India.

Historically, its antiquity could not be older than 1000-1500 B.C..

6. The earliest evidence of towns that we have come from Sonapur, Chiranda and others of early historical period. Houses of this time invariably were made of clay as there is no evidence of big houses during this period.
7. If the excavation is carried out properly in Ayodhya, one can know the political set up that prevailed during this period. But we have enough reason to believe that the rulers of this period came from the Ikshwaku dynasty and one could also suggest that around the original Koshal and Mithila, especially in the eastern and western regions, the population consisted of adivasis. Sita's abduction must have been carried out by Gond and Munda tribals. Ravan is still looked upon with the great reverence by these tribals.
8. The connotation of the term "Lanka" in Munda implies "very far" or "island". After departure from Chitrakoot, Ram had resided in this region and the original Lanka was situated somewhere near Amarkantaka or Jabalpur. In ramayana, one comes across enough indicationsof this from the conversations of monkeys and demons. Another evidence is the existence of sal trees in this area whose threads were used to tie Hanuman.

Ram and Laxman had far more effective weapons of bows and arrows compared to what were possessed by the adivasis in this area who used small and big rocks, trees and if they possessed bow and arrows, they were of an inferior variety.

This epic was first recited in a form of poem. Ram must have been depicted in this epic poem as a great warrior. There must be some references of Lanka in this poem. In any case, it appears that the poet has given an exaggerated version of the original story with extensive use of his fertile imagination. In this epic narration of Valmiki, a major focus was on Ram's single-minded devotion to Sita, Sita's incomparable love to Ram, and Laxman and Hanuman's supreme devotion to Ram, which made this epic poem extremely popular.

It is not possible to keep track of writings in Sanskrit on ramayan, or topics related to it. But there is no reference to ramayan or any direct or indirect reference to its main characters in the entire Vedic literature, the Vedic Sanhitas, Aranyakas or the Upanishads.

In several important Purans such as Vayu, Vishnu, Padma, Kurama, Shiva, Skanda, Bhagvat, Mahabhagvat and especially in Padmapuran, there is an exhaustive narration of ramayana. In these Purans one also finds an extreme form of presentation ranging from very aesthetic eulogization to extreme representation of its various perverse characters.

Sixteen out of the eighteen puranas (written between the 6th and 12th century A.D.) narrate the story of Ramayana - the most extensively written in Padmapurana with several editions and interpolations in Valmiki's Ramayana. Since Valmiki's volume was undergoing continuous revisions, some of these editions got incorporated in the original texts and have now become ingrained in the Hindu psyche. The ten heads and twenty arms of Ravan are first mentioned in the Vayupuran and it is the Skandapuran that makes Hanuman the son of Shiva as his incarnation and it is here that the lifelong celibacy of Hanuman is mentioned for the first time. Valmiki never mentions Hanuman as a brahmachari and in fact his house is described as teeming with beautiful women. Bharat gifts him with 32 women and he accepts the gift. Shivpurana makes Ram a devotee of Shiva and mentions the temple of Rameshwar built by him. There is no such thing in Valmiki's version. The Mahabhagwata Purana makes Sita a daughter of Mandodari. There are endless such editions and distortions in the purans; but then the purans were never highly rated by vedic pandits among the Hindus.

Hindus have a tradition of deifying human heroes and thereby creating more and more gods out of nothing. The process has been going on from the days of Ram to this very day when Saibaba and Santoshi Mata are being included in the ever expanding list of Hindus. Buddha and Mahavir have suffered the same fate. Even in the Ramanya, Ram is a rare specimen of human hero who chooses to suffer for following moral values and traditional virtues.

The story of Ram and the characters and incidents of ramayan proved to be a rich and ever attractive source for the creative writers of Sanskrit literature. So many dramas, poems and novels dealing with the theme of Ram have been produced by these masters that an exhaustive list of all of them would cover a volume.

Over and above the extensive literary products, the devotion to Ram has produced a flood of stotras, bhajans, padas and stutis that can hardly be compared or even listed.

The tremendous popularity of Ramayan encouraged the Jains to produce their own version emphasizing the volumes and concepts equivalent to their own creed. Most of the Jain Ramayan described the escapades of Laxman and Hanuman and portray them as womanizers. Vasudev Vahindi makes Sita the first child born to Ravan and Mandodari the one who was abandoned because she was declared to be inauspicious. She was put in a box and floated in a river where she was found by Janak.

But it was left to the Buddhist versions of Ramayan to take ramayan to the countries in East Asia. In most of the Buddhist Ramayans, Sita is the daughter of Dashrath and Ram has married his own sister.

The Chinese Ramayans are mostly translations of the Pali Ramayan but Japanese Ramayans are borrowed from the Chinese stories and hence are one more step away from the original story. In the Thai Ramayan, Hanuman is a very sexy philanderer and Ram ruled Thailand for 40 years. The Laos Ramayan is again a different version.

All such shocking versions of ramayan would stun the orthodox but they signify the spread of Indian culture in what is known as Greater India. To the scholars of ancient history, ramayan is still the living tradition in all these regions. Ramayan, of course, has been produced in all vernacular languages of India during the medieval period. These were not direct translations of Valmiki's epic but translations with considerable additions and distortions. The oldest such Ramayan is Kampan's Eramavatar in Tamil. For Kampan, Ram is the supreme deity and the creator, controller of the universe. Pampa Ramayan in Kannada is the oldest Ramayan in that language.

Ramayan tells the story of North Indian royalty but is far more popular in South India and vernacular Ramayans were first written in South Indian languages. The first vernacular Ramayan in India is Krittibas Ramayan in Bengali with several new incidents and episodes as compared to the Valmiki epic.

Hindi Ramayans came much later and the earliest of them was by Vishnudas of Gwalior, but the most popular is undoubtedly the Ramcharitmanas of Tulsidas which has now been the standard and most authentic text for the orthodox Hindu audience. Tulsidas is a great poetic genius and there are many other literary productions by him. Ramcharitmanas took many years in the making and Tulsidas has metamorphosed not only the content but even the format of Ramayan. The first two parts of Ramayan- Balkand and Ayodhyakand take up nearly two-third of his volume and he has deleted Uttarkand. Tulsi begins with the discussion between Shiva and Parvati but the threads are picked up by Kakbhushandi and once again the narration is picked up by Shiva. This may be due to the long span of time during the manas was being composed.[2]

There is a sharp contrast between Tulsidas' Ramcharitmanas and Valmiki's Ramayan. Valmiki's Ram is a person of rare virtues, a great person but still a human being with some inherent follies. There is no deification of Ram. But like purans, Tulsi's Ramcharitmanas also has totally transformed Ram and projected him as a supreme being, incarnation of Vishnu. In India, during the 5th and 6th century A.D. when feudalism was well established under the Gupta rule, one also finds the bhakti tradition flowering and the Nayanar and Alwar movements launched in South India. These saints made a profound impact in India, particularly in South India. Ram and Sita were popularized as the supreme beings and worshipped as such in the Bhakti movement. We find the extension of the same tradition in Northern India in Tulsi Ramcharitmanas and in other versions of ramayan.

Even Valmiki's Ramayan which is supposed to be the original version has also undergone drastic modifications over a long period. Valmiki portrays Ram as a person of extraordinary virtues, competence and compassion. His greatness is shown in terms of his commitment to his father's words, devotion to his mother, brotherly affection, single minded love and attachment for Sita, his great ability to sacrifice his right over his empire and acceptance of vanvas (exile in forest) for 14 years, his love and devotion for his people and also sympathy for Kaikeyi. But with all his greatness, Ram is also shown as a person suffering from or exhibiting other human weaknesses. Valmiki shows distrust of Ram for his father and brother, Kaikei's ability to manipulate Dashrath, also apprehension that Bharat with his newly acquired power as a king may harass Kaushalya and Sumitra and anxiety for Kaikeyi being wicked might poison his mother.

Even Sita displays suspicion towards Laxman when he initially shows hesitation in coming to the rescue of Ram. Even after her abduction by Ravan, Sita's first apprehension is that how it would be much easier for Kaikeyi now to succeed in her design to eliminate Ram.

Even with regard to the famous story of Ahilya and her past relationship with Indra, Valmiki has no pretention about Ahilya's ignorance or Indra fooling her. He holds that Ahilya also willingly surrendered and was fully satisfied with the act.

Valmiki's Ramayan in terms of poetic excellence and artistic narration has been far superior to most of the other Ramayans and especially Tulsi Ramcharitmanas.

Tulsi Ramcharitmanas projects Ram as a supreme being, divine incarnation, and in kaliyuga one can resolve all problems only by reciting his name and worshipping him. All sorrows, calamities, misfortunes would be eliminated and one could go straight to heaven. Similarly, Hanuman is also projected as an equally great supreme being and single minded devotion to Hanuman could put an end to one's worries.

In Tulsi Ramcharitmanas, one could also notice his if not contempt, but certainly very low opinion about women, their intelligence and their abilities and understanding. This is evident in his chaupais in Balkand, where Parvati while admitting her folly to suspect the greatness of Rama urges to Shiva suggesting that as a woman, as per the vedic principles, she has no right and she is a dasi in terms of man, karma and vaani but Shiv by grace should forgive her and be kind enough to recite Ram Katha to her. Similarly, Tulsi also exhibits his bias for Brahmin supremacy in Balkand chaupais where he suggests that because of tapa, Brahmins are always powerful and its not possible for anyone to withstand their anger. If you can please Brahmins then you can even please Brahma, Vishnu and Mahesh. The curse of Brahmins cannot be escaped.

Morari Bapu - A Profile

Birth and Family Background: Morari Bapu was born on 25th September, 1946 in Talgajarda (a small village near the port of Mahuva in the state of Gujrat, India) to Prabhudas Bapu Hariyani and Savitri Ben Hariyani. Morari Bapu has six brothers and two sisters. From the very beginning as noted, young Morari Bapu showed signs of extraordinary brilliance and spent most of his childhood under the guidance of his grandmother, often spending hours listening to folk tales of traditional India.

At the age of 5, Bapu began learning Ramayan (Ramcharitmanas) from his grandfather and guru Tribhuvandas Dada. A principled and learned scholar of the Ramcharitmanas, Tribhuvandas Dada would teach five chaupais (couplets) to Bapu each day, who then had to memorize them with their meaning throughout the day. The study of the Ramcharitmanas would take place on the site today known as Chitrakoot Dham in Talgajarda and has become a place of pilgrimage for thousands of people. Both Bapu's grandparents were the guiding force behind his upbringing and the most influential persons in his life in his early years. The nearest school was about 2 km from Talgajarda and Bapu would memorize chaupais from the Ramcharitmanas as he walked to school, often singing to the trees and plants on his path. On his return home, Bapu had to recite to Dadaji what he had memorized.

At school, his teacher Ram Shankar Bhatt remembers Bapu as a young boy who was "an introvert, quiet and independent student". The high school headmaster Narottam Kaka Mehta recalls Bapu as being an intellectual student with an unusually high regard for cultural and religious values and as a good student of the institution. Such was the relationship between the teachers and their pupils that in the monsoon months, when the river Maalan between Talgajarda and Mahuva became waterlogged and unpassable, Bapu and his school friends were encouraged not to venture home. The teachers would, instead, accommodate the young boys safely in their homes. Bapu often cites the journey to and fro from school which he says played an instrumental role in allowing him to sing and understand the depths of the Ramcharitmanas. Even today, when Bapu is at home, he walks the path between Mahuva and Talgajarda (now a proper road), where the village folk join him and talk to him about the issues concerning the village.

Born in the Vaishnav Sadhu Nimbark parampara (lineage), Bapu was also encouraged via letters from his paternal great grandfather, Mahamandleshwar Vishnu Giriji Maharaj of Kailas Ashram, Hrishikesh on the banks of the Ganges, to be proficient in the Bhagwad Geeta and the Vedas. At the age of 12, Bapu began to recite the Ramcharitmanas by heart. Bapu recalls the birthplace of his first recitals where he made a small platform out of mud and placed a portrait of Lord Ram and began to recite to a few herdsmen who had come to quench their thirst in the evening. The shrine today is commemorated in Talgajarda in a temple of Hanuman and named Ram Vaadi (meaning Lord Ram's orchid).

As years went by, Bapu began to attract the attention of the elder villagers who would test his knowledge of the Ramcharitmanas and on every occasion the young boy would leave the elders stunned. On completing secondary school, he started a teacher training course at Shahapur College in Junagad. Bapu today talks about his years in Junagad where he would sit with his mala (rosary) for hours on end and his room mate being concerned would complete the work on his behalf. Hence, Bapu jokes that he managed a hatrick by failing his exams three times. It was during this time that he spent his free time attending discourses by well known speakers and reading scriptures or singing chaupais of the Ramcharitmanas with music.

On completing his teacher training course he returned to Mahuva where he became a teacher at the J. Parekh High School teaching various subjects including English. During his 10 years as a teacher, Bapu often took time off to listen to prominent speakers and met some of India's most revered spiritual leaders, among them Vinoba Bhave, Dongreji Maharaj, Punit Maharaj and J. Krishnamurti. At the same time, Bapu's interest in Indian literature and poetry grew and he regularly attended sessions on various literary subjects by high ranking orators. Bapu often quotes some of the finest works by poets such as the nationally recognized Indian poet Zaverchand Meghani whose poem on Mahatma Gandhi inspired him tremendously. Increasingly, Bapu's quest for Ram Katha began to take precedence and he would sit in the Ram Vaadi in Talgajarda singing the Ramcharitmanas and interpreting its meaning to the villagers. Bapu's extraordinary command and oratory style quickly gathered crowds and the first ever Ramcharitmanas Maas Parayan (a month long discourse on the Ramcharitmanas) was organized at the Ram temple in Talgajarda in the Chaitra Month of 1960. People from nearby towns and villages flocked to this small temple to listen to Bapu whose popularity quickly spread and subsequently led to a number of month long discourses.

The first Navan Parayan (9 day discourse) was held in Gaandilaa in Gujrat in the presence of Ranfardasji Maharaj (revered saint from Gujrat) in May 1966. Morari Bapu's name and command of the Ramcharitmanas and his heart rending narrations brought people from all over India in thousands to listen to his Ram katha, often overwhelming listeners and organizers alike. This was the beginning of a reawakening of large numbers, in particular, of young men and women listening to Ram Katha. The era of listening to Ram katha in large numbers had begun in India and he lovingly became known as "Bapu" (father). The first ever recital by Bapu outside India was held in Nairobi, Kenya in 1976, when he was nearly 30. It is suggested that this was the beginning of Bapu's untiring quest to bring about a new upliftment among all living beings not only in India but throughout the world. A deep sense of pride in one's own religion reawakened people's belief. From 1960 to date, Bapu has recited Ram katha throughout India including places of pilgrimages like Badrinath and Gangotri. In 1984, preceding a recital in Bhavnagar, Gujrat, Bapu resided within the compounds of Bhavnagar jail to impart a spiritual message to prisoners and authorities alike. Soon Bapu started enlightening people in various parts of the world including the U.K. and the U.S.A..

He moves among people continuously, his spiritual practices are devoid of harshness. This way of living a life called Dharma has been a stable source of information to people from all walks of life, both in India and abroad. As he proclaims, his major objective is to bring different branches and sects of religion together. He stands for uniting not just one nation but the whole of the human race, while, at the same time preserving their individual fragrances. He addresses humanity for love and respect for each other because that is the only way to save the world from disaster and complete ruin.

Bapu is also eager to organize his Ram katha in Pakistan, one each in Islamabad, Lahore and Karachi. He is negotiating with the Pakistani government. This is consistent with his objective of promoting Indo-Pak peace. Two years ago he organized an Indo-Pak mushaira at the temple town in Pakistan which drew some Urdu poets from Pakistan.

Immediately after the 2002 Gujrat riots, he organized a peace meeting in Juhapura, Ahmedabad, at a time when other religious heads in Gujrat were completely silent. Pakistani singers like Ghulam Ali and Rahat Fateh Ali Khan have made it to his "gurukul" in Talgajarda village for live performances at the cultural festival that he organizes on Hanuman Jayanti every year.[3]

On the basis of the information given on the website of Morari Bapu, we have provided a brief glimpse of his profile right from his childhood to his education, career, katha recital and his varied interests, especially in literature and music. Even his grandfather Tribhuvandas Bapu was also fond of music and was quite conversant with classical ragas and musical instruments. Morari Bapu is not only a gifted singer but can also play tabla, compose ragas and would be at home right from folk to light to classical music. In his discourse, one can find a combination of all these. It's not surprising that wherever he goes for his katha recital, he is accompanied by a band of competent musicians well versed in different Indian musical traditions. As per the Indian tradition, even Hanuman is regarded as one of the pillars of Indian music. Morari Bapu articulated his love and appreciation for music in 1978 by initiating musical concerts in his village Talgarjarda at Chitrkootdham. Out of love and respect for Bapu, even the stalwarts of Indian music like Pandit Ravi Shankar, Ustad Bismillah Khan, V.G. Jog, Kisan Maharaj, Birju Maharaj, Pandit Jasraj, Bhimsen Joshi and Vilayat Khan have graced these musical festivals organized annually.

Apart from this musical festival, in 1997, Morari Bapu, on the occasion of Hanuman birth centenary, organized another interesting literary gathering in which prominent Gujrati singers such as Ramesh Parekh, Anil Joshi, Rajendra Shukla, Ramanuja and others participated. Since 1988, Morari Bapu also initiated a literary convention called Asmita Parva. Since then, Asmita Parva has become a regular feature and all prominent Gujrati writers, poets, novelists, literary critics, journalists, professors and scholars have participated in it. Morari Bapu has also instituted an award for Gujrati literary figures every year. Asmita Parva is organized for 3 days with workshops on important literary themes and dimensions ranging from dalit to new or recent trends in Gujrati literature. In the 11th Asmita Parva, the scale of celebration could be gauged from the fact that over 550 writers, poets, novelists, literary critics, painters, photographers, educationists, directors, editors, journalists and representatives of different media were present for the convention. Since 2008 it is being telecast live.

Morari Bapu is also fond of organizing mushairas which has attracted Gujrati, Hindi as well as Urdu poets.[4]

Morari Bapu himself has limited educational attainment but he is at home with the most brilliant writers, scholars, experts, artists, musicians, and corporate as well as political personalities. Bapu is also known for his simplicity, is easily accessible and hardly shows any pretention about his lifestyle, public image and achievements. He would not mind going to anyone's house in case somebody is sick or needs help. Even in his discourse in U.S.A, U.K. and African countries, he is very much at home with NRIs. He doesn't mind dialoguing with rationalists who have proclaimed that Morari Bapu is not superstitious and open to reason. He is known to have helped even enemies.

Bapu is also known for his extensive charitable activities right from donations to hospitals and natural calamities to rural upliftment, temple and toilet construction. Apart from this he has established his own gaushala. He also keeps very warm family ties, very much attached to his own children and also his brothers, at least two of them are working with him.

During his educational career, his teachers were also very impressed by his talent for performing in plays, which is still remembered by them. Bapu has also kept good relations with his teachers till date.

During the earlier phase of his katha recital, Morari Bapu used to dwell at greater length on the actual content of the Ramcharitmanas. He would portray the events, but since last two decades his focus has shifted from the narrative part of the acute content to the moral and philosophical aspects and current events.

We shall briefly refer to Morari Bapu's views about gurudom, literature, truth, Indian religious philosophy, devotion, miracle, his inner world and name recital (naam smaran).

As far as the role of the guru in his life is concerned, unlike the majority of saints who always praise their legacy in terms of their gurus and guru's guru, linking it with some prominent sect or tradition, Morari Bapu has no such pretention. In his life, his grandfather is the only guru and his present accomplishments are credited entirely to his grandfather. Apart from his grandfather, he has no other guru and he doesn't feel the need for any other proper guru from any other distinct legacy. He also cannot be compared with medieval saints who lived a very simple life. In contrast to them, he has lives in comfort with all modern amenities at his disposal.

With reference to literature, he suggests that any writing or artistic creation which has the three elements of Satyam, Shivam and Sundaram is literature. He doesn't read much. When a question is asked about his definition of sanatan dharma, his answer is that Ramcharitmanas itself is a very big religious platform. Non-violence and mercy both are religion, as is helping others and not condemning others. He suggests that truth, love and compassion are the three basic pillars of religion. Truth makes man fearless, love enables man to surrender, and compassion makes man non-violent.

With regard to the Vedas, his comment is that any perception or idea of Veda should be based on its closeness to people's life. In order to spread the Vedic teaching, it must be made acceptable and understandable, i.e., it should be something that people can consume as well as appreciate. With regard to devotion and favor, he suggests that favour is there with us all the time, but as we don't know how to have a proper devotion, we are not aware of it. He also suggests that he doesn't believe in "miracles" but would prefer self-realization. He holds that the whole world is a miracle. With regard to his inner world, he says that his grandfather repeatedly reminded him that he should not become susceptible to pride or egoism.

With regard to name recital (naam smaran), he says that he does not believe in a specific name. For him any name recited with love is a naam smaran.

With regard to his discourse in western countries, he thinks that by increasingly adopting the western culture, we have accumulated a lot of dirt in our society. The dirt of their gutters has been directed to our society.

There is so much demand for Morari Bapu's katha recital that one has to book much in advance, for at least two or three years. There is no guarantee that Bapu would accept the invitation, he has his own criteria for acceptance. In this context, people closer to him must also be instrumental in getting approval from Bapu. Bapu, as stated earlier, doesn't charge any fees for himself or for his institution for katha recital. But organizing Bapu's katha recital is a very expensive affair. We are just giving one illustration of his recital organized in Nairobi in September 2004. Bapu, in this discourse, invited various categories of people. There were several prominent Gujrati writers, political analysts and journalists, along with his band of musicians. He also invited his school teachers as well as various artists. Thus, it was a big caravan. The organizer is supposed to bear the expenses for this entire caravan, their accommodation, and other comforts for them. Obviously, they were supposed to stay in a very comfortable accommodation, with all their needs catered to. Apart from this, there were guests from other countries like U.K., U.S.A. etc. who were specially invited for this occasion. It is also customary to provide food for all those who come to attend this event. The number could easily cross thousands, often it crosses even lakhs. For nine days, the organizer must make arrangement to feed them. For such a huge audience, one also needs a huge pandal, T.V. cameras, electricity etc. Hence, the expenses could be in lakhs, may be upto a crore. It is a big festival, where in the morning, Bapu gives a live discourse for three hours, and in the evening, there are a variety of cultural programmes with participation of prominent writers, art critics, musicians etc inclusive of folk, light and classical music. Bapu's katha recital is also an entertainment programme in itself, because apart from narration of the Tulsi Ramcharitmanas, Bapu cracks jokes after every 5-10 minutes. This is accompanied by bhajans, songs, poems, often inviting well known singers to join in this recital. Bapu also freely makes use of film songs which he thinks convey the appropriate religious feelings.

While recognizing these distinct attributes of Morari Bapu, one finds a vast difference between him and the medieval saints of India like Kabir, Nanak, Dadu, and in Maharashtra, Varkari saints like Gyaneshwar, Eknath and Tukaram. Most of them came from the lower rungs of the society and also practiced ordinary low but honest occupations for their livelihood while conducting their devotional activities. They were different from the traditional upper caste or Brahmin pundits because they never preached in Sanskrit, they never quoted from classical religious scriptures like the Vedas or Upanishads. They rendered their discourse in local languages like Gujrati, Hindi or Marathi. Through their religious discourse, they enriched local languages. Their bhajan recital was a very simple affair where ordinary people from lower castes and ordinary women formed the major chunk.

They never ask for any fees nor were they accompanied by any professional musical band, nor did they organize food for the gathering. In fact, most of them avoided eating at anybody's house as they did not want to be a burden on them. They made religious worship a simple affair where women and all lay people could join without any pretention of acquaintance with classical religious scriptures. In order to make bhakti or devotion popular among masses, they made it very simple in terms of language and musical compostion. Hence, even illiterate women could also participate and enjoy. They challenged the monopoly of Brahmins over religion in priesthood and made religion widely popular among the masses. Many of them faced opposition from the Brahmins. Attempts were made to arrest them, to persecute, even at times to kill them. These medieval saints were not bothered about getting favours from the king. Some of them even refused to render their service to the palace. Some of them had to pay the price for such a refusal.

As a matter of fact, Kabir and several other North Indian as well as Varkari saints in Maharashtra were influenced by Siddha and Natha traditions that emerged during the middle ages of the Gupta period. Many of these Siddha and Natha exponents came from lower castes and evolved their own style of worship and also practiced their own style of mantras and tantras which were strikingly different from the Brahmin and Sanskritic traditions. Many of them were also instrumental in enriching scientific development in India. They contributed to the growth of chemistry, medicine and psychology. They could do it because Brahmin priests or upper caste people cut themselves totally from manual work while Natha and Siddha saints were deeply involved in practices like agriculture or other manual occupations. Discovery is possible only when you practice. Thus they also contributed towards the enrichment of Ayurveda.

As Prof. Romila Thapar aptly brings out, the cult of renunciation has been a part of Indian cultural and social development right from the earlier period. We have a tradition of Charwak and multiple religious sects strikingly different from the Vedic and Upanishadic tradition during the 4th and 5th century B.C.. Buddhism and Jainism emerged during this period and their debates have enriched our understanding of society, culture and human life. Their contribution in enriching Indian culture cannot be minimized.[5]

Nath and Siddha traditions, in a sense were a continuity of this legacy and the medieval saints of India were also influenced by this current which challenged the supremacy of Brahminism.

Surdas and Tulsidas in North India in a sense were two well known saints upholding Brahminic traditions. In Tulsidas's writings, there is ample evidence justifying Brahmin supremacy and their privileged position and running down of women and lower castes. In any case they also gained extensive popularity and support among the masses. Their style of rendering Ramayan and other scriptures in a simple, lucid, lyrical style has become widely popular since long and they have thus become a part of the folk culture and religious traditions of Northern India.

Morari Bapu, as most of the Indian godmen today, draws his legacy from Tulsidas and other such saints or the purans, justifying and rationalizing this upper class, feudal tradition, thereby following the interest of the establishment. Unfortunately, this is the dominant trend among the religious preachers in India today. Our next chapters will examine the various socio-economic, religious and cultural factors instrumental in popularizing such saints with specific reference to Morari Bapu.

Morari Bapu- Preaching and Practice

Morari Bapu, during his discourse on Tulsi Ramayan, focuses on moral and ethical values and according to him, Tulsi also advocates the prime requisite for basic human values as promotion of Sumati versus Kumati, i.e., good versus evil in society. In Ramcharitmanas too, Ram upholds these virtues of Sumati, that is, benevolent aspirations versus kumati, that is, moral degradation and selfish pursuits. Ram lived for others. He was an ideal son, a devoted husband and a true friend. Even while dealing with his foes, he always upheld moral values. In this context, Morari Bapu also stresses on samwad (dialogue). In one of his katha recitals in U.S.A., Bapu spoke of the urgent need for samvad to promote world peace by peaceful harmonius resolutions of conflicts among nations. Bapu draws a contrast between Ram's war against Ravan on moral grounds and the present war among nations for various types of greeds for land, metal, markets, wealth etc. Ram's messenger, Angad, even before the war, approached Ravan in order to prevent the war by persuading Ravan to return Sita. But the war was fought for moral grounds according to Bapu. Hence, Bapu suggests that one can still learn a lot from Ramcharitmanas and the ideals projected from the same could help in bringing peace and harmony to the nations. Hence, for the present world too, Ramcharitmanas has a lot to offer.

The inspiration which Morari Bapu draws from Ramcharitmanas is based on upholding moral principles like truth, love and compassion and non-violence. In this context, Bapu is not only a great admirer of Mahatma Gandhi but also subscribes to Gandhi's philosophy of non-violence, rural reconstruction through promotion of cottage industries, organic farming and the use of biomass energy. Bapu often refers to Gandhi's biography of experiments in truth.

Unfortunately, while proclaiming allegiance to Gandhian ideals, almost all these leaders are involved in brutal exploitation and oppression of the weaker nations and toiling strata in their own country. Obama, drawing his legacy from Martin Luther and ultimately Gandhi, while paying a rich tribute to Gandhi, doesn't hesitate to indulge in war crimes in Iraq and Afghanistan. Manufacturing of armament and their trade has become the major source of profit making for many of these so called developed countries, including USA. We are not primarily concerned with USA or other government policies, our focus is on Morari Bapu, and his preaching and practice.

Morari Bapu is also no exception to the practice followed by world leaders as well as our national leaders. This becomes evident in his silence on the ghastly Gujrat carnage in 2002 which resulted in massive destruction of minority property and loss of their lives in many parts of Gujrat. Muslims in Gujrat have still not been able to recover from these wounds inflicted on them. Though almost eight years have passed since the carnage, they still face boycott in villages, thousands have been rendered houseless, many have lost their occupations and many of them still live in refugee camps without shelter. Even now they face indifference and hatred from the majority community and this is still regarded as something quite normal in Gujrat. Morari Bapu and none of the other religious leaders raised a finger against these brutalities.

It is claimed that after this incident Morari Bapu joined some peace procession and organized a public meeting in Juhupura, the most thickly populated Muslim area for communal harmony. But here too while addressing them, the first sentence he said was, "Dil-e-nadan tujhe kya hua hai?" It places both the victim as well as the perpetrator of violence on the same footing, that is, both are to be blamed. It's surprising and shocking that people who upheld the Gandhian value of non violence like Bapu and many others have not even a word of condemnation for such a ghastly occurrence in Indian history. It is also shocking that nobody finds the need to even question them. It only shows the degradation of civilized society in Gujrat.[6]

In India, we are so used to the contradiction between preaching and practice by all categories of people, politicians, literary figures and academics as well as business people that saints like Morari Bapu could not be an exception.

A classic case of Morari Bapu shutting his eyes to state brutalities can be seen from his open support to the Gujrat Control of Organized Crime Act (GCOCA) [6]. This Act is far more brutal in terms of violations of human rights and is suggested for suppression of terrorist activity. But one overlooks the fact that in Gujrat as well as in other states, there was similar act called Prevention of Terrorist Act (POTA) and despite this act, terrorist attacks took place in Gujrat, Delhi and many other states. As per the report of the PUDR, both Terrorists and Disruptive Prevention Act (TADA) and POTA have only resulted in extensive arrests of citizens without any sound legal basis. For instance, between 1985 and 1995, over 77,500 citizens were detained under this act.

But only 1 percent of them could be sentenced as there was no basis for proving the others guilty. Despite this record, the advocacy of GCOCA in Gujrat only shows Bapu's bias and favorable inclination for Narendra Modi's BJP government in Gujrat.

As a matter of fact, Morari Bapu's subscription to Hindu mythology is nothing new. On the eve of the 1991 elections, Morari Bapu issued an appeal to those who love their religion and nation. He asked them to vote for those who are supporting the following issues of national importance:

1. Construction of Ramjanmabhumi temple at Ayodhya at the same place where the Babri masjid was demolished.

2. Deletion of Section 370 which separates Kashmir from the rest of the country.
3. Prohibition of cow slaughter.

He also said that martyrdom of those innocent Ram sevaks should not go waste. Such political overtones equating religion with nationalism became sharp during and before the elections.[7]

This contradiction in Morari Bapu's preaching and practice is a reflection of the hypocritic and intolerant civil society in Gujrat. It's not only the Muslims or the minorities who have become the victims of violence perpetuated by the majority. As a matter of fact, Gujrati society has become extremely intolerant of dissent, especially in the last three or four decades. Gandhi left Gujrat in 1930 and never returned. Gandhi's influence dwindled long ago. But the kind of intolerance we witness in Gujrat has become rampant since the last four decades. We can quote from our personal experience during the carnage of 2002 in Gujrat. We had formed a committee for communal harmony and against this carnage in Bombay. We had organized a meeting on 7th April 2003 in Ahmedabad. Iniative had to come from Bombay because in Gujrat and particularly in Ahmedabad, activists were scared of calling any meeting. We had called the meeting at Sabarmati Ashram at the initiative of Mridula Sarabhai and invited various groups, NGOs and activists working for peace. The meeting was very well attended. Medha Patkar, who also happened to be in Ahmedabad at that time insisted on coming for the meeting inspite of our request not to attend the meeting as the communal elements may use this opportunity to suppress the meeting. A mob of RSS-Bajrang Dal activists led by some of the notorious leaders were after Medha Patkar's blood because of her opposition to the Sardar Sraovar dam. They wanted to exploit this situation and with great difficulty Medha Patkar was taken out from the back door to prevent any calamity. Thus it's not only Muslims but anybody who opposes issues of development could be treated equally brutally. Thus intolerance is rampant in Gujrat.

As a matter of fact, brutal violence in Gujrat becomes evident in notorious anti-labor practices and violation of all labour security legislations. Surat, supposedly the most prominent industrial city of Gujrat, has acquired a bad reputation for the brutal treatment of workers. This is corroborated by a lumpenizing of employers, political leaders and criminal gangs that operate in the city indulging in violation of legislations like excise duty, income tax etc.

Gujrat is also notorious for its human rights violations. Social survey reports have brought out that in the land of Mahatma Gandhi, untouchability is still widely prevalent, especially in rural Gujrat. Similarly, the exploitation of the tribal labour coming from Dang in the sugar factories is brutal: inhuman living conditions, very low wages and insufficient protection. Similar is the plight of migrant workers working in industries in Surat and in the diamond industry.

Gujrat has been under the influence of the Mahajan culture since ages which traditionally had at least some human consideration. Relationships in commercial establishments though are based on a feudal culture of domination and subordination, also true of industrial establishments. With the recent phase of monopoly in finance capitalism, human considerations have disappeared and labour is treated like a commodity. This is practically true of the entire nation, but in Gujrat, it is far more dominant. With this dominance of commercial and financial culture, speculative aspirations acquire prominence. Gujratis' increasing interest in the stock market is clear evidence of such inclinations. Middle class people have also been influenced by this atmosphere, saturated with profit maximization. This culture based on middle class values has influenced practically all sections in Gujrat. Academic, literary figures, artists and other categories are all influenced by this dominant value structure.

As brought out so well by Kiran Desai, in Gujrat, most of the prominent writers, poets, playrights and others, coming largely from upper class backgrounds, have a limited vision, and also articulate the sentiments and problems of the small upper strata from which they have emerged. Obviously, in their literature, problems of suffering and exploitation of women, dalits and other deprived strata, tribals, toilers and minorities hardly find any expression. Hence, it's not surprising that many of them subscribe to the majoritarian Hindu ideology.[8]

This elaborate review of Gujrat's social and economic realities is imperative to understand how religious gurus like Morari Bapu and others find it convenient to build a rapport with them. One finds some kind of organic unity between these gurus and the literary and other people of Gujrati society.

The anti-Muslim sentiments, mainly among the Rajputs, Brahmins and Baniyas, have been nurtured since long by various political and cultural sources. They were especially nurtured by the Jansangh and RSS in the 1960s. It's not surprising that Gujrat has witnessed innumerable major and minor riots since the 1960s. According to official figures, there were as many as 2938 instances of communal violences between 1960-1969 in Gujrat. M.S. Golwalkar pleaded for the making of a "Hindu Rashtra", a concept on which there had already been an extensive discussion in Gujrat. The major thrust of the debate was that Muslims had destroyed Hindu culture and now enjoyed special favors in the country and that Hinduism was synonymous with Indian nationalism. The Congress was in power but it not only failed to control the riots but also shared a good deal of the communal Hindu outlook. They not only shared anti-Muslim attitudes with the Jansangh but also participated directly or indirectly in the strife, thus helping the party to expand its base in urban areas. In the 1980s too, Gujrat was once again engulfed by communal riots. The Hindu fanatics stressed the Gujrat identity with a view to bring all Hindus under one umbrella and project Muslims as outsiders.

The tensions between Hindus and Muslims were at an emotional peak in the late 1980s on the issue of Ramjanmabhumi. In 1989, the Sangh Parivar organized the Ramshila Pujan aimed at collecting and consecrating foundational bricks for the future temple in Ayodhya. Religious sentiments were fanned by recitals of bhajans, slogans, legends, myths, movies and rituals.[9]

The Sangh Parivar asserted that Ram was the life of Indian culture and Babar was an invader.

Thus, Morari Bapu, by joining this chorus around Ram, became instrumental in consolating and extending the hold of the BJP in Gujrat. His unreserved praise for the achievement of Narendra Modi's government and the development under BJP rule hardly leaves any doubt for his political sympathy for this majoritarian party.

Morari Bapu, in his discourse, is critical of superstition and irrational faith and also shares a platform with rationalist thinkers. As a matter of fact, he addresses the founder of Gujrat Rationalist Association Shri Raman Pathak as Raman Bapa. Morari Bapu, on their suggestion, removed the bow and arrow from the idol of Ram in his village temple (Talgajarda) as they signify violence. Often rationalists also feel that Morari Bapu shares their vision.

But if we examine Morari Bapu's ideas or preaching on Indian society, culture and people, and their achievement during this epic period, it becomes difficult to visualize how this guru could be ascribed any rational ideas. As a matter of fact, the tape we have of his discourse in USA on Ramcharitmanas, where his response to the doubts raised by some sceptic about Tulsi Ramcharitmanas's contention that Parvati (who was in a previous life married to Shiva and because of her folly of not recognizing the divinity of Rama, coupled with the insult and humiliation she suffered at her father's yagna and burnt herself) had the strong desire to marry Shiva in the second life. She is born as Parvati to Himalaya and thus did penance for over 25,000 years to marry Shiva. There are many such stories in Indian mythology, but no one takes them seriously. But Morari Bapu comes to rescue of Tulsidas and justifies this tale by stating that the epic period is a part of satyuga in Indian religious philosophy and during satyuga, man lived for one lakh years. Then in dvetayug, man lived for ten thousand years, in tretayug for a thousand years and in the present Kaliyug, man lives only for a hundred years. Justifying such an absurd contention is surprising and shocking, coming from a modern guru who otherwise shows contempt for superstitions.[10]

Similarly, in his interview on ZEE TV on Ram in Sri Lanka, he justifies the Pushpak Viman on the basis of the picture which the so-called Research Team in Sri Lanka just discovered from some Buddhist monastery, which shows a huge bird with flying wings and the space on the beak which could carry 3 three persons. Bapu suggests that the Pushpak in Ramayan could carry many more and Ram then travelled back on this Pushpak with several people to Ayodhya and returned this Pushpak to Kuber who is supposed to be the owner of this viman. He suggests that during this ancient period, when man has not discovered any metal and was struggling against nature for survival, Indian society had acquired such scientific knowledge to construct such a viman.[11]

In Sri lanka, this team has located several places:

1. Ashok Vatika, where Sita was kept by Ravan.
2. The stream where she bathed.
3. The location which Hanuman visited.
4. The passage which led to Ravan's palace from Ashok Vatika.

Apart from this, they also show us a plain ground which is suggested to be an air-strip where this plane could land, and also suggest a place on an unreachable mountain which is supposed to be the tomb where Ravan's body is still preserved.

As we have shown in our introductory chapter, archaeological evidence shows that during the Ramayan period when society was at a very primitive stage, travelling was difficult and the entire Ramayan episode occured in Madhya Pradesh. We have indicated the kind of simple lives people lived and that compared to Ram's weapons, the tribals who inhabited this area had weapons of an inferior level. As a matter of fact, there are innumerable Ramayans and legends even in a single state of Kerala. As Prof. Panikkar suggests, there are various texts of Ramayan found not in hundreds but in thousands. A.K Ramanujan, the renowned scholar is of the view that these are not the variant texts of Valmiki's Ramyana but largely independentt 'tellings'.[11]

Even in our age, when printing is widespread, Rama's story lives in people's minds through the chanting and singing of the story, such as the Ramleelas of North India and numerous folk dance in every part of the country. They have been formed as a result of the life experiences of the local community.

ZEE TV's telecast on Ram in Sri Lanka also raised an interesting riddle. As per the Tulsi Ramayan, Ram, through his multiple course of arrows, cuts several heads and hands of Ravan. But as per the Research Team, Ravan's tomb is located at some peak on some mountain in Sri Lanka. How does one reconcile this?

Morari Bapu's preaching and his extensive popularity have to be viewed in the context of the changing socio-economic and religious scenario in India, especially since the last four decades. The post 1980s witnessed a rapid rise in communal and religious movements and the culmination of this was the Ramjanmabhumi Yatra and the demolition of the Babri Masjid in Ayodhya in 1991.

Morari Bapu's appeal to NRIs in African and especially western countries, particularly in USA, should also be viewed in the context of the metamorphosis in the western world since the acceleration of globalization under the dominant influence of monopoly finance capital. Our concluding chapter will examine Morari Bapu's influence in the context of the new wave of religiosity experienced at a global level since the neo- liberal phase of capitalist development.

References

1. Hasmukh D. Sankalai: Archeology and Ramanaya based on his talk to Gujrat Vidyapitha Faculty, November 1972, Gujrat Vidhpitha.
2. Nagindas Sanghavi, unpublished article on Ramayana.
3. Bapu, Morari: Profile from website and his biography.
4. Chaudhari, Raghuveer; Biography of Morari Bapu (in Gujrat), Rangdwar Prkashran, Ahmedabad, 2008.
5. Thapar, Romila; An Ancient Indian Social History, PP. 63-104, Orient Longman, 1978.
6. Digant Oza and others; Letter to Morari Bapu dated 1/11/2008.
7. Shah, Ghanshyam; 10th Lok Sabha Election and BJP's victory in Gujrat, PP 109-203, Published in special issue of Islamic Perspective on 1oth Lok Sabha Elections, Editors Asgar Ali Engineer and Pradeep Nayak, Published by Ajanta Publication, Delhi 1993.
8. Desai, Kiran; Editorial in special issue of Literature in Gujrat.
   – Social Context In "Atharta" Journal brought out by Centre of Social Studies, Surat Jan- March 2010.
9. Shah, Ghanshyam; BJP's Riddle in Gujrat, Essay in "The BJP and Compulsions of Politics in India" Edited by Thomas Blom and Hansen Christophe Jefferlot, Oxford University Press 1998.
10. From DVD brought out by Shri Sitaram Seva Trust, Mahuva.
11. Tharuvana, Azeez; The Ramanaya of Wayanad from the foreword by Prof. K. N. Pannikar, Published by Vikas Adhyayan Kendra 2010.

7

Asharam Bapu

I: Modern Gurus in India; Historical Background-

Asharam Bapu - Profile

First we refer to Asharam Bapu's profile as provided in his website and publications. Sant Shri Asharam Bapu born on April 17th, 1941 and is referred to as a Hindu spiritual guru from India.

Family History

He was born in Berani village of Nawabshah District in Sindh (un-partitioned India). His father was a wealthy businessman. Asumal's family migrated from Sindh to Mani Nagar near Ahmedabad in Gujrat due to partition. He went to school in Mani Nagar but left his schooling after class tenth after his father's demise. His mother helped develop his interest in dhyan-bhajan (meditation and prayers) from his early childhood. Asharam lost his father at a very young age but grew more and more interested in pursuing meditation and spiritual matters. He finally left his family and travelled the country until he reached Vrindavan, the land of Lord Krishna. Here he was inspired to go to the ashram of the Guru Swami Shri Lila Shahji Maharaj. He had to wait for 40 days in the ashram to get a glimpse of the guru. There he stayed and served his guru with great devotion. Swami Shri Lila Shahji Maharaj made Asumal go through several hardships for another 30 days before

Asumal was blessed. Swami Shri Lila Shahji Maharaj then asked him to go back home and continue his spiritual practices at home.

While coming back home, he left the train and went to Moti Koral (a place in Gujrat). He had started spiritual practice at the bank of river Narmada and local saint Shri Lalji Maharaj was impressed by Asumal's interest to attain self realization. Lalji Maharaj made arrangements for Asumal to stay in Datt Kutir of Ram Nivas (Lalji Maharaj's ashram). When Asumal's wife and mother came to know that he was staying at Moti Koral, they went to visit him. They asked him to come back. Asumal refused to return until he completed the Anushthan. He successfully completed the Anushthan. The whole village including Lalji Maharaj came to the station to see them off to Ahmadabad. As soon as the train started moving from Miyagaun junction, Asumal jumped out and boarded a train towards Mumbai where he met guru Swami Lila Shahji Maharaj.

Self Realization

Swami was very happy to see his disciples' keen interest to attain the truth. Hence, on the second day of Ashvin month in Samvat 2021 at 2.30 pm, Asumal was transformed into Asharam Bapu by the blessings of Swami Shri Lila Shahji Maharaj. After this, Asharam Bapu went into samadhi for the next two and half days.

Swami Shri Lila Shahji Maharaj instructed Asharam to serve humanity by staying a householder. After self realization, Asharam Bapu stayed in solitude for 7 years. Asharam Bapu used to give religious discourse to all those who came to meet him. Bapu spent his solitude in various places like Disa, Nareshwar Dham, the Himalayas, Mount Abu and so on.

Life as a Householder

Asharam Bapu met Swami Shri Lila Shahji Maharaj in Haridwar in Vikram Samvat 1928, and by the commands of guru, in order to provide a good example to common householders, Bapu entered the life of a householder. It was the day of Guru Punam in Vikram Samvat 2028 when Asharam Bapu reached Ahmedabad after staying in solitude for 7 years.

Asharamji used a peaceful place in the Motera village on the banks of the Sabarmati. Later, some devotees constructed a small room for him known as "Moksha Kutir". Slowly, the number of devotees coming to Motera kept increasing and in a short time the place became a great spiritual centre. Today, Motera is the main spiritual centre for the devotees coming to Sant Shri Asharamji Ashram.

There are 350 ashrams working under the guidance of Ashram Bapu. These ashrams organize spiritual and social activities on a regular basis. Some of these activities include weekly satsang, distribution of Rishi Prasad and other spiritual publications like Divya Prerna Prakash. A live spiritual discourse is facilitated for more than 70 million sadhaks worldwide through the ashram website.

Shri Yog Vedant Seva Samiti

Over 1300 Shri Yog Vedant Seva Samitis are formed under the guidance of Bapu. These samitis carry out various social welfare programmes like tribal and backward class development, distribution of food-grains through ration cards, distribution of free buttermilk and water, de-addiction campaigns, centres for spiritual literature, video satsang centres, free food and financial support for the poor, programmes for prisoners etc.

Bal Sanskar Kendras

Bal Sanskar Kendras (BSK) are sessions and camps conducted for all round and comprehensive development of children-students. BSK is inspired by Asharam Bapu and coordinated by Bal Sanskar Kendra, Shri Akhil Bharatiya Yog Vendant Seva Samiti and Sant Shri Asharamji Ashram, Ahmadabad.

Institutional Activities

The major activities conducted by the ashram are:

1. Tribal welfare projects under the banner of the ashram and its allied institution Shri Yog Vedant Seva Samiti in Gujrat, Maharashtra, Rajasthan, Uttar Pradesh, Orissa and other tribal areas. Charitable activities such as distribution of food grains, clothes, blankets etc. and campaigns to liberate tribals from addiction and evil customs through spiritual and yogic experiments are also carried out.
2. In his satsang, through exposure to the horrible impact of addiction, Bapu makes people aware of the consequences of

addiction to liquor, nicotine, cocaine and other drugs. The ashram also publishes books and organizes exhibitions to make people aware of the dangerous implications of addiction.

3. Programs are conducted to remove evil customs among the backward sections of Indian society. Because of their ignorance there is extensive prevalence of evil customs around ghosts, superstitions, and apprehension about supernatural powers. They are exploited by false pandits. The ashram tries to expose such rackets and help people overcome such beliefs and evil practices.
4. The ashram and its sponsored committees distribute free medicines and food among the needy and the sick.
5. During epidemics of any type, caused due to floods, famine etc, such as typhoid, jaundice, cholera, ashram volunteers help the affected people physically, materially and emotionally. They also perform havans for purifying the environment.
6. The ashram has published over 175 books and booklets so far in Indian languages and also in English. The ashram also brings out a monthly magazine called 'Rishi Prasad' in three languages, namely Hindi, Gujrati and Marathi. Lakhs of people subscribe to this magazine and benefit from it in terms of physical and spiritual well being.
7. Bapu also conducts programmes for the present young generation who have lost direction by imparting knowledge of ancient Indian culture and religious traditions. Attempts are made to achieve an all-round development of young students. They are also taught yoga, and through satsangs and kirtans, their latent potential is given direction and expression.
8. Meditiation and spiritual exposure camps are organized throughout the year during different religious festivals not only in India but also abroad.
9. During summer, through various centres, ashram committees provide free buttermilk and cold water in various areas.
10. Gaushalas are organized in many parts of the country through different ashrams.
11. Lakhs of people have benefited from the ayurvedic dispensaries conducted by the ashram. Expert vaidyas take care of the sick

people in the ashrams. In the Surat ashram, devotees collect herbs from the forest and manufacture medicines at the ashram.

12. Maun mandirs (silent zones) have been regarded as very effective in the spiritual advancement of devotees. These maun mandirs enable devotees to have unique spiritual experiences. Such places with facilities of bath, food etc are provided to devotees, where they spend about a week and the door is locked from outside.
13. There are special meditation centres for devotees from other countries as well as India, where they can spend about 2 weeks or even months and can take advantage of the natural surroundings of the ashram and spend time in spiritual pursuit.
14. Shri Yog Vedant Seva Samiti organizes satsang gatherings in different parts of the country where lakhs of people come.
15. Bapu has established Nari Utthan Kendra. Women from India as well as other countries come and stay here. Bapu's wife, Lakshmidevi is in charge of this ashram. For all round physical, intellectual, mental and spiritual development of women, ashram provides training in yoga, meditation, kirtan and swadhyaya and through celebration of various cultural and religious festivals. All these activities are conducted by Bapu's daughter Bhartidevi.

    Women inmates of this ashram go to different cities and villages and spread Bapu's spiritual and religious message of Indian culture among rural women and guide them in their family life, child health, education, upbringing and nari dharma (women's spiritual obligation).
16. The Dhanvantari Arogya Kendra runs ayurvedic dispensary and also prepares ayurvedic medicine. Women vaidyas give free treatment to patients. They also plant trees. There are sadhna sadans and a swimming pool for women devotees.
17. Notebooks containing the essence of Bapu's spiritual message and Bapu's photographs are distributed among children.

Strength of Devotees

As per ashram records, , the total strength of devotees in 1995 in India as well as other countries was around 15 lakhs. Today it is impossible to enumerate the total strength, but it enumerates into crores. Various television channels regularly broadcast Bapu's discourses. As per ashram publications, thousands of religious discourses of Bapu have taken place in India and other countries. Of these, around 10,000 audio cassettes have been collected and made available to the ashram.

Asharam Bapu - Unique Saint of the Present Century

Asharam Bapu is unique in terms of his preaching and partly also practice from many other traditional as well as modern saints in India. The other saints in India either owe allegiance to a particular religious sect, or to some distinct religious or spiritual legacy. Many others have also specialized in religious discourse in terms of recital of some epic narration - we have scores of saints who have specialized and have become popular for the discourse of Ram katha. Most of these based their discourse on scripture like Tulsi Ramayan, Bhagvat Katha narration, Shiv Puran or Bhagwad Gita. In north India, with Mathura and Vrindavan, the focus is on Krishna devotion. But the theme of religious discourse is focused on Hindu religious idols such as Ram, Krishna, Ganesh etc. After independence, Swami Chinmayananda focused on teaching vedant and especially the Bhagwad Geeta. Quite a few saints like Chinmayananda follow Shankar's tradition of advait vedant. Most of these saints conduct their discourse in Hindi or their local mother tongues.

Asharam Bapu is unique from this whole galaxy of saints because in none of his discourses does he follows a fixed pattern, neither does he stick to any particular religious scriptures. He doesn't even casually mention them. If any reference is made, it is superficial and casual.

We provide here some titles of his major audio and video cassettes which would bring out the relevance of our observation. Some of the audio cassettes have interesting titles such as:

1. 'Madhur Jeevan Kaise Banayein?'
2. 'Jeevan Unnat Kaise Banayein?'
3. 'Sansar Musafirkhana Hai'
4. 'Geeta-Bhagvat Saar'

From these titles, there is hardly any reference to the actual teaching of the scriptures. There is another interesting - "Sanatan Dharma Anadi Hai" - which hardly gives any knowledge of either Indian religious traditions, their historical account or variations in terms of their continuity or discontinuity. There are also other titles like

'Moksha ka Marg' and 'Ishwar ki Ore'. These are interesting and thought provoking titles but in terms of content, Asharam Bapu has his own unique style of mixing fairy tales and common stories in his sermons, thus highlighting his own spiritual enrichment.

Similarly the video cassettes at our disposal have interesting titles. For example, we have a series of video cassettes on Mantra jaap. We may refer to them as follows:

1. Mantra se Labh
2. Mantradiksha se Jeevan Vikas
3. Mantra Jap Mahima.
4. Mantra Ka Prabhaav
5. Mantrajaap se Bhagyoday aur Swasthya Labh
6. Grihasthi mein Shanti ke Upay
7. Divya Prerna Prakash, Yuvadan Suraksha

If one goes through these video cassettes carefully, one can find that Bapu hardly refers to any religious scriptures to justify his preaching. He evokes his own unique style of preaching where he, for instance, mixes his own version of mantras with some well known mantras from the Vedas. For instance, some of the religious scriptures might have focused on the great merits of mantra recital. But when Bapu talks about mantras, his context is different and he usually starts and ends with his own experiments and experiences.

Bapu is like many other saints who seek to master the technique of hypnotizing their audience. They are so conversant with mass psychology or the audience's expectation is so high that they could play on their sentiments and easily bring them under their spell and hypnotize them. In this sense Bapu follows many other popular modern saints in India, but he is different because most of the other saints follow some tradition, established legacy or schools, and by and large try to be faithful to the preaching of religious scriptures. Bapu is unique because he doesn't follow any scriptures but makes his own. Even his formal adherence to any scripture is so incidental that one can't take any of these references seriously. In this sense, Bapu is either so clever, competent or shrewd in understanding the pulse of his audience that he consciously realized the futility of sticking to any particular religious scripture. He has his own ways of conveying the message and thus attracting the audience. In this introductory chapter we have attempted to place Bapu in terms of institutional proclamations and cursory critical observations of some of his publications and audio and video cassettes.

In subsequent chapters we shall attempt to highlight the other aspects of his preaching and practice as manifested through his ashram's activities in terms of their followers and disciples and the overall response to his and his ashram's activities in the last two decades.

Earlier we provided an account of the activities conducted by the ashram and a profile of Asharam Bapu as made available in his website and publications. As a matter of fact, we have also come across critical observations about this profile and ashram 3. 'Sansaactivities. We shall briefly refer to the observation made in the 15th July 2008 issue of the daily newspaper 'Gujrat Samachar', a very well established paper in Gujrat. As per the information provided in this paper, Asharam started his education in Ahmadabad but could not get through his matric examination. Subsequently, at a young age, he started his career as a mechanic in a cycle repair shop. It is reported that from a young age, Asharam exhibited a strong religious inclination and became a disciple of Lila Shah Baba. Lila Shah Baba's ashram is located in Adipur city of Kachh district which exists even today. As per the observation of Hemant Tolani, one of the prime devotees of Lila Shah Baba, Baba never accepted Asharam bapu as his disciple because Lila Shah Baba was not happy with his behaviour and conduct.

However, in 1972-73, young Asharam started his Ahmadabad ashram in the attractive, natural environment of the Sabarmati river. Asharam Bapu could capture his audience with his sweet tongue and powerful oratory and soon became popular among the people. Gradually, Asharam's fame spread to other parts of the country. One could say that he had now established his religious power all over the country. There are over 400 trusts in his empire, among which

Sant Shri Asharamji Ashram Trust

and

Sant Shri Asharamji Mahila Utthaan Trust

are very important, both located in Ahmadabad.

As per one estimate, the total wealth of these trusts is around Rs. 5000 crore. A monthly religious magazine Rishi Prasad and a fortnightly named Lok Kalyan Setu are published and their total circulation is around 14 lakhs. From these two magazines alone, the ashram earns around Rs. 7.50 crores annually.

Scandals around Asharam Bapu are not a new phenomenon. Since the inception of the ashram, the acquisition of the land and the construction of ashram buildings in different cities have been alleged to be illegal. We shall examine this issue more exhaustively in a separate chapter devoted to scandals around Asharam Bapu and his ashrams.

II Surat Ashram - Disciples and Followers

The focus of our study on Asharam Bapu was his well established ashram in Surat. The present Surat ashram is fifteen kilometers from Surat station. It is closer to the well known area Jahangirpura and Varial village. The ashram is spread out in around 25 acres near the bank of Tapti river. The location is very peaceful and pleasant.

The initiation of this ashram could be traced to 1985. When the ashram was started, it had only one room made of ordinary clay. Now it has become a huge place. It seems it started with the acquisition of government land and gradually the ashram encroached upon the farmers' land located in the vicinity. It is reported that land owned by the farmers in the ashram vicinity was captured by fair or foul means,. It is also reported that even at present, there are several cases going on in court, filed by farmers against the ashram for acquisition of the land by fraudulent means. Ashram people also have constructed a 60 feet long road from the main road which also seems illegal. Earlier this area was not within the limits of the municipal corporation but now since it is, there is a lot of pressure from different quarters for the removal of the illegal encroachment by the ashram. There are quite a few cases in the high court regarding this encroachment by the legal heirs of the families whose elders donated land for the ashram under the spell of Bapu's charisma. However, it is difficult to obtain any current information bccause people are scared of Bapu's political influence (the Advani connection). They also feel that nothing will come out of these court cases. Till almost the beginning of 1990s, this place on the bank of Tapti River was extremely isolated with hardly any human population. The land was uneven and full of pits and weeds. It is through the free labor of the people in the vicinity and devotees and followers that the land was made suitable for constructing this ashram.

Ashram

At the main gate of the ashram at the right hand side is a huge sales centre. In this centre one finds ayurvedic medicines, skin care ointments, shampoos and soaps along with miscellaneous items of daily household requirement such as fresh vegetable, seasonal fruits, incense sticks, fresh fruit juice etc. One also finds CDs, DVDs and 200-250 books on literature, spiritual advancement and home remedies.

Close to this sales centre is a homeopathy clinic and residential quarters for disciples and kitchens. There is also the manufacturing unit for ayurvedic medicines, a Shiv temple, a small garden for children, Bapu's cordoned cottage, two huge trees popularly called 'Vad Badshah' and 'Peepal Badshah', a huge prayer hall and a congregation hall which could accommodate over one lakh people and a huge garden where one can easily install tents to accommodate more people. There is also a Yagna Sanskar Kendra, a Saraswati temple, fruit orchards and vegetable gardens.

In any corner of ashram we visit, one would hear cassettes of Bapu's discourse or bhajans. During the day, about ten to fifteen thousand people visit the ashram. After 9 pm the ashram doors are closed, only the disciples can stay inside.

The ashram also generates a lot of income from the sale of vegetables, books, DVDs, CDs, medicines, fruits etc. Volunteers in-charge of these sale counters offer free service. Hence, the ashram dos not even pay for labor. The ashram neither pays tax nor any other kind of VAT to the government for the sale of the above. Disciples who offer voluntary service could expect peace of mind in return, moksha, or achievement of

shivtatva

or

brahmatatva,

and the biggest gain is obtaining Bapu's blessing. The architects of the ashram have kept in view its attraction as a picnic place which by itself can become a great source of income.

As our investigator reported, the ashram has been built at one place, without incurring any extra expenses, on somebody else's land, with a great pilgrimage spot in the form of two pious trees 'Vad-Baadshah' and

'Peepal-Baadshah', whose pradakshina is regarded as panacea for all problems.

Followers and Disciples

During our field study, we could interview around 26 followers as well as disciples. Of these 26, three were actual disciples who opted for lifetime devotion to Asharam Bapu. Of the 23 followers interviewed, 14 were female and 9 male. Of the total number of devotees and disciples, as many as 19 are from the OBC category and 2 from still lower castes. There was only one Brahmin lady devotee and one baniya devotee identified. A majority of them were either graduates or retired teachers. A sizeable number of the followers had their own business ranging from tailoring to mechanical goods and construction contracts. Almost half of the followers could be classified as rich or well settled. Only one or two could be classified as very poor. The rest would come under the category of middle class.

We also found that mostly the entire family members more or less express faith in Asharam Bapu and the ashram. Almost in all the cases, at least the husband and wife exhibited the faith. Some of the followers have been visiting ashram since almost its inception, that is, for the last 15-17 years.

We also observed that almost all those who follow Bapu had some religious background. They worshipped their local deities or in some cases, the local saints. Following Bapu did not stop them from worshipping their own local deities. The articulation of their faith in Bapu finds manifestation in their routine life. Almost all followers have kept Bapu's photograph in their house and they regularly worship the same. Apart from this, their involvement in Bapu and ashram activities finds different degrees of manifestation. Some of them are actively involved in various activities of the ashram. For instance, one old enthusiastic follower enrolled over 500 subscribers for Rishi Prasad, the monthly magazine of the ashram, and was also instrumental in popularizing Bapu's influence in his village and surrounding areas. He reported that over 3000 people have started worshipping Bapu in this area. Other followers normally help ashram by organizing a get-together of Bapu's followers in the area or participating in a *prabhatpheri*. They also actively canvas for subscriptions to Rishi Prasad and other magazines. One finds different degrees of participation among the followers, a few are active while others are satisfied by worshipping Bapu's photograph in their homes.

Almost all followers visit the ashram frequently and have invariably focused on the two pious trees. Almost all of them do a pradakshina of these trees for the fulfillment of their vows. Among these followers, there is variation in terms of practice, some do 11 rounds, while others do 21, 51, or even 101rounds. Some do it regularly while some do it only for a particular period. They do these rounds in case of sickness, family misfortune, marital problem, to find a suitable partner, to acquire a proper residence, or the most common occurrence being financial crisis.

Almost all the followers whom we interviewed, especially women, reported that by visiting the ashram, the two trees and because of Bapu's blessings, they have been able to resolve most of their problems. For instance, one follower reported that they were searching for a house because they did not want to stay in a joint family due to frequent quarrels. They did not have enough money. After visiting the ashram and praying, they found that they could obtain accommodation inspite of a shortage of Rs. one lakh. They explained their difficulty to the builder and he let them pay the remaining amount in installments. Similarly, one follower reported that a family was finding it very difficult to find a suitable match for their daughter due to lack of dowry. But with Bapu's blessings they found a very good boy from a nice family which did not demand dowry. They also insisted on a simple marriage. Similarly, one follower reported that their 70 year old mother who suffered from a serious eye ailment was not getting proper treatment and had started losing her vision. But when they visited Bapu, he blessed them and gave them an eye ointment and suggested some other household remedies, and within a fortnight or so, her vision was restored and she was free from the ailment. One lady follower reported that she used to be very short tempered earlier but after visiting the ashram and Bapu's darshan, she has become very calm and could make adjustments with family members peacefully. Apart from this, in a number of cases, respondents reported that after worshipping Bapu, they could overcome their financial worries, their businesses started flourishing, and their sons found better jobs. In case of some followers who are farmers, they reported that after coming to the ashram in the last decade or so, land prices have shot up so much that they have now become billionaires. Similarly the new cash crops like sugarcane that they cultivate give them great returns. One police constable was dejected because of his addiction. He used to drink so much that even his seniors had started treating him shabbily. He was humiliated in the office and was a liability for his wife and children. He even felt like committing suicide. Visiting the ashram and hearing Bapu's discourse on how to get rid of addiction influenced him so much that he could give up drinking and his life changed totally. He has not touched liquor for years. He has gained respect in the office as well as the family. Bapu's discourse proved to be a turning point in his life.

An old follower of around 71 years of age is so influenced by his visits to ashram that at this age too, because of the vibration that he derives from Bapu and ashram, he remains physically and mentally fit and participates in various activities of the ashram.

As far as participation in ashram activities is concerned, one finds varying degrees of participation among followers. The ashram conducts a number of activities along withcelebrating the main religious festivals like Holi, Guru Purnima and Diwali. When Bapu visits the ashram, there is a special programme where a huge gathering is present. Many volunteers are needed to take care of this gathering. Some followers volunteer during these festivals or do so regularly. However, we have also come across followers who don't even participate in Bapu's discourse and visit the ashram only once in a while. They are also not involved in any of the ashram activities in their day to day life. They only worship Bapu's photograph. However, almost all of them reported that they have found mental peace and relief from their worries and have been able to cope with their problems more effectively.

As far as Bapu's disciples are concerned, we came across three inmates who have been staying in the ashram for a long time. One old disciple aged 65 is a farmer and is staying in the Surat ashram for the past 18 years. As a matter of fact, he has donated his land to the ashram. The current value of this land would be almost a crore. His heirs are not happy with his donation. They want this land back in their custody but the respondent is firm and has absolutely no regrets. When he first came to the ashram, he wanted to stay only for a month, but then he continued because he found an irresistible urge and strong vibration because of which he is unable to go back to his family. He has seen Asharam Bapu very closely, because during the initial years, Bapu stayed in this ashram for a long time, when there was very little accommodation and also a few visitors. Bapu could spend more time with them then. Asharam Bapu is like God to him, but it's surprising that inspite of donating his land to the ashram, when he suffered from cancer, Bapu just gave him his blessings. The family incurred the entire treatment expense and he recovered with great difficulty. The ashram never provided for his expenses, yet he has no complaints. He keeps repeating that the kind of experience he finds here is so rare that it cannot be measured in terms of material wealth. And for this rare realization, crores of rupees would be nothing. By surrendering to Bapu, he is liberated from the cycle of birth.

Similarly another disciple from Madhya Pradesh had attended Bapu' discourse in his town and was so inspired that he expressed his desire to stay in the ashram as a disciple. Bapu encouraged him and he is staying in the Surat ashram for the past several years. He has brothers and a family. He comes from a poor farmer's family. He was not doing well in studies and was not finding a proper job. Even the family did not know what to do with him. After joining the ashram, he has not gone back to his family, nor does he want to. He too finds peace in the ashram and remains busy with the activities. He also holds the view that the family hardly has any relevance for him because now in the ashram with Bapu's blessing, he experiences divine grace and a kind of a rare peace of mind and self realization, some kind of a fusion with brahmatatva.

The third disciple we came across is from the Ahmadabad ashram who hails from Banaras. He is staying in the ashram for the past 10 years and participates in the various activities of the ashram. He is so busy that he has hardly visited any other place. He also has a similar response of finding eternal peace, divine blessing and liberation from the birth cycle.

It is interesting to note that when we conducted the inquiry in the Ahmadabad ashram, two children could not be located in the ashram premises and their bodies were discovered on the banks of the Sabarmati. They died under mysterious circumstances and the ashram authorities couldn't give a satisfactory explanation. The parents were well educated and there was a protest against Asharam Bapu and ashram authorities. As a matter of fact, the protesters entered the ashram and damaged ashram property. This incident was reported exhaustively in newspapers too. Most of the respondents were aware of this incident but by and large did not take it seriously. They also did not express any doubts about Bapu or the ashram authorities. They felt that it is false propaganda against Bapu. But we came across two respondents who lost faith in Bapu and in their residential area there were such protests against Bapu that it was difficult to re-establish faith in him. But this was incidental, a rare case. A majority of the people still believed in Bapu.

We have devoted the next chapter to the celebration of Holi in the ashram when lakhs of people visit the ashram and also stay there. The ashram festival goes on for about 3 days. This is a big event in the ashram.

III Celebrating Holi

We have provided an exhaustive account of the Holi festival celebrated in 2009 from 9th to 11th March in the Surat ashram. There are number of reasons for providing such an exhaustive account. This festival with a footfall of 1-4 lakh people is significant for a number of reasons. First, to organize such a huge festival and arrange for lakhs of people's stay of three days and to take care of all their requirements from food and sanitation to shelter is a huge task. Apart from that, even to make arrangements for lakhs of people to attend, watch and listen to Bapu's discourse from all corners of the hall and its adjoining areas is also a herculean task. People gather in large numbers from not only Gujrat but also from MP, Orissa, Maharashtra, Bihar and UP. Hence, one also has to arrange for parking these vehicles. The Surat Municipal Corporation has to organize routes to avoid traffic jams and to facilitate people's visit to the ashram. The Corporation also organizes 100-150 buses to ferry people. Even the ashram arranges for over 100 rickshaws especially for visitors with fixed rates.

It appears that this year special efforts were made to publicize the Holi celebration through banners, stickers in trains, hoardings, and posters on corporation buses. Religious television channels also did a lot of publicity for months before the festival. These special attempts were made probably to nullify the bad publicity the Ahmadabad ashram acquired because of the tragic deaths of two children in the ashram under mysterious circumstances and the resultant protest of people in Ahmadabad to the extent of observing Ahmadabad bandh and a protest march against the ashram authorities and the extensive exposure of this incident in the Gujrati media.

As observed by our field investigator who stayed in the ashram for a few days in order to properly appraise the event, preparations were started on a grand scale ten days prior to the festival. Arrangements were made for the stay of 2-3 lakh devotees in various types of tents. Food, utensils and carpets for over 4-5 lakh visitors were arranged as were various types of devices with string dividers to avoid crowding, audio-visual arrangements, and sanitation facilities. Parking was provided till 2-3 km by hiring farmers' fields in the adjoining area by paying Rs. 15,000-20,000 as rent. Tents, mandaps etc were erected on these premises.

Numerous committees were organized to take care of various requirements such as utensils, water for cooking, distributing food tokens by collecting money from the devotees, serving food, sanitation, shoe stands, parking, STD and ISD calls, security etc.

Women and girls from Surat and surrounding villages were mobilized to arrange food. For instance, in one tent, around 500-600 women devotees were only preparing chapatis. There were 10-15 such tents. There were huge furnaces where men and women were cooking chapattis. One furnace manned by 20-30 people could produce 50-60 chapatis in one second. 500-700 men and 200-300 women were actively involved in cutting vegetables.

Every morning devotees were served with a breakfast of upma or poha for which they were charged only Rs. five. For lunch they were served roti, vegetable, rice, pulses and farsan, the evening meal being khichidi, curry and papad, for which they were charged only Rs. ten. There was also a central organizing committee that would take care of the various committees and sub-committees. It is also significant to note that these hundreds of volunteers worked for days together for long hours without any remuneration.

From the main entrance of the ashram, one finds a large number of stalls on both the sides of the road, mostly for snacks, food (amla juice, amla muraba, gulkand, strawberry juice, farsan), books, CDs, audio cassettes, garlands, rudraksha, and naturopathic, ayurvedic and homeopathic medicines. These food stuffs were sold very cheap. For instance, batata poha at Rs. 5, khichdi and curry at Rs. 5, samosa, idli, sheera and upma at Rs. 2, ayurvedic tea at Rs. 4, pineapple and orange juice at Rs. 10 rupees and a variety of pickles at Rs. 75 per kilogram. Homeopathic doctors would examine patients, charging only for medicines. There used to be huge queues for visiting the doctors. The ayurvedic medicine stalls under the charge of one vaidya faced the maximum rush and sold around 108 varieties of medicine. There was also a free eye check-up centre which charged only for the spectacles.

One exceptional stall was of Narayan Sai (Asharam Bapu's son). The stall was from Madhya Pradesh where Narayan Sai's CD of *kukadlila* (tantric adventures) and other things were sold. That was his only stall but hardly 5-10 people were present.

It is also relevant to note that there was one special tent with a television and two huge screens. There were speakers around it as were various types of posters pertaining to *shishu sanskar*, that is, the ideal mode of bringing up children. Devotees were persuaded to spend at least one hour in this tent and were instructed on how to start such shishu sanskar kendras in their areas. The training essentially consisted of Bapu's views on shishu sanskar, a slide show on it which included tricks for improving memory, devotion to Saraswati and recitation of mantra-yantra and training for improving a child's performance through various yogasans, medicines etc.

Mantra Diksha

- Initiation Ceremony

The largest crowd was on the last day of the Holi festival since 7:30am. Bapu was to give mantra diksha. Hence, apart from the devotees, there was also a huge gathering of disciples desiring to obtain this mantra diksha. For this initiation ceremony, one form was distributed to each disciple, and ashram people charged 350 rupees from each disciple for this mantra diksha. Each disciple was provided with pooja material and mainly one photograph of Bapu. This time around 15,000-20,000 people took mantra diksha. The programme ended around 11 a.m as Bapu's satsang started at that time. Around two lakh people listened to his discourse. It is significant to note that in Bapu's discourse, one could not find any reference to either the Vedas, Upanishads, Geeta or any other important Hindu religious scripture. During his discourse of 2 hours, only in the initial 30 minutes did Bapu speak about the significance of Holi and its origin and the well known tale of bhakta Pralhad. After that, for the next one and half hour, he described the colorful festival, focusing on the *keshuda* flower (Holi color is prepared by mixing water with this flower's color).

On the day fixed for mantra diksha, the large number of people interested in taking diksha are made to sit in the hall since early morning. On this day, a disciple is supposed to observe fast but there are many who sit for mantra diksha without fasting. Bapu first addresses all these disciples and tells them about the great significance of the mantra which the guru imparts to his disciples. Then he himself goes for prolonged meditation. Subsequently he suggests ten other names including

om namah shivaya,

hari om,

jay shri krishna

and such other names. Disciples have to choose from one of these names. Bapu then pronounces each name and disciples have to raise their fingers when Bapu pronounces the name they have opted for. Bapu closely observes all these disciples during the process. Most of the followers opt for

hari om

because that is Bapu's pet name. After this ceremony, people are asked to stand in a queue and one by one, each one goes to Bapu and obtains his signature on his own photograph. Our field investigator suggests that at this particular moment when Bapu signs the photograph, through his hypnotic spell, he brings these disciples under his permanent influence. After that his disciples find various forms of god within Bapu. It has also been observed that disciples who don't stand in such a queue and are not serious about this ceremony do not get hypnotized or get the vision of Bapu as

bhagwan.

His discourse mainly consisted of different aspects of the keshuda flower such as its uses in curing skin diseases, indigestion and diabetes, cooling eyes, bringing peace to the mind etc. Between such an exhaustive narration he would shout "Hari OM!!" and expect people to repeat loudly. Another slogan was "Bapu ka bachha nahi rahega kachha" (any disciple of Bapu's will never remain weak). In between, he would ask devotees to raise their hands and intermittently join them to sing bhajans.

The climax of the programme was that after the discourse all devotees were organized in a huge queue and taken to the river bank. They were asked to stand up to play Holi. This place is 5-10 minutes away from the congregation hall but it took the disciples almost two hours to reach there. The ashram people had constructed a huge stage with a mandap and all devotees were divided into 3 different groups, one of men, one of women, and one joint group of men and women. On the stage there were huge fountains and with the help of a long pipe and a huge pump, Bapu sprinkled the color of keshuda flower on thousands of people. Devotees had special dresses of the same keshuda color. This programme went on for almost 2-3 hours after which the people dispersed.

According to our field observer, this Holi festival was a gathering of devotees but hardly a satsang. It was more like a get-together of devotees. The whole programme was organized in such a fashion that different age groups as well as men and women could relax and enjoy their stay. It was almost like a Diwali or summer vacation when people go to hill stations or other locations. Similarly, devotees visit this ashram for 3 days as if for a pleasure trip. The variety of food products, fruits, medicines and cosmetics at a reasonable rate was a major attraction. Secondly, the stay in open fields under tents was comfortable. The natural environment and the huge gathering were probably the great attraction. Playing Holi in such a huge gathering and along with darshan of the guru was a thrilling experience for the devotees. The whole arrangement is so inexpensive that any ordinary person can afford it.

If the stay was cheap and pleasant for devotees, for the ashram too it was a great source of income and instrumental for Bapu's publicity. Apart from this, such a celebration is also significant from the political perspective. For any politician, a gathering of 4-5 lakh of people is a big and important event, especially when the gathering is of people from different states as it becomes a huge vote bank.

For our modern godmen, it's also an effective weapon. Organizing such programs under the pretext of a religious occasion where lakhs of people participate, is, in a sense, a striking exhibition of their power or strength. It is also a challenge to other gurus in terms of their ability to cater to such a huge gathering.

Of course, for people who don't believe in such a celebration, it's a dilemma why people come in such large numbers for this gathering. But its political relevance cannot be underestimated.

Modern godmen derive very rich dividends from such celebrations. Such celebrations provide an opportunity to exercise political influence and enable such gurus to sort out their personal problems under this context. The government too, in one way or the other, protects and promotes such gatherings and activities. Political parties in power believe that the support of such a guru would be of great help in retaining power. Modern gurus also give importance to political leaders by providing them opportunities to address the gathering and publicly acknowledging their regard for them. In Gujrat, one finds a large number of such gurus who are quite influential and are able to get their legal or illegal activities approved by the state.

A striking example is the recent protest where a large section of people disillusioned with Asharam Bapu and ashram activities condemned the tragic death of 2 young children in mysterious circumstances in the ashram and expressed their condemnation by attacking the ashram and exposing the disciples. They also declared Ahmadabad bandh and wanted that ashram authorities including Bapu should be tried in court for the death of these children. Inspite of these huge protests, Asharam Bapu and ashram authorities could get away from any kind of punishment because the protection directly or indirectly provided by the state and especially Bhartiya Janata Party and Lal Krishna Advani who is stated to be close to Asharam Bapu.

In our concluding remarks, we would like to make some pertinent observations about the disciples, followers and the huge number of people who throng for such festivals. It seems to us that a majority of the disciples, as we noted earlier, come from OBC or even lower castes. Although our sample is very small, this seems to be the trend. Not only this, but many of these disciples and followers often come from rural or semi-urban backgrounds, follow traditional occupations and are used to the traditional mode of worship where saints or holy beings appear as a magnified form of tribal shamans, for whom Asharam Bapu could be an ideal substitute. Most of these followers have limited education. Even some doctors whom we interviewed came from a very traditional background. Thus, an overwhelming majority of those who come for Bapu's discourse, as far as our observation goes, are educated and semi-educated professionals with a more or less similar outlook and values. Asharam Bapu actually very cleverly articulates the popular beliefs, rituals and practices followed by or at least subscribed to by a majority of this gathering. Most of the godmen in India re-enforce feudal values, traditional family and caste institutions, popular religious beliefs, legends and other practices. Thus Bapu harps on purans, talks about traditional home remedies, ayurvedic medicines, family ties, kinship, subordination of juniors to seniors in the family, virtues of a joint family and traditional behavior patterns of daughters-in-law and sons in the family, hard work, honesty, morality and the ultimate possibility of redemption only through bhakti, recital of guru mantras, submission to supernatural powers and ability to win the guru's favour. Along with these sermons, Bapu also sings bhajans, though of course, devoid of any musical rhythm and cracks jokes, intermittently shouting "Hari Om!!" and demanding that the audience respond full-throatedly to his call.

We also found that the large number of volunteers, in hundreds, working from morning till night on seemingly tedious assignments such as cooking, looking after toilets, bathrooms, water, discipline, queues, serving food, and other such activities would have felt them to be monotonous, tedious and repulsive. But their total, enthusiastic involvement without any expectation of benefit in cash or kind seems a unique phenomenon. It is not easy to fully explain such a response, but it appears to us that the presence of such a huge gathering generates enthusiasm, spirit, sentiments and pride emerging from such collective participation for a noble cause. Not only that, these huge number of volunteers even look forward to such opportunities in the future. The explanation can probably be traced to the basic characteristic of human nature. Human beings left to themselves probably in their natural state of mind and also in terms of their biological and psychological makeup look forward to, or derive some inner satisfaction and joy by finding an opportunity to get involved in activities which give them such altruistic satisfaction. Human beings by nature are social and would find happiness in collective living and sharing the joys and sorrows of their lives. Probably, Asharam Bapu's Holi celebration on such a massive scale provides an opportunity to express such collective participation and natural human potential in a desired direction.

We would like to point out that as we found out, a majority of the respondents whom we interviewed found satisfaction and peace of mind and could resolve their worldly problems. Even the disciples staying in the ashram and doing routine and monotonous work found great pleasure and deep satisfaction as they felt that they are pursuing some noble path of redemption which will ultimately liberate them from the cycle of birth and death. Such an intricate faith appears to be the common characteristic among the disciples as well as followers whom we interviewed. Probably in the present capitalist acquisitive society where all individuals are exposed to cut throat competition, insecurities and hazards rooted in the market-oriented economy, these people find so little peace of mind that in such a collective gathering they can forget the external world joyfully and come together and participate in such celebrations, apparently without any greed. Thus, there are a number of factors which must be motivating such disciples and huge gatherings to come together and derive some unique pleasure and excitement in such a common celebration. This celebration is also in tune with the deep seated belief in observance of such traditional festivals which could also be a cause for inner joy and satisfaction. Thus, one may say that we are living in a modern Indian society, but these traditional ideas are so deep rooted that people in the rural as well as urban areas deeply share such sentiments and values. The question of overcoming these ideas doesn't arise because our government, the ruling strata and established institutions re-enforce such sentiments and values in every possible way.

Lastly, as we found out, most of the respondents stated that their material problems in terms of job, house, income as well as social problems like marital adjustment, finding a suitable bridegroom for a daughter, and even health related issues could be resolved by visiting the ashram and with Bapu's blessings. There is no point in refuting such facts or statements but these 20-25 people whom we interviewed got satisfaction and could resolve their problems. But we do not know whether the hundreds of others who visited the ashram found any relief in their suffering after performing such rituals and obtaining Bapu's blessings. Hence, it is difficult to generalize on the basis of the small sample we came across during our field survey.

IV Ashram - Scandals

Most modern godmen with their huge establishments have been also accused of scandals, corruption, crimes and violation of laws. For instance, Satya Sai Baba, ex-Swami Muktanand, Bhagwan Rajneesh, Pandurang Shastri, and even Shankaracharyas, Mahants and religious heads of *akharas* or religious organizations, especially in Ayodhya, have been surrounded by all kinds of gossip. This is true of other established religious sects like ISKCON and even Swaminarayan sects and similar other religious groups or organizations. Asharam Bapu and his ashram have probably surpassed many other modern godmen in terms of the notorious publicity and various scandals ascribed to them. We shall briefly refer to some of the major scandals around Asharam Bapu and his ashrams as it helps in understanding the role of such gurus in modern Indian society. There are scandals around the acquisition of land by his ashrams in different states, and around the mysterious deaths of young children in the ashram, as well as practice of tantric rituals and also sexual abuse. We are reproducing below some of the reports about such happenings, especially in Madhya Pradesh and Gujrat.

Chhindwara town of Madhya Pradesh, a backward tribal district, witnessed a serious outburst of public resentment on July 31st, 2008, arising out of the mysterious death of two children, on July 29th, in a residential institution in the town run by Asharam Bapu. Ramkrishna Yadav, a student of nursery standard was stifled to death in a hostel toilet. The dead body of Vedant Mourya, another residential student of KG, was also found in the hostel toilet on July 31st. Prima facie, the cause of death of both students was drowning in a bucket of water. Angry citizens of the town resorted to organizing protest meetings against the Asharam Gurukul. The CPI (M), Gondvana Gantantra Party, CITU and other organizations called for a bandh and demanded immediate arrest of the ashram in-charge and a CBI probe of the incident and immediate closing down of the ashram.

Another gurukul of the ashram at Ahmadabad also witnessed similar incidents of the planned murder of students on July 5th resulting in serial protests including bandh in Ahmadabad and elsewhere in Gujrat. Asharam's disciples physically attacked the protestors. The DIG who investigated the matter issued a statement that these were not normal deaths but seemed to be planned murders.

Similar doubts were expressed by a lady to the police regarding the first incident at Chhindwara. She went to the extent of pointing out a particular resident devotee as a suspect but nobody cared to inquire into her allegations. An investigating police officer was relieved of his responsibility midway and the task was handed over to the IG Police of Jabalpur who hastily announced the name of a student of standard IX, Rituraj, as the lone culprit involved in the serial murders. Rituraj was promptly taken into custody for 14 days.

The parents of Rituraj immediately objected to their son's arrest and described it as an unholy attempt to shield the real culprits. They told CPI (M) leaders that Rituraj is a patient of epilepsy and is taking treatment at Nagpur. Mentally he is not in a position to withstand the tension and anxiety. The police, the father claimed, took advantage of his crumbling mental condition and made him a scapegoat to be offered to the BJP which wants to bail the asharam out of this crisis.

The case of Ahmadabad deaths was also dealt with in a similarly one-sided manner. The police took several hours to reach the site where bodies of the students were actually found. The forensic team was not allowed to reach the place till the locked gate was opened by the management. The river water was allowed to flood the whole area. The chief minister Narendra Modi gave an empty assurance of bringing the guilty to book only in order to stall the anger and anguish expressed by the local people against the killings. After more than a month, the investigation could not even begin. Cases have now been filed in the Ahmadabad court by the parents of the dead children but one doesn't know the outcome. The BJP government of Madhya Pradesh proved even cleverer than that of Gujrat. In order to give a clean chit to the ashram, it appears that it preferred to fix the blame on a sick school student.

Corporate Asharam

This controversial baba's original name as reported was Asumal which was changed to Asharam, designated as Sant Shri (a religious person of repute). He was called Bapu (a fatherly person) to indicate proximity. One cannot be sure whether or not the earlier police file on Asumal as reported would be safe under the present regime, but his present day activities are no less controversial. There are hourly rates of his religious discourse. Sales proceeds from prasad, incense sticks and uses of erected canopy (pandal) etc are high. Bapu has himself become a corporate by establishing an extensive network of factories, schools etc. For setting up these, he successfully acquired thousands of acres of land made available by the BJP or at times even the Congress government, either free of cost or at nominal rates. There is hardly any town in MP and Gujrat where there is no ashram of Asharam Bapu. After getting the land he occupied neighboring lands as well on his own terms. This is the reason why almost all ashrams of Asharam are embroiled in land disputes. One who refuses to be a timid disciple is considered as an obstructive person and is dealt with accordingly. The government machinery has also been instrumental at times in teaching such a person a good lesson.

At Chhindwara, while local people were expressing their anguish and discontentment by participating in the bandh, some communal organization led by the RSS came out openly in support of Asharam. They designated the agitating people as anti-Hindu.

According to Vasudev Sharma, CITU Secretary, who was involved in the agitation, there are no 'rules and regulations' in the ashram to abide by. It doesn't adhere to a humanitarian approach in solving problems. The hostel meant for 70 students is occupied by 350 students. The institution (gurukul) doesn't have any teacher or employee on its records. They are all disciples (sadhaks) who follow the CBSE curriculum for examinations and teach rites and rituals as laid down by Asharam to innocent boys and girls. The fee starts from Rs. 35,000 per annum. An extra amount, non-refundable, is expected as a goodwill gesture. With such an affordable fee, the parents, despite being downhearted with the affairs, prefer to keep their children in the gurukul. An expression of discontentment, if any, is considered as an act of an atheist, non-believer and anti-Hindu. The parents of Ramkrishna Yadav were told by Asharam that Ramkrishna was bestowed with the age he lived to and has already been re-incarnated as a great man. One can very well guess the standard of refinement and cultural purification being imparted in the gurukul.

Vasudev Sharma complained that several truckloads of vegetables and forest produce from his premise have been sent to Gujrat to be used in Asharam's factories for pharmaceutical production. Absence of scientific quality assurance, safe manufacturing process and proven technology were brought to public knowledge by the recently conducted raids and surveillance by health officials. Students of gurukul are treated with this medicine.

Students as Guineapigs

Jasvinder Singh, CPI (M) state secretariat member, visited Chhindwara and enquired into the matter. Gathering first hand information from the students, their family members and local citizens, he expressed the apprehension that students are being subjected to experiments using this medicine.

Both at Chhindwara and Ahmadabad, the deceased students were found dead near water taps. One cannot rule out the possibility of adverse reactions to the medicines.

Medical Rackets

One ex-disciple also known vaidya Amrit Prajapati who served Bapu for almost two decades left the ashram when he came to know about the various scandals, especially sexual abuse of young women, especially by Bapu's notorious son Narayan and also Bapu himself. He worked selflessly for almost two decades and was in charge of manufacturing and networking for ayurvedic medicine in Bapu's ashram. According to him, Bapu's ashram indulges in this profitable business of selling ayurvedic medicines like churnas, gulkand and chyawanprash under the Rishi Prasad brand in over 1200 medical stores without any investment, only with the motive of making a profit. These medicines are prepared by women disciples in the Surat, Ahmadabad, Chhindwara and Delhi ashrams voluntarily without any remuneration. Vaidya Amrit Prajapati also, inspite of his long association with the ashram, has not been given any remuneration. Medicines are sold under the pretext of service to spiritual calls and devotees are almost persuaded to buy these medicines. Those who offer services for the sale or distribution of these medicines also work for free, the only remuneration they get is in terms of food and residence. Disciples are hypnotized under the pretext of convincing them that this too is service to god. Even the food in the ashram is provided free of cost by wealthy devotees.

Amrit Prajapati also was assured that the ashram would take care of his financial worries and help him start his own ayurvedic practice. But till the end he was not given any help. Prajapati states that of these 1200 stores which sell and make huge profits from this business, none of them maintain any account and no government official has the courage to ask for an account.

However, during recent times when the ashram was passing through difficult times because of the mysterious deaths of two children, troubles also mounted for the trust, when the Gujrat Food and Drug Control Administration (GFDCA) accused Bapu and 22 others, including Bapu's wife Lakshmi, in a Godhra court of distributing medicines without license. In the complaint, GFDCA officials said that a type of eye drop manufactured in Bapu's Motera ashram in Gandhiangar by an ayurvedic doctor, Nita Gaikwad, and distributed by Kanelav Lake ashram near Shehra in the Panchmahals district was not following any of the norms set by the body.

The case filed in the chief judicial court by drug inspector Pursnani stated that following a complaint by Godhra resident Pankaj Yadav who purchased the Santkrupa Netrabindu eye drops, the then drug inspector K.N. Ram visited the ashram on July 27th 2008 and seized 56 samples, none of which bore the manufacturer's name, manufacturing date or license number.

Bapu is also accused of giving shelter to law breakers in his ashram. A sting operation by Headlines Today caught him assuring a female fugitive from the US of not just shelter in his ashram, but also counseling her.[1]

Gujrat Samachar, a well known newspaper of the state, while referring to the mysterious deaths of two children in the ashram in its 15th July 2008 edition, reports that this is not the only time when Asharam Bapu is caught in the storm of such a controversy. In the past, the land disputes around Asharam's ashram in Ahmadabad had gone to court and some of the cases in this connection are still pending in the high court. First, the land on which the ashram is constructed is itself under legal dispute. The gurukul building constructed on the huge 15 acre land of the Ahmadabad ashram is challenged as an illegal construction and this has been publicized by many newspapers. This is also true of the ashram in Surat and Navsari. The case filed by the sarpanch of the village panchayat about illegal encroachment by the ashram authority of the village land has been approved by the court and ashram authorities have been told to clear the encroachment. In case of the Surat ashram too, around 30 acres of government land has been acquired by fraudulent means. The market value of this land today is around 125 crores.

Apart from this, the whole family of Bapu is entangled in a legal dispute for fraudulently acquiring land in the Pendmala village in Sabarkantha district. In this village, land has been acquired in the name of his wife, son, daughter and daughter-in-law under the pretext of declaring them farmers. This is also true of ashram land in Madhya Pradesh in Ujjain and Bhopal, in Rajoki village near Delhi and many other parts of the country, but it has hardly affected Asharam's popularity or his activities.

Cases also have been reported of ex-disciples who left the ashram because of their inability to withstand the malafide activities conducted in the ashram, and their receiving threats from the ashram authority for their physical alienation. It was reported in the Times of India that Mahendra Chawla, formal personal assistant to Bapu's son Narayan Sai, has been receiving threats to his life for lodging an FIR against Sai for forgery. Chawla had registered an FIR with the Virar police on 15th Aug 2008 against Narayan Sai, Hanumant Thakur and Rajendra Singh under sections 165, 168, 323, 507 of the IPC for faking his signatures on a property agreement. Since then, he has been threatened several times to remain silent. The alleged forgery was done in February 2005 for a 10 acre plot in Kumbharpada, Virar, when Chawla's signatures were forged without his knowledge to form the Shri Narayan Sai Trust. Chawla, aged 30, from Panipat, Harayana, who worked with Sai from January 2001 to August 2005, said "Only when the *gaushala,* which was on government land, received a demolition notice in July 2005 did I come to know my name was involved. I confronted Sai, and since then he has been threatening me to keep quiet. I quit immediately, returned to Panipat to be an insurance agent. However, Sai still threatens me on the phone. I fear for my life after news that follower Raju Chandak was shot in Sabarmati on Saturday. I lodged the FIR only 3 years later in August 2008 as I realized after the ashram deaths, it was necessary to expose Sai who is the main culprit." Chawla has demanded protection as he is afraid for his life.

The amount of money the ashrams make from the sale of so called ayurvedic medicines can be gauged from the fact that the extract of cow urine is sold in bottles ranging from price Rs. 350-500 and the daily sale is over 1500 litres with a daily earning of over Rs. 1,25,000. It is also reported that in the absence of proper distillation this urine extract also becomes harmful, but nobody bothers to check this.

Asharam Bapu himself is not much bothered about this bad publicity surrounding his ashrams. As reported by Amrit Prajapati who himself was an ex-RSS activist, Asharam Bapu told him that he should not be bothered because the police and the chief minister Narendra Modi are at his beck and call and even Advaniji also almost worships him.[2]

This somewhat exhaustive exposure of the financial and sexual scandals and criminal and corrupt practices of the ashrams becomes relevant for us when placed in the broader socio-economic context prevailing in India. Asharam Bapu's scandals should not be viewed as an isolated phenomenon as most godmen are surrounded by such publicity. Despite this, almost all of them have managed not only to survive, but also to flourish in the most pompous way without any trouble in conducting their activities. They have also received extensive appreciation from political leaders as well as corporate magnates. As a matter of fact, in the present era of monopoly finance capital, more and more wealth is acquired on the basis of financial transactions of a speculative nature, without any real roots in material reality. As reported, the nexus of politicians, businessmen and criminals dominate all financial and other activities. Our leading industrial tycoons have emerged on the basis of their political connections and also evasion of various types of taxes such as custom duty, excise duty etc. A striking example of speculative wealth is our stock exchange where share values sky rocket without any basis in its real book value. The sky rocketing land prices in Mumbai and most Indian cities is another striking case of this reality.

In the initial stage of capitalism, the system flourished on the basis of mass production, creating and adding to material value and also serving the needs of mass consumption goods. In the present stage of an exclusively market dominated economy, it is not the production of material value but the monetary gains based on various economic activities such as the service industry, tourism, entertainment, insurance, finance and other speculative activities that have become a major source of acquiring huge wealth. The wealth is acquired mostly by fraudulent means and in connivance with politicians and gangsters. Under these circumstances, it's not surprising to find that almost all political parties have a substantial number of elected leaders coming from a criminal background. Similarly, the corporate world also indulges in unfair practices. Thus, this nexus dominates society and all its institutions and most of the institutionalized godmen indulging in fair and unfair practices, acquiring huge wealth and having political and corporate connection ideally fit into the present scenario. Thus, the so-called spiritual or religious world of gurus can be only viewed as an organic part of the prevailing economic and political system based on the global dominance of monopoly finance capital.

V: Political Leaders and Hindu Saints to the Rescue

Religious revivalism has become a universal phenomenon for the last several decades. The Bush administration in the USA, for example, took to boosting Christian fundamentalism by extending support to orthodox religious movements such as the Movement for Moral Majority and also lending support to evangelists. Islamic fundamentalism has also become very strong in the last few decades and many Muslim states like Saudi Arabia, Pakistan and others seek to rigorously enforce orthodox Islamic laws. An extreme version is the Al-Qaeda established by Osama Bin Laden which has given rise to terrorist attacks in several countries under the pretext of defending Islam and punishing those who deviate from and oppose it. In India too, under the leadership of the BJP and its various offshoots such as the Bajrang Dal, Vishva Hindu Parishad, Hindu Sant Sammelan and others, serious attempts are being made to revive and strengthen Hindu fundamentalism in India. Since the 1980s, with the broadcasting of epic serials such as Mahabharat and Ramayan etc on television, and the launching of the Ramjanmabhumi movement culminating in the demolition of the Babri Masjid, this movement of Hindu revivalism has gained deeper roots in society. As a matter of fact, since the eighties, the two main political parties, the Congress and the BJP, have started competing with each other in lending direct or indirect support to the Hindu revivalist movement in India. Various other subjective and objective factors in India, especially since the 1980s, have contributed in strengthening the hold of the Hindu revivalist movement. The popularity gained by the plethora of modern godmen and other religious sects and cults in many parts of the country has to be viewed in this context. It's not only that the Hindu revivalist current has become strong but other revivalist and fundamentalists currents among the Christians and Muslims too have become fairly influential in the last three or four decades. In this context, the major political parties, especially the BJP, coming to the rescue of godmen like Asharam Bapu is not surprising.

Since 2008, the global economy is going through a serious economic crisis. There are no exceptions, even the advanced capitalist countries have been passing through severe economic constraint. In USA especially, the state has spent billions of dollars to salvage the corporate sector facing a severe crisis and disintegration. This has resulted ino ordinary people facing all kinds of economic and social problems. The problem of unemployment has become quite grave in many advanced countries, especially in USA where the percentage of unemployment has crossed 9%. In USA, the rate of bankruptcy has gone so high that lakhs of middle class people could not repay their housing loans and had to surrender their flats to the banks. The problem of homelessness in many cities in USA has become grave. Inspite of the state pumping in billions of dollars to rescue private sector corporations from bankruptcy, the economy still has not totally come out of the crisis.

Compared to the advanced countries, India and China have, as widely propagated, not experienced any economic crisis and the growth rate in these countries has been consistently high. India is thus presented as a model for ideal economic development in the world. Our political leaders are also not tired of always boasting about the Indian economy's high growth rate. While recognizing this factor of growth, one should not overlook the fact that the economic disparities prevailing in this country have been alarmingly, the difference between the earnings of the corporate sector and an ordinary migrant laborer in the city or agricultural laborer in the rural area is so vast that it brings out the hideous face of this development. We boast of our economic growth but conveniently forget that India's position in terms of the human development index is lower that even some of the poorer backward African countries. Our expenditure on health, education and housing and other social security majors is very low, with the result that the problem of insecurity in terms of health, housing, employment etc has aggravated in the last few years. The Indian state, which after independence proclaimed itself a welfare state, is fast withdrawing from providing these basic amenities. In this context of growing insecurity and instability, a vast majority of people find the struggle for existence so bitter and severe that they have hardly any hopes for a better future. Modern gurus come to the rescue of the state and the dominant strata which have immensely benefited from the recent economic reforms and policies by becoming instrumental in channelizing the growing discontent into spiritual and religious directions. This enables the state and the ruling strata to prevent a vast section of oppressed strata from taking recourse to struggles against their miseries or exploitation. Hence, all politicians of the ruling strata willingly come to the rescue of gurus and extend full support when they face any dilemma.

Our democratic institutions such as parliament, legislative assemblies, judiciary and executive have degenerated much in the last few decades. The contrast becomes so glaring when one compares this to the initial phase of independence. During this early phase, when Nehru was Prime Minister, the parliament and other democratic institutions functioned far more effectively. Even leaders of the opposition from left and other political parties contributed effectively by lively debate and meaningful contribution to the effective functioning of the parliament. Compared to that is the present debacle witnessed in the Lok Sabha and Rajya Sabha on the 3G spectrum scandal wherein the opposition did not permit parliament to function for the entire winter session. The degeneration of democratic institutions is also reflected in growing scandals, corruption and incompetence of political leaders and administrative heads and judiciaries. Scandals and corruptions are so rampant at the state and national level and their magnitude is so enormous that it becomes difficult to retain faith in the parliamentary form of government. It's not surprising under the circumstances that all major political parties have such large number of criminals at national as well as state level and elections are contested in such fraudulent and corrupt ways that one could easily suspect these leaders' moral authority to govern this country. Hence, political leaders at the national as well as state level coming to the rescue of godmen who also indulge in corrupt and illegal practices and scandals would not be surprising. Many corporate giants have also increasingly acquired wealth through political connections and fraudulent practices like tax and duty evasion. Thus, godmen occasionally indulging in corrupt or immoral practices no way form an exception to the rule. It looks as if all of them form an organic whole.

We now reproduce the observations made by different religious institutional heads, gurus, as well as political leaders in support of Asharam Bapu confronted with public displeasure and legal battles. In the concluding part of this chapter, we also refer to Hindu sants and political leaders coming to the rescue of Asharam Bapu after the recent scandals. This includes Shankaracharchya Jagadguru Sri Jayendra Saraswati of Kanchi Kamakoti Peeth, Sri Hariharanandji Maharaj of the famous Swaminarayan Mandir, Ahmadabad, Sadhvi Rithambhara, Morari Bapu, Shri Atal Bihari Vajpayee, ex-Prime minister of India late Shri Chandrashekhar, ex-President of India Late Shri K.R Narayanan, Shri Kamalnath, a Central Minister of the government of India, Shri Kapil Sibal, an important minister in the Central Congress government, Shri Ashok Singhal, president of Vishva Hindu Parishad, Shri Uddhav Thakre, executive president of the Shiv Sena, and lastly, Pawan Gupta, national president of Shiv Sena Hindustan.

It is also interesting and pertinent to note that a special *Rastriya Sant Sammelan* was organized on 19th October 2008, at Chhindwara, Madhya Pradesh in defense of Asharam Bapu in the context of the deaths of young students, both in Ahmadabad and Chhindwara ashrams. All sants from different parts of the country had assembled in large numbers and were unanimous in condemning people who held Asharam Bapu responsible for the children's death and were also critical of the malicious propaganda and conversion carried out by the Christian church in different parts of the country. It's not possible for us to summarize the speeches of all these sants who came to the rescue of Asharam Bapu. However, we find that the speech by Acharya Sunil Shastri Maharaj deserves special consideration.

He started his speech in a very queer manner. He argued that all sants who have assembled here have actually invited people to listen their message and also their warning. He said that sants have a special role, especially when the country is facing a great national calamity. They can always sense the possibility of coming storms. Hence, it becomes their obligation to warn people and give suggestions on how to face this calamity. He remarked that the attack on Asharam Bapu by the mischievous and anti-national elements is a sign of the gathering storm hovering over the Indian society and in order to counter this calamity, all Hindus must come together and jointly expose such attempts. As the guardian of Hindu *sanskriti* and traditions, and as a sant, it is his prime obligation to warn people and as Tulsi suggests in *Ramcharit Manas,* if sants don't perform such duties, they would go to hell. The attack on Asharam Bapu is an attack on Hindu *Samaj.*

It's a part of global conspiracy.

Sunil Shastri accused the Gondwana Gantantra Party, representing the interest of Gond tribals, of spreading the false news about Bapu. He also attacked Christian missionaries for spreading such false accusations against Bapu and burning his photograph and also probably behind burning the copy of the ramayan. He accused them of indulging in anti-national activities and questioned the sources of their finance. He suggested that this is a global conspiracy against Hindu society and saints, heavily financed by some global power. He questioned why the government of India was not taking any action against them. He also accused the central government of being dominated by a foreign lady and cited several examples of congress leaders of eminence including ministers who have Christian wives. Hence, missionaries get protection to continue with their anti-Hindu conversion. He threatened that if government or official agencies would not come out with the facts behind this conspiracy and the source of their finance, sants and Hindu society would jointly expose them and teach them a proper lesson. They should know Hindu strength and power. He also accused official agencies of expecting a code of conduct (*achaar sanhita)* only of Hindu saints and not for missionaries. He gave a call for unity of all Hindus and expose and punish those who attempt to divide Hindu society.

This trinity of Hindu saints, political leaders and the state with the implicit connivance of the corporate world coming to the rescue of Asharam Bapu is not an accident. As a matter of fact, the recent rapid growth rate of the Indian economy and the achievements of the country have been directly or indirectly attributed to the greatness of the ancient Hindu religious traditions and culture. This myth is perpetrated far more rigorously by our NRIs, especially those who are well settled in western countries and particularly in the USA. This sizeable section of NRIs, Indian elites abroad, has also been instrumental in sponsoring and spreading the influence of modern gurus in western nations. The recent judgment on *Ramjanmabhumi* in Ayodhya is a striking case where the judiciary too has no inhibition in accepting the legitimacy of the popular contention of the location of the birthplace of Ram in the vicinity of old Babri Masjid, despite the fact that archaeological findings do not support such an assumption. The two major modern gurus, Morari Bapu and Asharam Bapu, whom we studied in this monograph too have extended their open support to the Sangh Parivar in its battle for the construction of the Ram Mandir over the demolished Babri Masjid.[4]

With the passage of time, instead of moving forward towards a just, human, secular, egalitarian and democratic setup, the forces that drive India in a backward, unjust, authoritarian and sectarian direction have become far more powerful than we could ever imagine at the inception of the India's independence. Unfortunately, leaving aside even any radical movement of the left for the working class, gender justice, or struggle for the emancipation of the toiling and the deprived strata in urban, rural and tribal areas, we are confronted with a situation where even the very secular character of the Indian state is at stake. Progressive and liberal elements also find themselves quite weak to accept this challenge of Indian polity. The role and impact of the modern gurus on the present depressing scenario of the Indian society in terms of the plight of the minorities and other weaker sections in this country cannot be overstressed.

References

1. L Basham – Wonder That Was India, pp 164-166, published by Picadpr, London 2004
2. Romila Thapar-Ancient India Social Histroy, "Renunciation
   – The making of a Counter
   – Culture Interrogationn", p 63-104, Orient Longman Limited, 1778
3. Reprot from Headlines Today
4. Gujarat Samachar, July 2008
5. Dainak Bhaskar, Bhopal Edition, 3.8.2008

8

Aniruddha Bapu

SECTION - I

SHREE ANIRUDDHA BAPU - REINCARNATION OF SHIRDI SAI BABA

Shree Aniruddha Bapu is unique in the galaxy of the modern godmen we have come across in Indian society since over five decades. In a sense each godman or guru exhibits some unique traits and is not easily comparable with others. Each commands a following on the basis of some distinct traits, aura, attributes or achievements compared to others. Yet Aniruddha Bapu is still strikingly different from the entire range of godmen who have acquired recognition at state, acquired an excellent academic record and comes from a family of medical practioners. Dr. Aniruddha Dhairyadhar Joshi obtained his MD in medicine from Mumbai University and was a consulting rheumatologist who practised for several years in Parel before he decided to quit the profession in the late nineties. It seems that he was quite a popular medical practioner and had a good practice till he proclaimed himself as a reincarnation of Shirdi Sai Baba.

Unlike other godmen, Aniruddha Bapu does not claim to have any distinct religious affiliation nor has he acquired his initiation from any known or even unknown gurus. One hardly finds even a hint of his receiving any blessing from any guru. There is also no reference of his religious association with any particular sect or religious school. There are also no records of either he or his family having any inclination for the worship of Shirdi Sai Baba. Thus he emerges as a godman, a reincarnation of Shirdi Sai Baba and also of lord Ram on his own, without any spiritual lineage, a striking difference from other godmen.

Moreover, till he proclaimed himself as a reincarnation of Shirdi Sai Baba, one hardly finds even an inclination towards any religious or spiritual pursuit or interest in any devotional activities. It appears as if all of a sudden he declared himself as a reincarnation. We have given a more elaborate account of his emergence as an incarnation in the section devoted to his profile.

Not only does one not find any spiritual inclination in his earlier career, it's absent even in his routine activities or involvements to provide an indication of any such future possibility. If at all, it's his utter indifference towards any religious or spiritual pursuit. He used to smoke regularly for years, probably till he proclaimed himself as a reincarnation of Shirdi Sai Baba. This fact is noticed by practically all his colleagues. He was also known for his theatrical talent and liking for dramas. This gift of being a good actor probably enabled him to perform his new role more admirably. This is probably true of all godmen - known for the trust they command and admiration they receive from their huge number of followers.

Of coursé, one distinct characteristic he displayed and noted by his old pals was his prolific reading and thinking with a varied interests apart from medicine like literature, politics, history and philosophy.

His appearance as a godman is also deceptive as unlike other godmen who invariably don saffron or white, colors symbolically attributed to both present and past saints or gurus, Aniruddha Bapu puts on white half sleeve shirt and black trousers and has a huge moustache which demarcates him from the rest of this crowd. Similarly, unlike other godmen, he addresses his gathering sitting comfortably in a posh chair, that too for a short time and only in Marathi. No wonder that he is essentially a Marathi godman with an almpst exclusively Maharastrian following of the elites and upper castes.

Unlike other recent godmen, especially in Gujrat and the northern states, sizeable number of them who come from the lower or other backward castes, Aniruddha Bapu is a Brahmin godman highly conscious of his caste and the distinct caste attributes.

Similarly, Bapu also differs from the rest of the godmen in terms of his training programme, activities and style of functioning. We shall briefly refer to this aspect in a separate section for this purpose in this essay.

Unlike other godmen, Aniruddha Bapu is known not only for his religious or spiritual eminence but also as a visionary who is extensively interested in analysing the national and global political and economic scenario, international correlations of power blocks, and especially his writings on the third world war, its first initial spark in the Palestine-Israel war, ultimately all major powers joining this global war and India, i.e., Bharat joining, leading and ultimately emerging as a victorious power in the final scenario. Aniruddha Bapu also drops hints of the possibility of him playing a major role in terms of guiding and providing an effective strategy for winning the battle, the comparison obviously being with Krishna who led the battle of *Mahabharat* resulting in the *Pandavas'* victory over the *Kaurav*s. We have also briefly summarized his views and findings and the effective strategy he provides for the final outcome of this world war. As a matter of fact he has published an interesting volume of the coming third world war and its outcomes.

Further, Bapu also has no hesitation in openly advocating the supremacy of the Brahmin caste. He firmly believes in the exceptional abilities, merits and the distinct contributions of the Brahmins in evolving and enriching Indian traditions, culture and civilization. He believes that it is because of the superior intellect and merits of this caste that India could effectively respond to the periodical challenges posed before its society and culture. In his address to the national Brahmin caste conference held in Poona in 2008, he mentione that this distinct role and contribution of the Brahmins is not only for India but also global advancement. We have also dealt with his views in a separate section devoted to this purpose.

Finally, Aniruddha Bapu not only claims divinity for himself but also elevates his wife and a close associate and disciple Suchit Dada to a superhuman status. His wife is equated with *Sita* and Suchit Dada who is also a doctor and his junior identifies himself with Laxman with Bapu projected as Ram. Thus, three idols of Bapu, his wife and Suchit Dada are prominently displayed in his Khar house which has become a pilgrimage centre for his devotees. Even their foot prints are prominently placed and all devotees are expected to touch them and seek their blessing.

Aniruddha Bapu is different from other godmen also because he hardly seeks to gain prominence by the use of any media, either print or electronic. He is also equally indifferent to giving interviews or seeking publicity through any covert or avert device. One does not find him on any TV channel devoted to religion.

Similarly, one wonders why Aniruddha Bapu opted for being a reincarnation of Shirdi Sai Baba. There is also hardly any evidence of his visit to Shirdi or any explicit evidence of his inclination for Baba's worship during the earlier phase of his life. We have devoted a small section to the interviews with Mr. Dabholkar whose house has been traditionally recognized as a place for worship of Shirdi Sai Baba.

One striking feature which Aniruddha Bapu shares with the rest of the godmen, a universal device found among practically all such classes, is their mode of raising money from their devotees, by marketing various products they manufacture for selling through numerous stalls for visitors and followers during celebrations. The range of products usually includes food, snacks, herbal health and beauty products, candles, their idols, notebooks, photos, books, pens and such other items with their image. All of them usually raise enormous amounts of money by marketing their products among their followers. Usually no receipts are given for the sale of these products. The entire transaction takes place without following any institutional accounting.

Aniruddha Bapu has actually evolved a unique device which could serve a dual purpose of making money as well as raising the intensity of devotion - his special Ram Naam notebook. This Ram Naam notebook is sold for Rs. 20 and has 150 pages. Each page is to be filled with the names of gods like Ram and Krishna, and the last few pages are devoted to writing Jai Jai Aniruddha Hari. Each devotee after filling up one note book is supposed to deposit it in Aniruddha's Universal Bank of Ram Naam and would become an account holder in the bank with an account number. He is supposed to fill 150 such books that would obviously demand money as well as several hours of writings daily. This would take at least a few months, even if followed regularly. Submission of these duly filled in notebooks would entitle the devotees to the privilege of Bapu's direct darshan. This is indeed a unique device enthusiastically followed by devotees.

This essay, as indicated earlier, is divided into five sections. The first section is devoted to Bapu's profile, brief narration of his emergence as a reincarnation of Shirdi Sai Baba, his childhood, educational career and his other interests and activities. This section also provides a brief narration of Bapu's profile in his new image as reincarnation, the various activities initiated by him, his devotees, and such other narrations as we could obtain from his website.

The other sections are devoted to the other distinct contributions of Bapu, his unique training programme of disaster management, his medical camps in interior tribal villages in Kolhapur, his commitment and glorification of Brahmin contribution to Indian society, his unique appraisal of the possibility of the Third World War and the distinct role of Bharat in this global war, and finally our concluding observation about Aniruddha Bapu's role and relevance as a godman and its implication for Indian polity and society.

Disaster Management Training Course

SECTION - II

As we mentioned earlier, one of the unique features of Aniruddha Bapu's activities is his comprehensive and effective training manual on disaster management.

Aniruddha's Academy of Disaster Management has published a manual based on the workshop on disaster management conducted by Bapu's Trust from February 15, 2002 to February 27, 2002. The training was imparted by well known experts from various branches of medicine to fire management and civil defence. The workshop also covered the role of the police and media in disaster management. The academy has also published a book titled Textbook of Disasters and their Management in 2002.

Promptly after the institution of the Academy, the first project taken up was the compilation of a comprehensive textbook, a treatise, a user's handbook on disaster management. It is with the help of this textbook that till date the Academy has trained over 45000 citizens recruited from all over the country in the basics of disaster management, absolutely free of cost. Of these, more that 25000 have become Disaster Management Volunteers (DMVs) of the Academy.

Volunteers of the Academy are visible in major festivals like Ganpati immersion, Durga Puja, Navratri etc for maintaining discipline and promoting peace and harmony. They also promptly reach during any kind of disaster such as fire, flood, epidemic, famine, earthquake and even communal riots. The state administration utilizes their services regularly for such eventualities.

Aniruddha Bapu's medical camp in remote tribal villages such as Pendakhale (taluka Shahuwadi) in Kolhapur district also deserves special consideration. We are reproducing below the details of the camp conducted from 8th to 10th February, 2009. Bapu himself was also present during the camp.

We have provided an exhaustive coverage of the training programs, approach, conceptual framework, vision, activities and achievements of the Aniruddha's Academy of Disaster Management and also of the medical camp. The main purpose of this appraisal is to highlight how Bapu's approach and activities differ sharply from other godmen who are by and large devoid of any scientific or even systematic understanding of any disaster or the health problems and requirements in such situations.

Bapu himself being a medical practioner has a different approach, and also probably large number of ex-colleagues willing to help. Thus, Bapu's religious bias or understanding has not come in the way of his tackling human or social problems of varying categories and magnitudes. We will reserve our critical observation about the apparent contradictions in his preaching and practice in our concluding observations.

Multlingual Brahmin Convention

SECTION - III

This is based on Aniruddh Bapu's address delivered to the Multilingual Brahmin Convention held on 24th January 2009 in Poona. This address clearly brings out Bapu's die-hard faith in Brahiminic supremacy and its exclusive contribution in enriching Indian culture and civilization, and maintaining its legacy since its inception to modern age.

Bapu begins his address in a way similar to that of the convention held in Parbhani two years earlier. His address begins with the glorification of the past and Brahmins' role in creating Indian culture. Bapu harps on the role of the present Brahmin leadership in not only preserving but further promoting and enriching this tradition and rightfully assuming its leadership at the national and even global level.

Bapu focuses on their two major contributions to Indian culture: Indian culture's potential for perennial growth and enrichment and secondly, its ability to modify itself in response to the historical challenges it has faced since its inception to modern age. Brahmins alone exhibit the competence to incorporate innovations, meet the new challenges posed by modernization and scientific advancement, and provide global leadership in the further development of humanities.

Bapu's justifies Brahmin supremacy with the following belief: The religious and spiritual diversity of the Indian (Hindu) legacy in terms of sects, deities and gods, languages, customs, modes of worship, rituals, competitive rivalry of Gods' supremacy, temples and their architecture, etc is of bewildering complexity and can be harmonically united only by Brahmins. But for Brahmins, India's sense of unity, harmony, or cultural and religious synthesis would have been impossible. In terms of numerical expression, he attributes a hundred and eight percent credit to Brahmins. He assigns this percentage as the number one hundred eight has religious significance in Hinduism.

Similarly, he traces the unity of all Brahmins, located in any part of India in terms of all of them observing some common vedic rituals, mode of worship, beliefs and other practices. While tracing his own family genealogy of the last fourteen generations, he claims that in his blood there is an ideal fusion of Brahmins of great variety, Gujrati Audich Brahmins, Karnataka Pandits, Maharastrian Brahmins and some others.

Aniruddha Bapu himself is trained in karate and is a strong advocate of violence. He publicly declares that if someone verbally abuses you, you must retaliate by breaking such a person's bones and should never spare any abuse from any quarter.

Bapu also believes that if Brahmins are to retain their supremacy, they must respect and value India's democratic set up. They must participate actively in electoral processes and should play an active role in Indian polity. This is crucial to retain their supremacy in Indian society.

During his discourses he refers to his medical qualification several times as well as his children's' brilliant academic achievements - his son too being a doctor and his daughter with an excellent academic record being married to an equally eminent person. His children also follow Indian religious and cultural traditions and take pride in using Marathi as a language of communication in spite of being educated in a highly respected convent school.

In his concluding remarks, he openly declares his brotherhood with Kashmiri Brahmins and assures them that in this life only he is committed to their settlement in Kashmir with the comforts, privileges, and eminence they had enjoyed in Kashmir in the past.

We reserve our critical remarks on his speech in this national Brahmin convention for our concluding observation.

(Ref " star vrut ") Daily newspaper Published by Narendra. R. Hadkar Mumbai Friday. 27th Feb 2009, pp. 4x6.

Third World War

SECTION -IV

"Third World War" by Dr. Aniruddha D. Joshi published by Lotus Publication Pvt. Ltd., Mumbai, First Edition: 23rd December 2007.

The book begins with the message that war cannot decide who is right, it only decides who is left. This book is a compilation of a regular series of articles written by Aniruddha Bapu in their daily 'Pratyaksha' over a period of time, culminating in an exhaustive book published in 2007.

We are reproducing the introductory note to this book before a more exhaustive summary of the book.

'The Third World war authored by Dr. Aniruddha Dhairyadhar Joshi. It is a collection of a series of studied and thoughtful articles that appeared in the columns of the daily 'Pratyaksha'. The work does not dwell only on the causes and possibilities of war, it also discusses several issues that are, as a matter of fact, real, a part of history. Moreover, the common person, not necessarily acquainted with the details, events and causes behind the previous world wars should indeed read this work.

There is no doubt that over the next twenty to twenty-five years, conflict will become an aspect of everyday doings and in every region an earth, values based on theory or principle will have no place whatsoever in this conflict. Survival of the fittest will, on the contrary, be the only commandment. Political games and secret conspiracies too are likely to be sure directives. Quantitative powers that can resort to aggression, violence and extreme restlessness are going to prove more dominant and successful in the conflict and for a long time to come.' These words, part of the prologue, are a strikingly realistic comment on the general circumstances that prevail. We also become aware that with modern techniques changing the face of war, battles between two nations are no more restricted to the battlefield. Now the fury of war has engulfed every region. War is no longer fought between good and evil. It is but a violent eruption, entirely immoral. Pulling us out of our secure cocoons, the work bears before us this and other such blatant realities. This is indeed the strength and also the success of the work.

The work makes profound yet sharp observations about the history of the Jews, the birth of Palestine and Israel, Osama bin Laden, the Al-Qaeda and other terrorist organisations, the conversion in Africa, Saddam Hussain, the I.S.I., the double standards of the U.S.A., Pakistan's hatred for India and the shelter it offers to terrorists, Iran and terrorism, the current situation in Bangladesh, Taiwan, Cuba and also in the Indian subcontinent.

By no means a prediction of the future, this thoughtful presentation of history and the present also gives, to a certain extent, a glimpse of the 'calendar' of the third World War. Pure democracy is capable of watering down the horrors of war but the stream of democratic thought is weakened in most nations due to the struggle for power and religious mindsets. Yesterday, it was a cruel tyrant by the name of Hitler, today it is a bin Laden. As for the mastermind behind the Third World War, we are in the dark about him, at least for now.

This highlights the paradox of a man who exhibits a rational mind visible in the disaster management manual, but has no hesitation in glorifying Brahmin supremacy and his own divinity, presenting himself as a reincarnation of Shirdi Sai Baba and also Rama and Krishna.

We present below a brief summary of Bapu's book on the Third World War. It indicates a sharp mind given the vast amount of data collected, and an ability to visualise future events, although it is impossible to agree with any of his major formulations of world events, correlation of global power blocks and the eventual outcome in the form of the war, which as per his prediction should have started in 2006. This time too was presented in his equally mystical prediction as (6.6.6.) i.e. 6th June 2006.

Third World War: A Brief Appraisal

The book not only deals with the Indian polity but is also an attempt to comprehensively appraise the political history and future of the major countries in the world.

Aniruddha Bapu thinks that the Third World War has already entered our doorstep wearing the mask of peace. He has divided this work into eighteen parts. These parts provide detailed accounts of the first two World Wars, their beginning, causes and outcome. It also deals with terrorist organizations and their mode of operation in different countries.

This book also deals with the impact of the Third World War and weapons that would be used to win the war. He classifies them in the following categories:

(i) Chemical warfare
(ii) Biological warfare
(iii) Oceanic warfare
(iv) Desert warfare
(v) Aerial and galactic warfare
(vi) Guerrilla warfare
(vii) Psychological warfare

He strongly believes that China and Pakistan pose a serious threat to India which should thus cultivate friendship with Afghanistan, Nepal and Sri Lanka; China joining hands with Pakistan would make all attempts to confront India.

Let us briefly refer to Bapu's understanding of global wars.

He refers to the Vedas to trace the beginning of world wars which have mentioned "Dasratu war". According to him, the Mahabharat is a glaring incidence of a World War during the epic period, a major devastating war of early history. According to Aniruddha Bapu around 11 crore people participated in this war and led to the destruction of wealth and resources and annihilated mankind on a global scale. Bapu also proclaims that on behalf of the Kauravs, Afghanistan (Ganakar), Iran, Babylonia, Java, Greece, Germany, Egypt, Arabsitan and other countries participated with their royal heads, and other provincial states in India were involved too. The Mahabharat war led to global destruction but India paid the heaviest price.

On the basis of his study of the two world wars, Bapu argues that ordinarily a world war would imply theinvolvement of at least 20 nations. On the basis of his appraisal of the present global situation, at least 90 nations would be directly involved in the coming world war. Bapu also predicts that in the coming period, India would witness the maximum terrorist attacks. Initially it would not be involved but would be drawn in in the final phase. Initially it would also be at the receiving end as it would not get any help or cooperation from its neighbouring nations. In order to counter China and Pakistan effectively, India must help Nepal and Burma (Myanmar) in restoring democratic rule.

Bapu subsequently traces the history of the first two wars, how they were initiated, who led these wars, nations that benefited and those who lost. In this context he comes forward with an exhaustive appraisal of Germany - its defeat in the First World War, the later emergence of Hitler, his techniques and ideal fusion of religious and political ideology, his targeting of Jews and recourse to fascist rule.

Bapu holds the view that a handful of followers misinterpreting the original teachings of Islam are misguiding the world and preparing the ground for the Third World War in the name of protecting and promoting Islam. He traces the beginning of this coming war in 11th September attack on New York and strongly advocates a collective and powerful response by attacking Islamic terror centres all over the world. He also warns that one should not underestimate their influence as thier image as religious crusaders has made a deep imprint on Muslim populations all over the world.

Further he highlights the role of Pakistan in encouraging terrorists and their organizations.

Initiation of the Third World War

Aniruddha Bapu predicts that the initiation of the Third World War can easily be traced to the present conflict between Israel and Palestine. He even argues that there is close collaboration between the Hamas and Al Qaeda. Once the war between Israel and Palestine begins, oil free friendly nations upholding the cause of Palestine and also Muslim countries around the world would openly declare support to Palestine. Obviously USA would come to the rescue of Israel. This would be followed by five terrorist organizations from the friendly countries of Palestine launching a powerful attack on UK and USA. This spark will light a fire all over the world.

This Great War would continue uninterrupted for some time. During this period Jews all over the world would come under one banner and create a strong secret network. Its headquarters would be located in USA, obviously with state approval. The second important centre would be located in Russian.

Bapu actually predicted that the Third World War would be launched on 6th June 2006 and that the secular state of India would be forced to enter this war in the final stage. By 2012, the flare-up would spread all over the world and culminate into the Third World War. The final phase of this war would be approximately in 2018.

India would play a leading role during the final phase. This country with its great legacy of an ancient culture, civilization, and a value system based on religious tolerance and non-violence would play a leading role in putting an end to this global war, promoting peace and harmony in the world, and contributing to the onward march of humanity. Bapu traces the massive global destruction with the outcome of the Mahabharat war and subsequently the world witnessing a new dawn of mankind.

Bapu also refers to Nostradamus who predicted a thousand years ago that in the midst of such a war, a great leader called Chiron (pronounced *Shyrun)* would emerge who would travel all over the world and would be a leader to mankind.

In Bapu's formulation (which according to him is Nostradamus's prediction) from the aquatic triplicity shall be born one who shall make Thursday his holiday. Bapu too has chosen Thursday as his day. His discourses are invariably held on Thursday. Thus he indirectly traces a link between him and Nostradamus's old prediction to promote the notion thathis own greatness should not be confined to his contribution to india but that he should be recognized as a great world leader who would ultimately play the role of the saviour of mankind.

Concluding Observations

Aniruddha Bapu's profile, his emergence as an incarnation of Shirdi Sai Baba, his institutional activities, style of functioning, appearance, mode of discourse and operation, outlook and behaviour pattern differentiate him from most of the godmen of the twentieth century. In this context he can be compared to Rajneesh, also a modern Guru - highly educated, philosophically profound, radical in outlook, with an infinite capacity of experimentation, exposure to both western and Oriental, especially Indian philosophy, commitment to a religion with his own distinct interpretation and ultimately his degeneration due to his lust for power, ego-centric personality, increasing insecurity and isolation, an obvious outcome of his obsession to retain his supremacy as an undisputed monarch of his institutional set up, and the consequent moral degeneration of his subordinates as well as his own, and the ultimate withering from this universe with hardly any impact. Aniruddha Bapu is also a modern godman but the contrast between the two is sharp. Aniruddha Bapu too is highly qualified, with a good command over English, Marathi and Hindi. He has studied Indian scriptures, modern medical science as well as international and national politics, the history of different civilizations, as well as the back drop of the two World Wars. His scientific approach and rational thought is visible in the systematic training course and standard textbook on disaster management. One may disagree with his appraisal and understanding of the causes and consequences of the World Wars and could have reservations about his prediction of the third, its beginning, the power blocks involved, the global correlation of political and economic forces and their equations etc. However, his rigorous intellectual exercise, exhaustive narration of the events preceding and subsequent to the wars, and even his presentation of the present global political scenario is admirable. Such an appraisal coming from a guru who proclaims himself to be a reincarnation of Shirdi Sai Baba is surprising and certainly impressive in its presentation. His contrast with Rajneesh is sharp because Rajneesh was a modern guru, liberal and in some respects strikingly radical. He possessed an understanding of the bold experiments conducted by western Freudian and especially post-Freudian psychoanalytical schools which were introduced to his Indian followers with minor modifications making them more palatable to the Indian psyche. Introducing such experiments in a traditional, conservative Indian setting, that too from a platform of a religious discourse was a remarkable advance over all his preachings and practices.

In contrast to Rajneesh, Aniruddha Bapu is highly traditional, orthodox in his outlook, in his interpretation of the Indian scriptures and dogmatic, pro-adherence and pro- Brahmin supremacy. Bapu is not traditional because he too stands for social reforms in Hindu society by promoting widow remarriage and inter-caste marriages, and opposing child marriage. He encourages marriage among his followers, irrespective of caste, language or even regional boundaries. But unlike Rajneesh who was far more radical in his approach to sex, caste, religion, Bapu is more conservative and openly upholds Brahiminic supremacy. He believes that he is naturally gifted with the qualities and competence required to dominate the world, ideologically and culturally.

But Bapu is a truly modern when it comes to training volunteers for disaster management, in his medical camps, and his support of modern education, sports etc.

Even the place from where he operates cannot not be compared with any traditional or modern ashram in any sense of the term. He operates from a residential building of around six floors totally occupied and owned by him in Khar, a Mumbai suburb. This place with its several floors looks more like a bureaucratic set up with different departments and personnel conducting administrative activities. Bapu probably stays on the top floor. Nobody knows how he operates, what does he do the whole day as even his followers cannot access him. He stays with his family, daughter and son, like any other householder.

Its is also interesting to note in this context that Bapu regularly visited Appaji Dhabholkar's house, which is traditionally recognised as a Sai Baba temple, for three years from 1993 to 1996. In 1996, he suddenly demanded that Appa Dhabholkar return the three articles Sai Baba had entrusted to their family till his reincarnation claims them. Even after receiving these articles, Aniruddha Bapu had strictly adviced the Dabholkar family to keep this a secret. Two years after getting these sacred articles, he closed his clinic, gave up his profession and became a full time guru, operating as Shirdi Sai Baba's reincarnation. Even then in his only interview he gave to a journalist sometime during this period, he off hand remarked that he does not claim that he is reincarnation of Shirdi Sai Baba, and his findings of these articles could be an outcome of his three years' close acquaintance with Dhabholkar family and his casual enquiry about whether they had any articles that Baba might have gifted to them because of their long association. Dhabholkar suddenly realized that only Aniruddh Bapu can be the reincarnation of Sai Baba, and that is the only reason why he claimed these articles. Thus, Bapu at times maintains that he is an ordinary householder, unlike other Gurus who live alone and hence are called sanyasi. It is not surprising that when we interviewed his ex-colleague in 2009, who knew Bapu from his years of service in Nair hospital, the said person was forth right that he or other colleagues had never thought that Dr. Aniruddha would one day emerge as a reincarnation of Shirdi sai Baba. He also has pleasant recollections of his friendship, Aniruddha's cheerful nature, regular smoking, avid reading of history, politics etc, and popularity as a good medical practioner. He was known especially for his liking for dramatics and his good performances as an actor. There was no inclination towards either religion or even spirituality. Surprisingly he also mentioned that he is still in touch with Aniruddha Bapu, and usually calls him every two to three months like old friends. He has not attended any of his religious discourses or visited him in the last several years. It sounds a little surprising and also somewhat shocking that the modern Sai Baba talks to his old friends or gossips with them as if no serious transformation has occurred or that he is now a different, divine being.

Any way, it appears to us that Aniruddha Bapu's initial reservations about his new role must have probably passed through several phases till he finally chose to present himself as a reincarnation of Shirdi Sai Baba - he instructed the Dabholkar family keep it a secret for two long years, and then comes his declaration of being a reincarnation. One does not know what transpired between his family and close friends in these two years till the declaration of his reincarnation.

Further, we also strongly feel that one cannot take seriously his contention that he has never claimed to be a reincarnation - he has not missed any opportunity of getting worshipped by his devotees who eulogise him as God and also as a divine reincarnation. As a matter of fact, it becomes apparent once you enter his building that every attempt is being made not only to accept him as the reincarnation of Sai Baba but also that of Vishnu or Ram. Even his wife and a colleague call themselves divine beings. Even the magazine Kripa Sindhu regularly published by his disciples is full of incidents where Bapu has involuntarily come to the rescue of his devotees in their troubles such as illness, depression, loss of confidence, family quarrels, financial crisis etc.

These make believe acts of Bapu and his other pursuits are paradoxical and without rational explanation. But so are Indian minds, especially of eminent personalities. This apparent contradiction is not only astonishing but shocking. All his discourses are based on the purans and Indian mythology, which do not even align with the six major schools of Indian philosophy. In his public discourse, he is no better than an ordinary semi-literate or literate hordes of gurus one comes across in many parts of India.

Partly it is a clever device to play upon the sentiments and beliefs of ordinary people. All god men liberally indulge in such practices and Aniruddha Bapu is no exception. As a matter of fact, Bapu surprised other godmen by openly inserting his wife and colleague whose names are also included in the arti sung by devotees every day. Aniruddha Bapu expects his devotees to chart his name along with the Hanuman chalisa as he has declared himself to be an incarnate of Ram and Vishnu too. Thus he projects himse

lf as a divine being come to earth to deal with all its material miseries.

Bapu's projection as God is also strikingly evident in all his religious discourses and publications. But devotees, even highly educated people, accept and worship him as superhuman. This raises a crucial question about our intellectual convictions, mindsets and beliefs. An average Indian, especially our intellectuals, scientists, medical practioners, leaders and professionals, exhibit a strong faith in mythology, idol worship, and performance of religious ceremonies. All important events right from birth, marriage and death to bhumipujan are carried out as per religious guidelines. There are temples constructed in each caste locality and even communities dominated by professionals, scientists and such other luminaries. They also like to have temples of their traditional god in their residences and worship in these temples regularly. Even after independence, right from the late Pandit Jawahar Lal Nehru to late president Rajendra Prasad, leaders display no hesitation in participating in religious functions even in their official capacity. Another contention is that an average Indian has multiple levels of existence. It seems there are blocks in our mind, closed from each other like water tight compartments where one can indulge in activities that may not fit into or may be totally alien to the framework of another block. We are accustomed to live with these multiple levels of existence, without bothering our conscience about such contradictions. This has become such a normal practise that hardly anyone questions it.

The prevalence of such a situation on an extensive scale leaves enough room for Aniruddha Bapu and several others belongings to this group to prosper.

Appendix to Anniruddh Bapu

— By Roozbeh Gazdar.

An accomplished medical doctor, Mumbai-based Aniruddha Joshi is today revered by millions as the reincarnation of the Sai Baba of Shirdi. Credited with having performed many miracles, he nevertheless advocates a practical blend of spirituality and science. Aniruddha Bapu's charitable activities, conservation, inter-faith beliefs and scientific attitude blend seamlessly.

Aniruddha Bapu's blend of spiritual wisdom and pragmatism appeals in today's material world with its fast pace and slackening spiritual mores.

'Digambara, digambara, shripad vallabh digambara...', a bhajan plays on. It is 7:30 pm on a chilly December evening as I wait in the compound of the New English School in Kherwadi, Mumbai. People have filled the ground in front of an elaborately decorated stage; beyond, separated by a grill, the school's lobby is packed to capacity. I am lucky to be here; many others have had to be accommodated inside the school building, and will only witness the evening's proceedings courtesy close circuit television. Others have settled outside the compound walls, on the footpaths and in an open ground across the road, eyes glued to a big screen put up for their benefit.

Around 7:50 pm., the excitement among the gathering is palpable. Suddenly, the blowing of a conch shell causes a stir in the crowd. All eyes expectantly turn towards the path leading to the gate. A whisper rings through the throng: "Bapu *aale, Bapu aale*." A pair of turbaned, traditionally dressed musicians march stiffly blowing on *tutaris* (wind instrument), followed by a pair of similarly dressed sentries. Behind, walking briskly, casually waving to the crowd, in white shirt, black trousers, and leather *chappals,* is a fifty-something man, tall and athletic. The people in the audience bow in reverence, hands folded. He responds drooping moustaches accentuate a friendly smile, his eyes twinkle; he seems to greet some individually. For the lakhs of his devotees assembled here, he is Aniruddha Bapu, the reincarnation of the Sai Baba of Shirdi.

Born in 1956, Aniruddha Joshi studied at a school in Parel, before following in his father's footsteps and opting for medicine. A brilliant student and gold medallist, he gained his MD, specialising in rheumatology. A lecturer in Nair Hospital till 1985 he later started his private practice in Dadar and Parel, which he continued till 1998.

A married man with two children, Dr. Joshi led a normal life, until around 1981, when he started studying *Ayurveda* from *Vaidya Antarkar* and experienced a radical shift in his thinking. This doctor began to realise the superiority of this system over Allopathy. It also made him mull over what had gone wrong with the system - why had ayurveda stopped progressing? Looking for answers, he had an insight into the role of spirituality in society. Social progress, he realised, was hindered as spiritual values ceased to be important.

But the transition from Dr. Aniruddha Joshi to Aniruddha Bapu has an interesting story behind it. Before taking samadhi in 1918, the Sai Baba of Shirdi had given three of his personal belongings to Govind Raghunath Dabholkar (also known as Hemadpant), a close devotee of his, assuring him that he would return one day to claim these articles. The articles, a shaligram (holy stone used in Puja), a small trishul and a rosary passed on to Hemadpant's son Gajanan Govind Dabholkar, who in his last days gave them to his son Govind Gajanan Dabholkar also known as Appa Dabholkar. This fact was, however, a closely guarded secret, known only to the family.

Sai Niwas, the ancestral home of the Dabholkars in Bandra, has always been associated with Sai Baba. The Sai puja, held here daily since 1911, draws hordes of devotees. Dr. Joshi, himself a Sai bhakt, thus came first to Sai Niwas in 1993. Known then to the Dabholkars as an eminent doctor, he immediately impressed them with his modesty, simple and joyful ways and his profound yet lucid explanation of religious scriptures.

On May 27, 1996, Dr. Joshi went to Sai Niwas and asked for the articles belonging to Sai Baba. "We were stunned. We bowed in reverence as we saw him manifest in the form of Shirdi Sai Baba," recalls Dabholkar, whose wife and children were also present to witness the event. However, they were asked to keep this encounter to themselves till Bapu gave them permission to talk about it in 1998. "This was not the first occasion on which Bapu declared his divinity. It had been predicted to his great-grandfather that Lord Vitthal would take birth in his home and thus his family was always aware of his divine status," maintains Dabholkar.

As word spread, believers started flocking around Aniruddha Bapu or Sadguru as he came to be known. Today, lakhs of devotees in and outside Maharashtra and even abroad consider him to be the avtar of Mahavishnu. Nandmata, Bapu's wife, is also worshipped as Laksmi avatar. A former student of his, Dr. Suchit Dada's clinic draws many patients seeking a cure and Bapu is supposed to work his miracles through him.

For various devotees from all walks of life, Aniruddha Bapu has proved to be a turning point in life. "It is as if a miracle has taken place in my life," says Sandhyaveera Jaikar, who is actively involved with the movement. "I have been attending the *pravachans* (discourses) and taking an active part in the various socio-cultural activities. I have been exposed to a world beyond the four walls of my house. My life has taken such a turn for the better," she exclaims.

For the Dabholkars, their devotion to Sai Baba had borne fruit. The Sadguru had once again entered the lives of the family in human form. 'He is full of *prem* and *karuna* and forgives easily. He teaches that though men make mistakes, they can always be corrected. He remembers the name of every devotee he meets, even children, whom he especially loves. Not only humans, even animals are drawn towards him. Cows come to him when he calls them by name and when he talks to them, they have tears in their eyes. Today we are privileged to experience God in human form," Dabholkar says.

Sadhnatai Upadhye retired as the head of the Marathi department in Wilson College. 'When my husband died,' she recalls, "I had lost all hope. Confining myself in my house, I just used to read my books. Meeting Bapu helped me to open the windows of my heart, and I started attending his discourses and participating in his activities,' she says.

'He has come to remove the decadence that has set in the world today. He works day and night for the people. When others see the work he is doing, they are also inspired to dedicate themselves to his service. Working for Aniruddha Bapu, I feel that I am working for society and the nation."

In fact, Sadhnatai had been first graced with his darshan when during her pregnancy in 1964 she used to visit the Vitthal Mandir in Wadala. There she once met a small boy with a happy smile who gave her a peacock feather and touched her belly. A woman accompanying the boy remarked then that her baby had been blessed by Lord Vitthal himself. Years later, when he himself reminded her about the incident, she realised that the child was none other than eight year-old Aniruddha himself.

Dabholkar has an interesting observation to make. 'In the Sai Satcharita, Sai Baba has said that he would take rebirth when eight years of age. This refers to his age when the outside world would first experience his grace, just as Sadhnatai did,' he explains.

Dr. Santosh Salagre, a lecturer in medicine, is also sure that Bapu has come to alleviate the ills of the world. "We see such lot of the effects of kaliyug today. I realised that just like Shri Ram and Shri Krishna (before him), Bapu too has taken birth to solve the problems of our world," he says.

Dr. Keshav Narsikar studied with Dr. Joshi in Ruia College and later in Nair Medical College from 1972 to 1979.

'He was exceptionally brilliant and could cite from any textbook, even giving cross-references off hand. This is not possible even for an above average student," he recalls. "He was interested in dramatics and was famous for his excellent oratory and mimicry. Always cordial, he would go out of his way to help others. His entire outlook, even as a student, was very different," reveals Dr. Narsikar. Though clueless about Bapu's spiritual credentials, he says: "I always respected him and found consolation in his company." Today he has no doubt that his former classmate is indeed a Sadguru.

'Thousands of people have experienced sudden transformation, some experiences cannot be explained by material sciences,' he explains, adding that he makes it a point to regularly attend the evening discourses.

Filmmaker Shrabani Deodhar, though spiritual from a young age, "did not fancy the worship of human beings". She went to Bapu's programme out of curiosity while working on a TV serial about Shirdi Sai Baba. She says: "I am not from a background where I get carried away easily, but I was soothed and felt very strongly drawn to Bapu." Suffering from health problems as a result of work pressure, she met Dr. Suchit Dada at his clinic who assured her that she would be completely cured. Thereafter she was privileged to have a personal meeting with Bapu which she describes as an intense psychoanalytical session. "I had a lot of fear inside me, such as the fear of death that I was not even aware of. During the session all this came out as I learnt how to fight my fear-psychosis. And from there my life really took off. I feel he has come into our life in a big way. He is really our sadguru," she says. "The whole approach taught by him has made life so beautiful."

However, Bapu himself has never claimed to be an avtar. In fact, he denies the new role thrust upon him, repeatedly pointing out that Sai Baba was a brahmachari while he himself is a family man. In an interview with the Marathi weekly Lok Prabha, incidentally the first and only press interview that he agreed to, he explained the claim of reincarnation, 'I had casually asked Appa Dabholkar if he had in his possession any articles given to his grandfather by Sai Baba.'

Whether an enlightened doctor preaching spiritual values or an avtar of Sai Baba, going by the phenomenal numbers that flock to his discourses held every Thursday evening, Mumbai has given its heart to the sadguru who even dresses in the city's own cosmopolitan garb.

One reason for this, according to Wing commander (retd.) Ravindra Parasnis is that Bapu, even before he came to be known as sadguru, was a competent doctor with a reputation for curing many incurable conditions. Again he has always been involved in social work and has successfully brought back people who had gone astray, such as drug addicts and alcoholics. "Also, as a guru he is great and gives practical and good advice,' he feels. Though personally not sure about his divinity as an avtar of God, he says: "I definitely respect him as a guru. I have attended only a few of his pravachans but I like what he preaches."

Wing Commander Parasnis has a point. Instead of an abstruse philosophy that can be comprehended by few, Bapu's teachings boil down to common sense, pure and simple. While teaching bhakti (devotion), he stresses sincerity and awareness.

'For naamsmaran (recitation of the name of God) any name will do, but with awareness,' he says.

'If pressed for time, it is okay to perform puja without taking a bath, rather than not doing it all,' he clarifies. Disapproving of those who renounce their domestic duties in the pursuit of God, he preaches that a few minutes spent daily thinking about God are sufficient.

Harking back, perhaps to his training as a doctor, Bapu strongly advocates an intelligent and scientific approach to life. This blend of spiritual wisdom and pragmatism especially appeals in today

's increasingly materialistic world with its fast-paced schedules and slackening spiritual mores, and perhaps explains the presence of a large number of youth among his devotees.

A crusader against superstition and blind faith since his medical days, another facet to Bapu is his role as a social reformer. He has often spoken about the need to eradicate social ills such as caste discrimination and the low status accorded to widows, even declaring that if Manusmriti (Manu's Laws) cannot benefit all, it must be discarded. At the Ramnavmi mahotsavs organised by him, the puja is conducted by volunteers, including members of the lower castes. Widows, traditionally debarred from religious ceremonies, also take part in auspicious rites.

'What Bapu preaches, he himself practises and even the last rites of his parents were conducted by volunteers from amongst his devotees,' confirms Sunil Mantri, a devotee.

Bapu exhorts his disciples to read Sai Satcharita, Sai Baba's biography written by Hemadpant. To ensure the scientific study of this message, he introduced the panchsheel examination: a set of five exams including practicals at the final level, held twice each year for which thousands of students appear. Dr. Salagre refers to the exams as "milestones of my spiritual progress."

In 1999, Aniruddha Bapu established a gurukul at Juinagar for the propagation of ayurveda and mudgal vidya, the martial arts of ancient India. The Govidyapeetham established in Karjat near Mumbai aims to study the rearing and breeding of cows, combining modern veterinary science with ancient techniques.

For the establishment of 'Ramrajya' by year 2025, Bapu instituted the Aniruddha Samarpan Pathak and the Sadguru Shree Aniruddha Upasana Trust (SSAUT). Inspired by his words "Tu ani mi milun ashakya ase hya jagat kahihi nahi" (There is nothing that you and I together cannot achieve), volunteers involve themselves in social work including rehabilation of leprosy patients, holding blood donation camps, working for the blind, running de-addiction centres and hygiene awareness. A welfare centre for earthquake victims opened in June 2001, in Kharoi village, Kutch, with a team of volunteers, including qualified medical professionals administering treatment. As part of the rural development scheme, a few villages in Dhule, Maharashtra have been adopted by the SSAUT.

'Bapu teaches us different responsibilities, including our social responsibility,' feels Mantri, himself a volunteer and member of the Aniruddha Samarpan Pathak. A unique '13-point programme' was announced by Bapu on October 3, 2002. Its aim: to achieve 'Samartha Bharat', a strong and self-reliant India.

The discourse delivered, it is well past midnight as Bapu walks down the path leading to the gate. I had come here full of questions. Does God walk the earth as a man? Wear a shirt and pants? Go to medical college? I am still not sure I have the answers. But what the heck, I think. Heaven alone cannot lay claim to God. What about His work? People being taught the right path, rediscovering their spiritual selves. Volunteers committing themselves to the uplift of society. Youthful lives rescued from the clutches of drugs and alcohol. Needy students given the chance of a better life. If there is God, then He is here. On earth, among us, wherever his work is.

The crowd picks up a chant. Egged on by Bapu, it grows louder.

'Waheguru Ji Ka Khalsa! Waheguru Ji ki Fateh!

' Originally a Sikh salutation, the words

'Hail the Khalsa (pure) who belongs to God! Hail God to whom belongs to victory!' ring loud in my ears as I make my way home.

CONSLUSION : Religion, Globalization and Alienation

India has witnessed a massive upsurge of a multitude of religio-mystical cults of godmen, swamis, gurus, shastris, bapus and bhagats after independence, particularly during the last three decades. Some of these cults are local while some have established an extensive network at the national as well as international level. What is being witnessed by this country is not an isolated phenomenon. As so aptly pointed out by Meera Nanda, globalization is making the world more religious, and all religions more political. Even as people are drawing closer economically, people all over the world are becoming more self conscious of their religious and civilizational heritage. Globalization, it seems, has been good for Gods. Meera Nanda sums up this development as follows:

1. As India is liberalizing and globalizing in its economy, the country is experiencing a popular tide of Hinduism which is leaving no social segment or public institution untouched. There is a surge in popular religiosity among the largely Hindu middle classes as is evident from a boom in pilgrimage and invention of new and more ostentatious rituals.
2. This religiosity is being cultivated by the emerging state-temple corporate complex which is replacing the more secular public institutions of the Nehruvian era.
3. Aided by the new political economy, a new Hindu religiosity is getting evermore deeply embedded in the everyday life, both in the public and the private spheres. Use of explicitly Hindu rituals and symbols has become so common that Hinduism has become the de facto religion of the secular India.
4. Given India's growing visibility in the global economy, Hindu religiosity is getting fused with feelings of national pride and dreams of becoming a super power. The country's economic success is being attributed to the superiority of Hindu values and India is seen as entitled to the "Great

Power" status. Thus, the hardwork and achievements of all of India's diverse traditions and cultures are being absorbed into the religion of the majority community.

5. This new culture of political Hinduism is both triumphalist and intolerant in equal measures. While it wants the entire world to admire the superior tolerance and non violence of Hindus, it tolerates intolerance and even violence against religious minorities at home.

On the basis of the material obtained from the mass media, opinion polls, government reports, research reports of think tanks, and websites of temples and ashrams, the author draws the following inferences:

1. The newly prosperous middle classes are turning away from the more philosophical, new Vedantic form of religiosity and embracing a more ritualistic and superstitious form of Hiduism centered on temples, pilgrimages, and popular saints or godmen. The signs of the rising religiosity are all around us. There is a boom in the construction of temples and mega temples, some of which house gentrified gods and goddesses while others offer newly invented or ancient rituals. The number of people following rituals is rising.
2. This religiosity is becoming more and more public and political. Religious observances like homas (yagnas), jagrans and kathas that used to be relatively simple domestic affairs are becoming more expensive and public. In addition, religious rituals like yagnas and yatras (pilgrimages) are becoming mobilizing tools for political causes of all sorts, from benign ones like protecting the environment and preventing AIDS to the more sinister shobha yatras and samaj mahotsavs (social festivals) which are meant to consolidate majority Hindu consciousness.
3. The rise in religiosity has the support of the leading institutions of the state, temples and the business sector, often working in a three-sided partnership.

This rising Hindu religiosity is explained by suggesting that Indians are innately more other-worldly and that Hinduism is a total way of life, in which spiritual motives cannot be separated from the other spheres of life. While the rest of the world might be expected to become less religious with modernity, India will always be religious.

Meera Nanda treats religiosity as any other cultural phenomena with pros and cons and changing with time. She describes that the rise in religiosity can be explained by the emergence of the state-temple-corporate complex that is filling the space that the "socialist" state of the Nehruvian era has ceded to the private sector.

In a sense, the existence of the nexus between the state, temples and the private sector is nothing new, the supposedly secular state of India has never been inhibited in celebrating Hindu religious symbols in a public sphere - all in the name of propagating Indian cultures. Merchants and business houses too have a long history of sponsoring temples and monasteries devoted to their own Gods or gurus.

But the present neo-liberal economic regime is bringing the state, religious establishments and the business-corporate elite in a much closer relationship than ever before. As the Indian state is withdrawing from its public sector obligations, it is actively seeking partnership with the private sector like tourist facilities and other social services. As a result, public funds earmarked for creating public goods are increasingly being diverted to facilitating the work of these private charitable institutions which bear a distinctly Hindu traditionalist bias. This is helping to modernize Hinduism. Many of the newly minted English-speaking and computer savvy priests, astrologers, vastushastris and yoga teachers, who service the middle class's insatiable apetite for religious rituals are products of the nexus between the state, corporate sector and temples.

The rising religiosity among Hindus is not an isolated phenomenon. As a matter of fact, Hindutva neo-liberals are the closest ideological cousins of, as Meera Nanda suggests, American religious neo-conservatives, the "theocons" who justify their fervent American nationalism and their ardent admiration of capitalism in a theological world view derived from the natural law traditions of Roman Catholicism. Unlike the main line protestant denominations who accept (at least in principle) the fundamental American creed of church-state separation, American theocons see the very idea of secular society as an abomination and the primary source of the cultural pathologies of the American society. Theocons, who have provided the philosophical justification for George Bush's so called "faith-based initiatives" insist that Christian faith is the pre-condition of the American nation and the pre-requisite for the functioning of capitalist free markets.

The Indian theocons or Hindutva neo-liberals also insist that Hinduism is the pre-condition for the Indian nation and a pre-requisite for the proper functioning of Indian capitalism.

These theocons such as Subramanian Swami and his fellow Hindutva neo-liberals insist that the state should have a minimal role in economic affairs but maximum role in the propagation of Hinduism. The state is exorted to teach the "correct" reading of history which makes India the homeland of Aryans and to bring science and Hindu spiritualism together in classrooms in order to promote an indic model of education.

The new Indian middle class composed of white collar workers in the new internet enabled global service industry - banking, accounting, insurance, hotels, tourism etc, although numerically smaller than the traditional middle class of shopkeepers, businessmen, government officials, teachers, and land-owning farmers, exercises tremendous influence and is much admired for putting India on the global map as an emerging world power.

Estimates about the size of this so-called middle class vary, but the two most important surveys put the numbers anywhere between 60 million and 300 million. According to the Indian National Council of Applied Economic Research, the term middle class applies to those earning between Rs. 200,000 and 1000,000 annually. By this definition, about 6% of 1 billion Indians were middle class in the year 2000-01, with close to 22% being the "aspiring class" that expected to catch up in a decade or so. But middleclassness is measured by the ownership of middle class goods - telephones, motor vehicles (two-wheeler or four-wheeler), television sets etc. Close to one-fifth of India was already middle class in 2007 as the State of the Nation Survey by CNN and IBN revealed.

Going by the recent Pew Global Attitudes Survey, the new middle class in India is overwhelmingly pro-free markets. A solid 89% of Indian respondents supported free trade, 73% welcomed foreign companies (comparable figures for the US bastion of unrestrained capitalism are

59, 45 and 70% respectively) and a solid 76% were in favour of free markets.

The Indian elite and middle classes exhibit a high degree of tolerance for the inhuman levels of poverty and deprivation all around them and the trait could well derive from the Hindu concept of karmic justice and the individualistic concept of salvation (moksha) in Hinduism.

The new middle class also shows equally promptness to drop another plank of the Nehruvian project - secularism. An overwhelming majority - 92% at the Pew Global Attitudes Survey mentioned earlier, claims that religion is very important to them. The educated and privileged sections of Indian society have never shown even the most mild resistance to the close involvement of elected leaders and government functionaries in their official capacities sponsoring and celebrating religious rituals in public. There is no sign of public protest against using government funds to support denominational schools, pilgrimages, yoga camps, yagnas and kathas. The only time anyone gets agitated about state support for religion is when the religion in question is someone else's religion such as Islam and Christianity. It's not surprising that the middle class share of votes for the BJP has been growing through the 1990s while the support for the Congress has been declining.

One important cultural trait of Indian classes which deserve consideration is their understanding of their religiosity and their view of modernity and science. Indian middle classes see themselves as modern under the pretext of rejecting blind faith. But scientific correctness, as Meera Nanda suggests, is the exact opposite of what the advocates of rationalism have in mind. Rather than developing a habit of critical thinking which subjects metaphysical assumptions to scientific scrutiny, educated Indians have shown great inclination for pseudo-scienticism as taught by Neo-Hindu philosophers, modern gurus and the peddlers of new age spiritualism. All the metaphysical concepts of traditional Hinduism - such as the existence of an all-pervasive notion of atman, shakti, or prana, survival of the soul after death, efficacies of yagnas in influencing human affairs; correspondence between the movement of stars and planets and the human life - are accepted as if they are backed by scientific evidence. This kind of Vedic-Hindu scienticism appears to have a wide appeal for educated and modern Indians.

The findings of reliable surveys conducted in India also seem to support that globalization is facilitating the spread of religiosity in India.

1. According to the 2007 State of the National Survey conducted by the Centre for the Study of Developing Society (CSDS) for IBN-CNN-Hindustan times, "Among Indians, the level of religiosity has gone up considerably during the last 5 years. While 30% said that they had become more religious, only 5% mentioned in negative."
2. The same survey findings also reveal that education and exposure to modern life will make Indians more, not less religious: "Urban educated Indians are more religious than their rural and literate counterparts. Religiosity has increased more in small towns and cities than in villages."
3. Hindus are not the only ones becoming more religious. The same survey shows that 38% of Indian Muslims, 47% of the Christians and 33% of Sikhs, as compared to 27% Hindus, claimed to have become more religious in the last 5 years.
4. It is also pertinent to note that according to the same survey, over one third of the respondents stated that religiosity had increased among their family members and the educated. The proportion of religiousity is higher particularly among those educated above secondary level and also the upper castes (27%) and peasant proprietary castes (25%). Both among Hindus and Muslims, the upper class are more religious than the poor. So it seems religiosity is a pastime of the high and the rich.
5. The number of registered religious buildings in Delhi grew from a mere 560 in 1980 to 2000 in 1987, with similar trends reported from other parts of the country.
6. In his widely acclaimed book, Being Indian (2004), Pavan Varma reports that around the turn of the millennium, the country had 2.5 million places of worship, but only 1.5 million schools and barely 75,000 hospitals. His observation is based on data from the 2001 census.

7. Another measurable indicator of growing religiosity is the tremendous rise in pilgrimages. According to a recent study by the NCAER, religious trips account for more than 50% of package tours, much higher than leisure tour packages at 28%. The most recent figures show that in 2004, more than 23 million people visited the Balaji temple at Tirupati, while 17.25 million trekked to the mountain shrine of Vaishno Devi.

The phenomenon of rising religiosity in this period of rapid technological innovations and economic growth is neither particularly new nor uniquely Indian. Religions everywhere seem to have learnt to coexist with the infrastructure of modernity. But Indians are, as Meera Nanda argues, well known for being harmonius schizophrenics who live in many different worlds at the same time. Most educated Indians seem to switch effortlessly from the profane to the sacred, from the lab to the temple and back, without being troubled by the contradictions between the operative beliefs in the two spheres. As a scientist once said, many of us are double people. As scientists we are rational, but when we leave the laboratory and go home, we behave differently.

This phenomenon of keeping modern ideas and religious traditions in two separate compartments as suggested by Milton Singer and mixing them as and when required to basically validate and uphold the superiority of tradition is nothing new. What is new now is that the contents of the compartment marked the "Great Tradition" of Hinduism are being re-ritualized and re-enchanted.

The earlier generation of Indians defined the essence of Hinduism in Neo-Vedantic terms while re-emphasizing rituals and temple worship in favor of "rational" mysticism centered on philosophical reflections and meditative contemplation of the impersonal Brahman. The rituals, pujas, pilgrimages etc. were by and large left for the domestic spheres of wives and daughters.

This tendency to downgrade the popular ritualism in favor of scriptural is actually the legacy of Hindu Renaissance that started in the 18th century but continued well into the 20th century. It should also be noted that the Indian social reformers of the 19th century, right from Raja Ram Mohan Roy, Ishwar Chandra Vidyasagar, Ranade and Gokhale were influenced by the western, democratic and liberal value system but upheld Indian Vedic traditions. They only suggested that in

Vedic times, Indians too practiced such values. Thus, they were in favor of imbibing western liberal values and democratic traditions for Indian society while defending the Indian Vedic system. This was also true partly of humanists and rationalists like Jawaharlal Nehru, while B.R Ambedkar, M.N. Roy and Bhagat Singh were very critical of Hindu legacy and institutional structure.

India's modern gurus with their urban middle class followers go to the other extreme of rejecting western culture, liberal values and other legacies of enlightenment and blindly uphold Indian religious traditions, and these are not even the Vedic or Upanishadic concepts of atman and Brahman and their fusion but the traditional rituals, festivals and other activities based on superstitions based on the blind faith.

Thus, the earlier philosophized or secular-humanist version of Hinduism that appealed to the earlier generation of elites doesn't seem to satisfy the religious cravings of contemporary middle and upper classes. They are instead craving for jagrit Gods who respond to their prayers and fulfill their wishes - the kind of Gods who are personal, caring and loving. As Meera Nanda suggests, the textual or philosophical aspects of Sankritic Hinduism have by no means diminished in cultural prestige; they continue to serve as the backdrop of "Vedic Sciences" and new age spiritualism, and continue to attract a loyal following of spiritual seekers from India and abroad. Nevertheless, what is changing is simply that it is becoming fashionable to be religious in the theistic (sagun bhakti) tradition of popular Hinduism and to be seen as being religious in this manner. The new elites are shedding their earlier reservation about openly participating in religious rituals in temples and public ceremonies like kathas, jagratas and yagnas. The ritual dimension is thus becoming more pronounced.

It's not easy to generalize about the religious behavior patterns of people in a country as vast as India. But what appears to be apparent and more pronounced is the invention of new rituals and new gods. Old gods are getting a face lift and new gurus are mixing spiritualism with capitalism, consumerism with often blatant Hindu chauvinism.

Hindutva Ideologs and Modern Gurus

Supporters of Hindutva are fully aware of the usefulness of the new gurus for the cause. In the words of Swapan Dasgupta, an ex-

Trotskyite historian who now supports Hindu nationalist causes, "the real energy of contemporary Hinduism doesn't lie in Brahminical institutions like the Shankaracharya of Kanchi." What drives Hindus are either venerated temples or individual preachers and "living saints". They are to Hinduism what evangelical preachers are to Christianity and Dasgupta urges the leaders of the Sangh Parivaar to invite them to lead the Hindutva cause.

There is a thriving tradition of what can be loosely called evangelical Hinduism. It comprises the likes of Asharam Bapu, Morari Bapu, Baba Ramdev, Ma Amritanandmayi, Satya Sai Baba, Shri Ravi Shankar and many others who feature on the various religious channels on television. They are the Pet Robertsons & Billy Grahams of modern Hinduism. They are able to inspire and motivate individual Hindus far more successfully than purohits and pontiffs. The failure of organized Hindu nationalism lies in not being able to link the congregations of individual evangelists with bodies like the Hindu Acharya Sabha.

The Sangh Parivar seems to have paid heed to this advice. There were reports that the VHP listed Shri Ravi Shankar, Baba Ramdev, Morari Bapu, Asharam Bapu and Pranav Pandya of the Gayatri Parivar to create an allaince that would marry political, religious, and environmental causes in the run up to the 2009 elections. As a matter of fact, all these gurus, with the exception of Shri Ravi Shankar, were members of the VHP's Dharma Raksha Manch which campaigned for a Hindu vote bank and the BJP in the 2009 elections. Rather than embark upon communally charged yatras over the Ram temple and other such issues, they encourage "constructive agitations" around issues of cleaning the Ganga, saving Adams bridge, and "saving" temples from government interference. The objective is to use the goodwill these gurus have among the middle classes to reach out to moderate Hindus who may be fed up with the Ram temple but may be more open to concern about the environment and temple affairs in general.

One inference that can be safely drawn on the basis of the survey of new religiosity is that education and upward mobility do not necessarily lead to any serious questioning of the reality of supernatural beings, powers, the possibility of miracles or the efficacy of rituals and prayers. In this sense, even middle classes challenge Max Weber's assumption of being modern leading to disenchantment. The Indian middle class, as a matter of fact, is indicating that one can very well make a good living out of mastering modern technology and education, and still continue to have recourse to magical belief for resolving worldly problems.

The popular assumption in the west that religiosity is adversely related to income, because the poor show greater inclination for worship than the rich, doesn't seem to apply to the Indian situation. Here we have a case of rising religiosity among the already wealthy and upwardly mobile, whose level of material well-being is fairly decent even by western standards. Clearly, the gains in existential security from improved material well-being are not translating into a decline in religiosity in India.

Even the explanation of religiosity, as provided by Pavan Verma, the author of the much cited 'The Great Indian Middle Class' as a refuge for the alienated and lonely urbanites, uprooted from the old warm little communities they left behind in villages, doesn't seem to be very relevant. Verma simply assumes that modern life in the cities must be traumatic and drives the new middle classes to seek the consolation of God in the company of fellow believers. Even Achin Vanaik suggests a more simplistic explanation for middle class receptivity to Hindu preachers as a "balm for the social despair due to loss of dignity and typically self respect," which comes from neo-liberalism.

Social despair doesn't seem to be the soul of or a significant explanation for the new middle class to opt for greater religiosity. There is anxiety and insecurity even among the newly well-to-do as they face increasing competition in an economy with declining job security. But as Meera Nanda suggests, there is also a sense of expanding horizons and multiplying opportunities. It is not despair or alienation but rather ambivalence over the new-found wealth that seems to give a better explanation of the growing religiosity. Like in other religions, there are contradictions between Hindu theology and the actual social practices. While Hindu philosophical traditions degrade materialism in favor of renunciation, popular Hindu traditions worship wealth and material riches. Even when Indians are acquiring wealth at an unprecedented pace, it seems they are doing it with a bad conscience, as if they are violating the basic moral goal of their culture. Even while they certainly do not practice Gandhian philosophy by any stretch of imagination, they still like to glorify Gandhian simplicity as a cultural ideal.

In this context, it seems modern gurus are coming to the rescue of Indian middle classes to help them overcome this ambivalence by giving new wealth a divine stamp of approval. "To be rich is divine" appears to be the message coming from the modern gurus who cater to the upper crust. "The Bhagwat Geeta and yoga sutras have been turned into self-help manuals for making money and achieving success." While blessing this worldly pursuits and pleasures, the new gurus also help their followers to overcome guilt by teaching them how to balance it with spiritual aspirations. For example, gurus like Mata Amritanandamayi preach that western consumerism creates a bad karmic burden which can be negated, or at least "balanced" by performing some of the rituals and pujas she prescribes. As Meera Nanda suggests, this amounts to flippancy - the cure for shopping is more shopping, but this time for spiritual products and the services of gurus and priests. Surely, a win-win situation for all involved.

In her concluding remarks, she observes, "There is, however, another factor that is making public expressions of religiosity fashionable, namely the rising level of nationalism." Indians top the list of all nations when it comes to a sense of cultural superiority. The 2007 Pew Global Attitudes Survey brought out that as many as 93% of Indian respondents, the highest in the world, agreed that "Our people are not perfect but our culture is superior to others." In comparison, the Chinese, Japanese and American public opinion was far more self critical and ambiguous over the superiority of their culture. Being used to a staple diet of religious, media and other cultural discourses as the essence of Hindu culture, it has become almost second nature for educated Indians to mix the two. As India is becoming a significant player in the global market, there is an increasing tendency to ascribe the country's success to the superiority of Hindu values. This sentiment is being aggressively promoted by gurus and tele-yogis. Indeed, the public sphere is replete with such messages of becoming more Hindu in order to become more successful in the global race for money and power.

Nevertheless, it would not be correct to interprete the picture presented here as a proof that Hindu Indians are "naturally" more spiritual than other people. On the contrary, as Meera Nanda suggests, the explosion of popular Hindu religiosity is a result of the open and often hidden support that Hinduism has received and will continue to receive from the supposedly secular Indian government and India's corporate sector.[1]

Morari Bapu's popularity in the west and his increasing identification with the Hindutva brigade has to be understood in the context of the rising wave of Hinduism in the west as well as in India. Reports of Morari Bapu's recent Ram katha in New Jersey as part of the Swarnim Gujrat celebrations amply justify our above contention.

Apart from the major thrust on ideals such as truth, love, compassion and non-violence, Morari Bapu focuses on upholding traditional values cherished by patriarchal joint families. This is true of practically all Hindu saints who preach about Indian culture and values. The relevance of this teaching consists of upholding family honour, subordination to family elders, women's role being in the kitchen and serving the family, youngsters' obligation to their parents and elders and promoting the Chaturvarna system as advocated in the Bhagwad Geeta. This kind of moral sermon ideally suits the mindsets of Hindu NRIs settled in the USA. Many Indians settled in the USA since long have experience identity crises. It's neither easy for them, nor are they inclined to accept western democratic liberal values based on individual freedom to choose one's career, marriage partner, and to stay independently from the family right from adulthood. The apprehension regarding the younger generation's exposure to western education and culture of becoming independent and the possibility of their raising their voice against family heads in all important aspects of their life encourages NRIs to fall back on our traditional values and uphold unity and harmony in the family institution. The apprehension of revolt by the younger generations must be pulling them back to their traditional moorings. This identity crisis is an old phenomenon but this vigorous Hindu reinforcement is something new. As we suggested earlier, the downgrading of western values and culture among Indians is a new phenomenon. Morari Bapu strengthens and consolidates this position.

This trend is not confined only to USA. In India too, our modern gurus, irrespective of religious forum, opt for consciously upholding and propagating these feudal values and institutional structure. The message imparted is of domination of elders and subordination of juniors in the family and especially encouraging the submissive role of women, their ideal forte being the kitchen and family.[3]

This trend of dominance and subordination is not confined to the family - blind submission to authority has become the dominant trend in Indian society. In political life too, we see the domination of leaders and some families, and blind submission to authority. This is an extremely common phenomenon. Hence, the paradox of Indian democracy, that although the prevalence of the caste system is supposed to be the antithesis of democratic values, yet the casteist and communal hold over politics, instead of declining has continued to grow and dominate politics for decades. Thus, this upholding of feudal values is conducive to our leadership.

Modern gurus harp on the need for personal honesty and integrity and the indispensability of these virtues for one's spiritual happiness. But this exclusive thrust on personal honesty and integrity, with total indifference to the Indian reality, makes the whole exercise meaningless. Personal integrity and honesty become meaningful only when they are harnessed to the task of achieving the happiness of the world in which we live. If we remain blind to the miseries and sorrows of the overwhelming majority of our toiling population, and the causes that contribute to their problems, one's craving for individual happiness becomes meaningless.

The Upanishadic Rishis, and centuries later Shankara preached that man must release himself from the temptations of the flesh, from personal desires and attachments, and such disentanglement from worldly life leads to bliss or liberation, but for whom? Their reply was clear that categorical release from worldly involvement was for one's own happiness, one's own bliss, and one's own salvation. It had nothing to do with liberating society from toil and misery. Society was out of the picture. The ethics of the individual were not concerned with it. Hence it is suggested that such spiritual ethics are essentially egocentric ethics.[3]

Hence, both Buddha and the Lokayats rejected any supernatural origin of the universe. They accepted the reality of the world. They clearly recognized the misery and sorrow of the common people. Buddha's message was of love and compassion for the common people. The Lokayat creed was of protest and denunciation of the arrogant, the duplicity and the oppression of the gullible masses by the higher orders. It was the priesthood that led a parasitical life of peace and comfort, rendering little useful service to society while moralizing pompously on the pure ethics of spiritualism.

Prof. K.M. Pannicker, while referring to the massive upsurge of gurus and other religious activities in India since the last 4-5 decades, suggests that India has witnessed a rising religiosity and comodification of religion in the last few decades.[4]

This concept of comodification of religion is rooted in the concept of alienation, especially as defined by Karl Marx. Marx's concept of alienation has four main aspects:

1. Man is alienated from nature.
2. Man is alienated from himself (from his own activity).
3. Man is alienated from his species (from his being as a member of the human species).
4. Man is alienated from other men.

While commenting on Marx's concept of alienation, Erich Fromm says that Marx could foresee with amazing clarity how the needs of man in an alienated society would be perverted into his true weaknesses. In capitalism, as Marx understood,

'Every man speculates upon creating a new need in another in order to force him to a new sacrifice, to place him in a new dependence, and to entice him into a new kind of pleasure and thereby into economic ruin. Everyone tries to establish over others an alien power in order to find the satisfaction of his own egoistic need. With the mass of objects, therefore, there also increases the realm of alien entities to which man is subjected. Every new product is a new potentiality of new deceit and robbery. Man becomes increasingly poor as a man; his increasing need of money in order to take possession of the hostile being. The power of money diminishes directly with the growth of the quantity of production, that is, his need increases with the increasing power of money. The need for money is therefore the real need created by the modern economy, and the only need which it creates.'

Alienation is a sickness of the self, as Fromm suggests, to be at the core of the psychopathology of modern men even in those forms which are less extreme than psychosis.[5]

During the time when Marx lived, the problematic of the human situation was expressed mainly in terms of economic exploitation under the then capitalism. The new type of capitalism contains an almost irresistible tendency towards the universalisation of alienation. It tends to convert, in other words, "the totality of the social life and existence into an object of domination, with the intention of transforming all subjectivity and activity into reified objectivity". A process which previously had been more or less restricted to the sphere of market relations and had not penetrated private life. The present monopoly finance capitalism has turned all human beings into passive spectators of their own alienated existence. As a result of this process involving the progressive integration of the social whole, the growing interpenetration of the base and super structure, and the increasing diminution of the individual psychic space, it follows, as Marcuse put it in 1932, "The situation of capitalism is not only a question of economic or political crisis, but (is) a catastrophe of the human essence."

Thus, probably the main factor for the growing appeal of religion could be attributed to this root cause of total alienation of man in modern society. Alienation is so total that there is hardly left anything to the privacy of individual life. Monopoly finance capital has made such a deep inroad in individual life today that man has almost totally lost control over his real needs, aspirations and ambitions. The comodification of man is so deep that individuals in all walks of life - artists, sportsmen, actors, professionals, literary figures, academics - have become marketable commodities. Modern advertisements are glaring examples of the way in which the best of artists or sportspersons are being used as marketable commodity. This process creates an inner void for everyone in modern society. This total alienation from your real self paves the way for succumbing to all such appeals, especially religious appeals.

Alienation is a phenomenon being experienced by the rich as well as the poor. Reification is an all-pervading phenomenon affecting the upper as well as lower sections of society. Thus, the root cause of the miseries or spiritual void or craving for self realization, futility of existence, can be traced to this dominant phenomenon of monopoly finance capital. The solution lies in dealing with this phenomenon rather than rushing to gurus.

1. Nanda, Meera; Based on findings and observation in "The God Market- How globalization is making India more Hindu", Published by Random House India, 2009
2. Bapu in America; Internet Report
3. Fromm, Erich; Beyond the Chians of Illusion, CREDO PERSPECTIVE, PP 51-53, 1962
4. Pannikar, K. M; Ungodly Men, Unholy Activities, Godmen in Society compiled by Ram Puniyani, Vikas Adhyayan Kendra,
5. Brown, Bruce; Marx, Freud and the critique of everyday life, PP 13-14, 1973

Marx and Engels in their concrete appraisal of the role of religion through the ages highlighted its contradictory functions, its positive as well as negative significance. While indicating that historically the primary function of religion world over had been to sanctify repressive institutions, they have also brought out the fact that rebellious movements, among the oppressed in pre-bourgeois periods and even subsequently, the aims and aspirations of social agitations have also found expression in the needs and expectations of the insurgent masses.

Such observation also throw new light on Marx's dictum that religion is the opium of the masses, which is generally presumed to mean that religion is a drug which enables the toiling strata to bear their miseries by losing themselves in dreams that deprive them of the capacity to revolt. This is the conception of the Enlightenment philosophers and it is undoubtedly a good deal of what Marx meant, but it is not all that he meant. Immediately preceding his famous sentence is the sentence 'Religious distress is at the same time the expression of real distress and the protest against real distress. Opium dream could rouse to protest and struggle, could stimulate as well as stupefy.[2]

However, it should be pointed out that Engels thought that since the French revolution, religion has become incapable of serving any progressive class as the ideological vehicle of its aspirations. This is not true as borne out by the heroic contribution of liberation theology, particularly in several Latin American countries, in strengthening and extending the struggles of the oppressed and exploited against the ruling oligarchy. Similarly the role of the Catholic Church in the Polish liberation struggle and the solidarity movement of independent trade unions cannot be brushed aside as reactionary by any stretch of imagination. It has also been reported that Buddhist theology made a significant contribution in the heroic Vietnamese liberation war against American imperialism.

In this context, it should also be noted that the persistence and spread of religious influence in so called socialist countries as well as advanced capitalist nations do not disprove the validity of the Marxist observation on religion. As indicated earlier it was Engels who first suggested that till men acquire control over social forces (which would not be possible in all class societies), religion in some or the other form would persist. In this sense, it is neither in U.S.A. nor U.S.S.R, or for that matter even in China or in other countries, that the so called working class, toiling people have acquired command over social forces, nor has the exploitation or oppression of man by man has come to an end. This generates a climate of uncertainty and increasing insecurity leaving enough space for the flourishing of religious influences.

Religion in Modern Indian Society

As indicated earlier, India is experiencing a new wave of religious revivalism, especially since the last three decades. What is being projected as Hinduism in recent years is a novel concept based on a crude amalgam of various contradictory sets of beliefs, rituals and practices.

As pointed out by Romila Thapar, "The New Hinduism which is being currently propagated by the Sanghs, Parishads and Samajs is an attempt to restructure the indigenous religions as a monolithic, uniform religion rather than paralleling some of the features of semitic religions. Further, "Hindu" sects unlike Buddhism or Islam are characterized by a distinct and independent origin connecting them to a particular founder or text. Only at a later stage were attempts made to assimilate some of these sects into dominant sects. What has survived over the centuries is not a single, monolithic religion but a diversity of religious sects which today have been put together under a uniform name."[3]

Frequent reiteration by upper caste elites these days that Hinduism has passed through very severe persecution for the last thousand years conveniently ignores the fact that in the history of the last thousand years, Hinduism has witnessed the establishment of the powerful Shankaracharya Maths, ashramas and similar institutions attempting to provide all ecclesiastical structures to strengthen conservatism, the powerful Dashnamis and Bairagi religious orders, the popular cults of Nathpanthis, the extremely significant sects of the major Bhakti teachers such as Tukaram, Namdeo, Vallabhacharya, Chaitanya, Dadu and Kabir, not to mention Guru Nanak. Given that the establishment of these sects was accompanied by wealthy patronage, accounting for the prosperity of temples and institutions, the last thousand years have actually seen a most assertive thrust of the major 'Hindu' sects. As a matter of fact, the non-violence of Hinduism is a nineteenth century myth, largely invented as a response to the requirement of nationalism stressing the spiritual superiority of Indian culture.[4]

Romila Thapar has aptly coined the new tern 'syndicated Hinduism' for modern Hinduism. According to her, "Syndicated Hinduism draws largely on Brahminical texts, the Gita and Vedantic thought, accepts some aspects of the Dharma Sutras and attempts to present a modern and reformed religion. It ends up inevitably as a garbled form of Brahminism with a motley of 'values' drawn from other sources, such as bringing in elements of individual salvation from the Bhakti tradition of some puranic rituals. Its contradictions are many. The call to unite under Hinduism as a political identity is anachronistic. [5]

This new Hindu phenomenon has acquired strength as result of the widening of the social base of political Hinduism in the post-independence period. The backward castes or more appropriately 'the other backward classes' who benefitted from the initial phase of agrarian reforms have now entered the socio-religious spheres which were till recently preserves of the upper caste Hindus and have developed stakes in them. This phenomenon is also described as a process of political Sanskritization. Large scale mobilizations such as the Ekatmata Yagya and the Ram Janmabhoomi Andolan in all probability would not be possible without the actual involvement of this enlarged base. Moreover, the following observation deserves attention: "The closing of ranks between the upper castes and the backward castes in recent times seeks external enemies in order to consolidate its somewhat uneasy solidarity. Hindu communalism directed against minorities and scheduled castes is one of the outcomes".[6]

Nineteenth Century Religious Reform Movements and Modern Hinduism

The chauvinistic thrust of the new Hinduism becomes strikingly evident if one compares it with the dominant spirit of the religious reform movement of the nineteenth century and the Bhakti movement of medieval India.

The modernization introduced by the British despite its distorted nature encouraged a secular and rational outlook, scientific knowledge and technical skills, new ways of thinking and self-reliance. It was a process by which men began to break away from medieval customs and superstitions and the fatalism based on traditional beliefs in *karma, maya* and transmigration of the soul and by which new occupations and new relations among men began to emerge.[7]

As brought out by the late Mr. Damodaran, "The 19th century thinker though could not completely free himself from the concept of the supernatural but he began to interpret karma creatively instead of in its totality. The concept of karma underwent a radical change. Fatalism gave way to a new sense of strength and confidence. The new thinker asserted that caste distinctions, priests and animal sacrifices and customs like sati and child marriage were not ordained by God or karma, but were created by man's ignorance."[8]

Raja Ram Mohan Roy inaugurated the modern age in India. He opposed the caste system, idol worship, religious separatism, child marriage and the practice of sati. He advocated remarriage of widows, inter-caste marriages, English education and freedom of speech. He founded the Brahmo Samaj, the teachings of which are summarized as follows:

"The wide universe is the sacred temple of the Brahman, of the supreme being. The pure heart is the place of pilgrimage. Truth is the one eternal scripture. Faith is the foundation of all religions. Love is the desire and the only form of ascetic renunciation recognized and proclaimed by the members of the Brahmo Samaj."[9]

Further, "This universalism appears to be a synthesis of the best elements of the Upanishadic teachings and the ideas of Islam and Christianity".

Ranade also being inspired by the teachings of the Brahmo Samaj proclaimed intense faith in individual freedom and human dignity. He insisted that revival was impossible and that reform was the only alternative open to sensible people. The emphasis in life was no longer on mundane existence but the freedom of the individual was now interlinked with his social and political emancipation.

"In the middle ages," as so aptly argued by the late Damodaran, "Self-emancipation was interpreted as an escape from the idea of sansara, i.e., from social life. The ultimate aim of life was to end the cycle of births and deaths, to liberate the atman from the physical body and the material environment. But to the modern age the concept of self-realization assumed a new meaning. The self was no more abstracted from life. The self was the social life, the self was that could find the fullest being only in social life. Self-realization as the realization of the identity of the individual self with the universal self meant the identification of oneself with the whole of humanity. Man could realize himself only in another man, in the totality of human existence that is Brahman." Vivekananda himself explained this truth as follows:

"The individual's happiness is the happiness of the whole; apart from the whole, the individual's existence is inconceivable. This is an eternal truth and is the bed-rock on which the universe is built".[10]

As a matter of fact, freedom, democracy and human dignity were the values of the 19th century. Old values of renunciation, denial and withdrawal began to give place to social action. Concepts like *karma* and *dharma* assumed new meaning.

Nevertheless, inspite of the distinct contribution made by the 19th century religious reform movements, one should not overlook the fact that the Bengal renaissance as well as its counterpart in Maharashtra were essentially sponsored by upper caste elites who were initially exposed to western liberal ideas, values and aspirations based on democratic and scientific spirit. Although they came in sharp conflict with Sanatani orthodox Hindu religious protagonists, their impact was by and large confined to certain select intellectual circles.

In sharp contrast to this elitist movement, it is argued that the movement led by Jotirao Phule through the Satyashodhak Samaj founded by him in 1873, stood for a revolutionary transformation as against revitalization of the old social order sought by the former under the pretext of modernization.

As pointed out by Gail Omvedt, "Their identification was in the Hindu cultural system and as modern intellectuals concerned about the Hindu religion, they developed an ideology which sought to use a revitalized Hindu tradition as the spiritual and moral centre around which the liberal modernism of the West could be created".[11] This is also dubbed as "Eastern morals and Western science'. Upper caste elites accepted the "Aryan theory of race" which had the implication of identifying them ethnically with their British conquerors rather than a majority of their countrymen, which traced civilization in India from the Aryan conquest, and which provided a new pseudo-scientific justification for the caste hierarchy. They also developed an economic theory which looked to the capitalist development of India freed from the destructive bonds of British imperialism. Hence, they opposed foreign exploitation without considering the exploitation of workers by native capitalists or that of peasants by landlords and the lower bureaucracy.

It is further argued that the majority of Indians were dark-skinned non-Aryans. The majority of Indians were peasants and had no hope either in the near or distant future of becoming members of the bureaucratic elite or capitalist, large or small. The liberal modernization of the Hindu culture and the capitalist development of India did not conform to their interests. Peasants, tribals, workers, lower castes and untouchables were all adversely affected by the colonial regime and responded like the upper caste elites, lacking access to education, lacking control over communication, with both renaissance and rebellion. But their ideology and organization remained a mere incipient, crude, localized and incomplete form. Nevertheless it may be said that with Jotirao Phule, the lower caste, non- Aryan, peasant masses of India came into consciousness.[12]

While taking note of the fact that Dayanand Saraswati's version of Aryan culture was not racial as he stressed on acquisition of virtues of ideal Vedic practices and rejected birth as a determinant of an individual's status in society, similarly Vivekananda called for the liberalization of women and ending of Brahmin superiority even as he bitterly attacked "Westernized reformers". Gail Omvedt along with several others holds the view that these religious leaders sought to harmonise the early emphasis of liberal and conservative Brahmins. They argued that the Hindu nation must be considered holy, but insisted as well that the social evils of the present day, including caste, were not ancient religious customs. They formulated a revivalist nationalism that was to have dangerous anti-Muslim aspects.[12]

Totally dismissing the dominant religious traditions of India, Phule accepted the assumption that something had to be put in its place, that 'Even a revolutionary culture required a moral religious center.'[10] Hence he never rejected the idea of Dharma but rather attempted to establish a universal one. It is suggested that Sarvajanik Satya Dharma expressed this concept completely, implying that the moral basis of society has to be centered on truth or rationality and it had to be one that unified all men and women as equals. The world was regarded as good and holy in contrast to the Vedantic projection of it being an illusion.

Further the same author remarks that Phule's thinking does not show the Indian tendency to the reconciliation of opposites and is based upon the principle that an irreconcilable conflict of interest existed between the Brahmin elite and the non-Brahmin masses. Secondly, Phule's theory of exploitation focuses on cultural and ethnic factors rather than economic and political ones. Although he displayed great concern for the economic and political aspects of exploitation, Phule's ideology, in short, was based on identification with the peasant masses and on attachment to the revolutionary values of equality and rationality. Such concern for the poor farmers also reflected in his projection of Baliraja as a peasant god, drawing on the image of the common man and his focus on the plight of women and the untouchables. [13]

The basic question posed in this context is about the appropriate center of a "national culture." If the focus is on Sanskritic Hinduism, Vedic culture, Vedantic philosophy and the epics of Mahabharata and Ramayana, this implies a bias in favour of the upper castes and towards indirect support of the caste system and geographically in favour of north India. If the emphasis is towards non-Vedic culture, towards traditions of religious cultural revolt running through Buddhism and the Bhakti cults, then the bias is socially in favor of the masses and geographically in favor of the outlying linguistic regions of India. Given the scholarship and nationalist thinking, the bias till now has been towards a sanskritic and therefore elite basis to Indian culture, but in fact non-Sanskritic traditions have as much claims to an all-Indian spread."[14]

The non-Brahmin movement or what was also popularized as the self-respect movement in Tamil Nadu under the leadership of Periyar had a powerful emotional appeal for the masses. Periyar preached a new secular form of marriage which would have no priest of any caste. Idol-breaking, removal of casteist name plates (particularly those of Brahmins), propagating the eradication of superstitions, beliefs and practices, burning the copies of Ramayan and the Purans and demanding the expulsion of the Brahmin from Tamilnadu were his major programs of anti-Brahminism. Periyar's popular methods of communication and the programs adopted by him created the popular stream in the elite N.B.M. in Tamil-Nadu.

Both these protest movements against Brahminism and domination by landlords and the money-lenders' exploitation of poor farmers in Maharashtra later degenerated into casteist and elitist movements utilizing the anti-Brahmin platform for sub-serving the interests of the vocal and affluent sections of backwards castes. In a sense, over a period, they started articulating the aspirations and interests of the rich farmers and intermediate caste elites that had begun to emerge under the British patronage and the socio-economic changes brought about as a result of the British conquest of India. In the case of Tamilnadu the movement was dominated by the elites right from its inception.

As a matter of fact, the resent aggressive version of Syndicated Hinduism is jointly sponsored and articulated by the upper and backward castes. As observed earlier, backward caste have acquired a wider social and political base as a result of the first land reforms introduced after independence.

As we can see, the major focus of the religious reform movement, particularly in the nineteenth century, and even of the much more radical pro-poor movement led by Phule including the non-Brahmin movement in Tamil Nadu, was on propagating liberal values and a rational outlook and these were essentially directed against orthodox Brahminic rituals, undesirable customs such as sati, child marriage, prohibition of widow-remarriage, superstitions, monopoly of priesthood, and untouchability and for the spread of education among women, towards the improvement of women's plight and their rehabilitation against a monolithic, aggressive, highly authoritarian new version of Hinduism as projected by the upper and backward castes in recent years.

The progressive liberal character of the nineteenth century religious reform movement, though dominated by the upper caste affluent section and despite its very limited impact, could be seen in its re-interpretation of traditional religious ideals. 'Tatwam asi' was re-interpreted as self-realization in terms of striving for the collective happiness of the Indian humanity. The late Damodaran while tracing the genesis of the post-independence resurgence of religious revivalism remarks, "Millions of people had hoped that political independence would lead to a new social order which would abolish poverty, unemployment and human degradation and guarantee opportunities and freedom for every individual to build his personality. But all these hopes were belied in practice.[15]

The widespread poverty, unemployment, exploitation and squalor leading to human degradation torments sensitive hearts. Corruption, bribery and black markets have generated a "get rich quick" mentality and abominable success ethics have begun to dominate society. Moral values are sacrificed at the altar of profit. The individual regards his own interest as something opposed to the interest of the people. This exaggerated pre-occupation with one's own person vitiates and distorts all human relations. It is only natural that under such conditions man is encountered with a sense of insignificance and powerlessness. He is subjected to feelings of isolation and abandonment. This situation has already produced a crisis of cultural and spiritual values leading to frustration and despair. People are left with a feeling of emptiness. The turmoil and the squalor, the anxieties and the anguish, the anarchy and the violence created by the capitalist path of development makes life untenable and miserable".[16]

The vast bulk of the toiling classes, the petty bourgeois and others gravitate towards religion out of a sense of sheer helplessness and apathy. The ruling classes, by effectively playing on this sense of frustration and helplessness among the masses, have whipped up religious propaganda which has already become instrumental in dividing and generating animosities among the different sections of the Indian population on communal lines.

As a matter of fact, the ruling classes in India, as have since Independence evolved a dual policy which may appear contradictory but has proved extremely effective in perpetuating their rule and consolidating and expanding capitalist development in this country. In economic, administrative and legal spheres they have evolved a logical, rational and worldly approach that could result in maximization of economic gains to the bourgeoisie. While in the social and cultural sphere they have encouraged feudal institutions and traditional, religious values which has succeeded in stupefying and confusing the masses and generating a pessimistic, fatalistic outlook among them. With increasing political instability and the aggravation of economic crisis as reflected in growing unemployment, widespread industrial sickness, increasing papurisation of masses, rising inflation and the total bankrupcy of the ruling party and the state in resolving them, the dominant classes are desperately seeking to regain their credibility by increasingly relying on the whipping up of religious sentiments in order to retain their hold over people in recent years.

In this context, it is interesting to note that the material conditions created as a result of the introduction of modernization by the British in the 19th century paved way for the emergence of the religious reform movement which in a sense also articulated the aspirations of the rising bourgeois. The decadence and utter bankrupcy of the capitalist system in resolving any of the basic economic, political, social or cultural problems faced by the Indian society and the resultant crisis of legitimacy have created a new, aggressive religious fundamentalism particularly since the last decade.

As pointed out earlier, the modern version of Hinduism itself is based on concoction and distortion of earlier historical traditions and an unfortunate identification of nationalism with Hinduism since the 19th century (an outcome of the peculiar historical situation) with sufficient room for future distortion. Hinduism as popularly projected toady is a downright reactionary formation and rules out any possibility for the emergence of any form of any liberation theology within its fold.

Buddhism in its formative stage was certainly far more liberal and progressive with a dialectical orientation compared to later Vedic or Upanishad traditions. Under the circumstances, Dr. B. R. Ambedkar's protest against Hinduism took the form of a call to his followers to en-masse convert to neo-Buddhism.

It is also suggested that by focusing on the dynamic elements of earlier Buddhism, certain sects of medieval Bhakti movements, radical aspects of Satyashodhak Samaj and other non-Brahmin movements, one can evolve a liberation theology which may prove quite effective in mobilizing the oppressed and exploited classes and ultimately might pave way for a just and egalitarian social order free from all forms of exploitation.

Unfortunately the entire history of social movements is based on caste and sectarian loyalties drawing inspiration from some of the above traditions and does not leave much room for such optimism.

In this context, it is interesting to note that the material conditions created as a result of the introduction of modernization by the British in the 19th century paved way for the emergence of the religious reform movement which in a sense also articulated the aspirations of the rising bourgeois. The decadence and utter bankrupcy of the capitalist system in resolving any of the basic economic, political, social or cultural problems faced by the Indian society and the resultant crisis of legitimacy have created a new, aggressive religious fundamentalism particularly since the last decade.

As pointed out earlier, the modern version of Hinduism itself is based on concoction and distortion of earlier historical traditions and an unfortunate identification of nationalism with Hinduism since the 19th century (an outcome of the peculiar historical situation) with sufficient room for future distortion. Hinduism as popularly projected toady is a downright reactionary formation and rules out any possibility for the emergence of any form of any liberation theology within its fold.

Buddhism in its formative stage was certainly far more liberal and progressive with a dialectical orientation compared to later Vedic or Upanishad traditions. Under the circumstances, Dr. B. R. Ambedkar's protest against Hinduism took the form of a call to his followers to en-masse convert to neo-Buddhism.

It is also suggested that by focusing on the dynamic elements of earlier Buddhism, certain sects of medieval Bhakti movements, radical aspects of Satyashodhak Samaj and other non-Brahmin movements, one can evolve a liberation theology which may prove quite effective in mobilizing the oppressed and exploited classes and ultimately might pave way for a just and egalitarian social order free from all forms of exploitation.

Unfortunately the entire history of social movements is based on caste and sectarian loyalties drawing inspiration from some of the above traditions and does not leave much room for such optimism.

In this context it is worthwhile to draw a contrast between the dominant Hindu religious traditions and early Christianity. Jesus Christ was literally a messiah of the poor and the oppressed and he upheld their cause and ultimately was criticized for this 'crime'. The heroic martyrdom of Jesus for the proletarians of his time leaves enough scope for future inspiration. Secondly, the missionary traditions in the church of working with the poor, coupled with the peculiarly oppressive and suffocating conditions in most of the Latin American countries could give birth to liberation theology. In India, conditions are quite different in terms of the nature of capitalist development, political set up, astute leadership of bourgeois, and even in terms of the history and traditions of the country. It is not surprising that one of the main architects of Indian liberation theology had to admit that as far as India is concerned, liberation theology is likely to be low key in the years ahead due to the specific conditions existing here. As he further remarks, "The parties of revolution have been tamed and absorbed into the bourgeois politics of power and expediency to a point where they scarcely differ from the parties of order. Gandhism is today a spent force, being no more than a convenient ritual. The prospects of fresh revolutionary energies springing up from the subterranean consciousness of the masses are not bright. The power of the establishment to neutralize dissent knows no bounds."[17]

References

1. Siegel, Paul N; The Meek and the Militant, pp. 21-26, Oxford University Press 1987, pp. 21- 26.
2. Ibid.
3. Thapar, Romila: The Hindus and Their Isms - Syndicated Moksha? p. 14, Seminar, September 1985, p.14.
4. Ibid, p. 15.
5. Ibid, p. 22.
6. Mukherjee, Nirmal & Banerjee, Ashis: Neo-Nationalism. p. 26, Seminar, September 85, p. 26.
7. Damodaran K: Man and Society, Delhi 1970, pp. 75, 84.
8. Ibid.
9. Ibid.
10. Ibid.
11. Omvedt, Gail: Cultural Revolt in a Colonial Society, Bombay 1976, p. 99.
12. Ibid, p. 99-115.
13. Ibid, p. 104-105.

14. Ibid, p. 108.
15. Ibid, p. 112-115.
16. Damodaran, K. Op. cit p. 88.
17. Kappen, S: In Search of a New God, Illustrated Weekly, June 9, 1985, p. 27-28.

Index

B

C

N

O

P